The Wolf in the Parlor

The Wolf in the Parlor

THE ETERNAL CONNECTION
BETWEEN HUMANS AND DOGS

Jon Franklin

Henry Holt and Company ◇ New York

Henry Holt and Company, LLC
Publishers since 1866
175 Fifth Avenue
New York, New York 10010
www.henryholt.com

Henry Holt® and ⬚® are registered trademarks of Henry Holt and Company, LLC.

Distributed in Canada by H. B. Fenn and Company Ltd.

Library of Congress Cataloging-in-Publication Data

Franklin, Jon.
  The wolf in the parlor / Jon Franklin.—1st ed.
    p. cm.
  ISBN-13: 978-0-8050-9077-2
  ISBN-10: 0-8050-9077-0
  1. Dogs—Behavior.   2. Human-animal relationships.   I. Title.
  SF433.F73 2009
  636.7—dc22

                                                    2009002227

Henry Holt books are available for special promotions and premiums.
For details contact: Director, Special Markets.

First Edition 2009

Designed by Meryl Sussman Levavi

Printed in the United States of America

2 3 4 5 6 7 8 9 10

To Lynn

The love of my life

When the Man waked up he said,

"What is Wild Dog doing here?"

And the Woman said,

"His name is not Wild Dog any more,

but the First Friend,

because he will be our friend

for always and always and always."

—RUDYARD KIPLING

ACKNOWLEDGMENTS

To say that this book is a product of ten years of research and pondering is accurate but fails to credit what came before. By the time my attention was drawn to the wolf in my parlor, my questions were automatic, the result of fifteen years of interviewing, reading, and generally integrating myself into the culture of science and, in particular, that of brain science, anthropology, and related fields.

By this I mean I attended press conferences and training courses and, of course, schmoozed like a good reporter ought to. At scientific meetings, for example, I hung around the hotel bars because sooner or later almost all the big dawgs ended up there, and scientific salaries being what they are, most were happy to have a free drink, courtesy of my publisher. Alcohol, as all reporters know, loosens the tongue.

The late Victor Cohen, medical writer for the *Washington Post*, once said that scientists are to science writers as rats are to scientists. Very, very true. So I played anthropologist. In the process I naturally picked up a lot of useful information from sources as varied as Nobel Prize–winning scientists to anatomy department dieners, but information is not the heart of science. Science is a culture, made up of distinct subcultures, each with its own attitudes, prejudices, and perspectives on the world, in this case, of biology.

It was great fun, I must say. But when it comes to acknowledgments, I am at a loss. Decades have passed, and their faces blend together and I can't remember who taught me what. In regard to brain science, though, some names are indelible. The late Paul MacLean, the premier comparative brain anatomist of his time, taught me to think of mind and brain evolving together. Solomon Snyder and Candace Pert, the Johns Hopkins scientists who discovered the opiate receptor and opened the way to brain science as we know it, devoted hours and hours of their precious time to make sure I understood what was going on. To them, and the culture from which they spring, my deepest thanks. It has been a privilege to share their company.

For information and wisdom directly pertinent to *The Wolf in the Parlor* I am indebted to a number of experts. Some of them I interviewed directly, some I interviewed by e-mail, and others contributed through their books and scientific papers.

One of the latter instantly springs to mind: Juliet Clutton-Brock, at the Natural History Museum in London, who wrote the book (several, in fact) on the domestication of familiar farm animals. We played phone tag for a while, but I never actually talked to her. Her work, however, was clear and self-explanatory. Most notably, she coined the phrase "walking larder" for animals early humans captured but didn't need immediately. Dr. Clutton-Brock hypothesizes that these early people, lacking refrigeration or any other means of preservation, just tethered the wild animals and took them with them.

Maciej Henneberg, professor and head of anthropological and comparative anatomy at the University of Adelaide, South

Australia, was critical to the book. He confirmed, once and for all, the diminution of the human cranium at the end of the last ice age. Nancy Rawson of the Monell Chemical Senses Center undertook to educate me in the cellular nature of smell.

Other knowledgeable and helpful scientists include Alan Beck, director of the Purdue vet school; Marc Bekoff, professor emeritus of ecology and evolutionary biology at the University of Colorado, Boulder; Andy Blaustein, professor, department of zoology and director of the environmental sciences graduate program at Oregon State University; author and trainer Ray Coppinger; Darcy Morey, professor of anthropology at the University of Tennessee at Martin; the late Stanley Olsen, professor at the University of Arizona at Tucson; James Serpell, director of the Center for the Interaction of Animals and Society at the University of Pennsylvania; Forrest Smith, professor at the University of Akron.

It's customary to acknowledge experts and then emphasize that any mistakes are the responsibility of the writer, not the source. That's doubly necessary in this case since the basic thesis of this book will be controversial and none of these scientists can be assumed to buy into it. They will probably say, as I would have said: Speculation!

To that I plead guilty, but then so much of paleontology, for example, is speculation. Its history is one of controversy and disagreement in the absence of fact. Given that absence of fact it is only human to wonder, to try to put together the pieces, and perhaps, as in *The Wolf in the Parlor*, to emerge with a conclusion that is too important to the human race to be ignored. But for better or worse, that's my conclusion, and nobody else's; its worth will be determined by the reader.

And in this case, the book was helped along by many experts on dogs who were not scientists, at least formally, but were scrupulous observers of human-dog interactions. That includes such dog-world figures as moviemakers Charlene and Glenn

Dunlap and breeder Nancy McGee. Nancy is a perfect example of a breeder who successful breeds generation after generation of standard poodles with impeccable temperaments. With each one, she does a good deed to the human race.

I also owe a debt of gratitude to Ginny Reinhart, a first reader and enthusiastic supporter. I am especially grateful for the support of Tom Kunkel, until recently dean of the Philip Merrill College of the University of Maryland; and to the indomitable Gene Roberts, a fellow professor at the college, former managing editor of the *New York Times*, executive editor of the *Philadelphia Inquirer*, and of course a Pulitzer winner.

Last but not least I am grateful to my wonderful agent, Geri Thoma of the Markson Thoma Literary Agency, and to Mark Kramer, who introduced us. It was Geri who introduced me to Marjorie Braman, editor in chief of Henry Holt and Company. Marjorie, with her magic touch for word and phrase and her skill as a diplomat, has finally tamed this editor-bashing writer.

Finally, my everlasting thanks to my wife, Lynn, who stood by me as editor, reader, instructor, and friend throughout the preparation of this manuscript. And, of course, to Sam and the ghost of Charlie.

JON FRANKLIN
Calvert County, Maryland

The Wolf in the Parlor

Chapter One

To live the considered life is to dwell in an enigma. Nothing is truly as it seems. The certainties we hold when we are twenty-five have become absurdities by fifty. In the process, we have to nose along through the clamor and smoke of existence, trying to understand what is *really* going on as opposed to what only seems to be going on, struggling to separate the vagaries of the moment from the constants of existence, to eliminate the obvious irrelevancies that so many people get hung up on, like fashion and, oh, I don't know . . . dogs. Dogs are a good example. They are there, for some reason, and can be enjoyable creatures, but the why of it is not worth our time and energy. Alexander Pope said as much: "The proper study of mankind is man." Man, not cats or rabbits or hyenas or aardvarks. Or dogs.

Eliminating the trivia, clearing our minds of chaff, allows our attention to fix on the things that really matter. Then sometimes those things, things we otherwise might not even notice, can stun us with their relevancy.

The element of surprise adds to the power of such moments. As scientists like to say, serendipity is often the crux of discovery. In my case it all started thirty years ago or so, in an instant burned forever into my mind.

I was sitting in the northeast corner of the Baltimore *Sun* newsroom, feet propped on my desk and a cold cup of coffee by my elbow. I was opening mail, which, for me, was like a hound hunting rabbits. I would patrol the mail, ruffling my nose through the news, never sure what would emerge from the next envelope I slit open. So it was that one day in the late 1970s, I opened an envelope and pulled out a photograph that would forever change my perception of myself and set me on a journey that has consumed much of the rest of my life since.

They called me a science writer, but I thought of my beat as Truth and Beauty; and, yes, in my heart of hearts, I looked down on other reporters. All they got to cover was the everyday trivia of city hall, elections, the machinations of administrators and officialdom, fires and floods and homicides and growth plans and school budgets and cats stuck in trees—this and all the other superficial stuff that seemed relevant to the dullards on the city desk. Everything else—the whole, magnificent, unfolding panorama of scientific endeavor, from the moot to the apocalyptic—belonged to the science writer. Me!

Think of the great imponderables of existence. The mystery of the quasars, shining so brightly at the far horizon of time. The enigma of what makes a volcano explode, or a tornado germinate. Why butterflies flutter and fireflies blink and black carbon fuses together to make glittering diamonds. Fruit fly genetics. The denning behavior of Asian bears. The molecular machinery of the red blood cell, the burial preferences of ancient Micronesians, the tidal motions of the Bay of Fundy, the sex life of the lesser kudu, the quixotic search for the ivory-billed woodpecker . . . what is science, anyway, if not a living compendium of ballads, mystery yarns, and shaggy dog stories?

And there was always more, and more, and more. The forces of history shifted with the avalanche of discovery and invention, and the hard realities that shaped life came less and less from the political process and more and more from the laboratory. Everywhere you look, you see the results of science: The hydrogen bomb, the birth control pill, the computer, the Internet—science is everywhere. Science has become the primary driving force of modern existence. And politics? In modern times, politicians are almost always behind the game. Science acts. Politicians scramble to react but by the time they do, the science is usually a fait accompli.

Drama, meanwhile, does just what it always it did, which is follow reality. When the stirrup was invented, allowing armored warriors to balance themselves on horses, the balladeers strummed their lutes and sang of knight and fair damsel. A few centuries later, when a spacecraft blew up or a researcher died in pursuit of knowledge, you had a tragedy with Shakespearean possibilities. When biologists tracked down the cause of a disease (or when one of them phonied up a journal article) you had a detective story Sir Arthur Conan Doyle would have killed for. When a team from France and another from the United States raced to find the cause of AIDS, it was mano a mano à la Ernest Hemingway, even if the fight was set in the barroom of the mind. Sometimes, as when ulcers turned out to be caused by bacteria that thrive in the hot acid of the stomach, you had a delicious surprise ending. Other times, as when beasties were found living happily in the throats of undersea volcanoes, it was pure science fiction—a bad phrase, probably, considering that the science had long surpassed most of the fiction built on it.

It isn't all that much of stretch to connect science with art. If science is based on process and obscured with unfamiliar words, it nonetheless grew out of a fundamentally human, childlike curiosity. What makes the sky blue, why does ice float, what is "blood," how does the mind work? What child fails to ask those questions? And what child fails to try to draw what she sees, or sing what he knows?

As curiosity morphs into science and the powerful new instruments come into play, the questions go deeper and the fascination quotient goes up. Look close enough into the cell and the gooey protoplasm turns into a churning mix of little gizmos. Suddenly the living cell is crisscrossed with highways, all crowded with trucking engines carrying supplies in and out of the industrial areas near the center of the cell. There are factories and recycling plants, entry ports and guarded secure zones. Or you can look through the other end of the microscope and focus your mind on the realities of black holes, supergalaxies, and parallel universes that go on and on beyond the meager limits of our comprehension.

◇

In the middle decades of the twentieth century, physics and astronomy were the *real* sciences. But as the century proceeded the best stories were happening in biology. Once it was the purview of rich men with butterfly nets, physicians with leeches. By the 1970s, when I was earning my spurs as a science writer, biology had turned into Big Science, complete with million-dollar budgets, interdisciplinary research teams, and instruments that examined molecules as small as the galaxy was large. Medicine followed right behind, beginning its historic transformation from art to science. Brain scanners were on the horizon. Psychology, which I had long considered only slightly more credible than voodoo, would evolve into a hard science. I was in the audience of a press conference Johns Hopkins held in 1973 to publicize a paper one of their professors had written about the breakthrough he, Dr. Solomon Snyder, and his postdoctoral partner, Candace Pert, had made. They'd discovered that the human brain contained receptors—tiny ports on the surfaces of brain cells—that were built to attract and hold opium molecules. I thought that sounded bizarre. If the receptors were there, did that mean the brain made its own opium? Was that why people became addicted to opiates like morphine and heroin? What on earth was the purpose of that?

Trying to write the story of the discovery for the newspaper, I read the scientific paper again and again and reviewed my notes. Piece by piece, it came together. If the brain had opium receptors, that must mean it made its own opium. If so, I could only conclude that these powerful secretions were the source of good feelings, and that we were hooked on the behaviors that produced those feelings. You didn't have to reach far to conclude that the human mind was therefore a chemical process, explainable in chemical terms—really, in natural addictions.

Motherly love, for instance, would be a woman's addiction to her own opiates. Her baby smiles; she gets a fix.

The more I puzzled over the implications, the more it seemed to me that Snyder and Pert had just handed us the keys to the kingdom. We had a way, now, to truly understand ourselves. A few steps down the scientific road and we'd have a new and very specific grasp of the mechanism of yearning, the metabolism of love, the chemistry of all human compulsion. It was a glimmer of a different future.

There is nothing more fundamental to our worldview than our attitude toward the mind, the seat of the self. Now, in a couple of hours, the foundations of how I saw myself and the human race had been deconstructed and restructured. I was left in the state of shock and confusion that follows any major psychological realignment. The enigma had rolled over on me, the world was different than I had thought it was. The only thing I understood clearly was that I was in on the ground floor of a revolution in biopsychology that would ultimately change everything from the depredations of mental illness and addiction to our view of our own history.

Much has been written about the explosive chain reaction of knowledge that happened in the following decades. It started in brain chemistry and spread rapidly to neurophysiology. New generations of brain scanners appeared. Now, with our first glimpses of the thinking human mind, the revolution spread further: to psychiatry, to social science, and to anthropology. Every new discovery in brain science seemed to reinforce the thinking in anthropology, which fed back to suggest new experiments in the flux rate of neurotransmitters.

It stands to reason that all the really important scientific papers on the brain went back, one way or another, to Darwin. The premise of the new brain science was that the brain had evolved to produce thought, emotion, and behavior—and in those terms, the discoveries were often understandable even to the layperson.

Why did we have opium receptors in the brain? Obviously, to make us feel good. When you were a student, and you did a math problem properly, you felt good. So you did it again, and again, and again. Enough of that and you'd be addicted to numbers and formulas for life.

The brain had other uses for opium as well. As the story unfolded the "runner's high" was also laid to natural opium. Other receptors and messenger molecules were discovered and linked with everything from anger to self-hypnotic states.

With specifics such as these, the ancient philosophical questions of existence seemed to pass from philosopher to scientist. For the first time, we could focus the armamentarium of science—scanners, giant computers, statistical models, and large-scale collaboration—on the ancient questions of who we are and where we came from. There was an intellectual juggernaut rolling straight toward the center of the human universe and that inner singularity for which we had no other word but "soul."

◇

Even the non-laboratory sciences were coming along, albeit much more slowly. Anthropology had grown into a sort of a science (and never mind the pseudoscience around the edges). As a result we now knew some of our evolutionary history. We knew, for example, where the road had forked and our ancestors began making stone tools. That change separated them from the rest of the apes and sent them down the evolutionary road that would lead to modern humans. Half a million years ago, they mastered fire, and the tree branched again. By a hundred thousand years ago, having spread across the face of the old world, they were recording the birth of human imagination in rock art. They did not yet produce what we would call architecture, but they had definitely learned to impose their will on the most fundamental and resistant material in their world: rock. Their flint edges were as sharp as scalpels. I happen to know this because I once wrote a story about a surgeon who made and used stone knives to operate. He claimed they cut cleaner than steel, though they dulled faster.

By some point late in the last ice age our ancestors had become anatomically modern. They looked like us. Put them in neckties or pantyhose and you wouldn't have noticed them on the subway—at least, not to look at them. But however modern they might have appeared, they remained among the animals. Their numbers remained small and the populations of competing animals did not shrink. Humans remained part of the ecological balance. They built shelters but they did not settle in them, and they did not even dream of cities. They harvested, as the other animals did, only what nature planted. They hunted and killed, but did not domesticate. Depending on which archaeological calculation you believe, they remained that way, fairly static, for a hundred thousand years or even longer.

Then, twelve thousand years ago, as the ice age ended,

something truly extraordinary happened and the human race simply . . . changed. Exploded. Blossomed. Suddenly and inexplicably we began to herd, dig, build, draw, plan, and invent on a scale only hinted at by our earlier existence. In an evolutionary heartbeat we became the uncontested masters of the planet. Twelve thousand years Before Present is a date that evokes the human enigma itself.

The changing perception of human evolution is itself a study in the evolution of ideas. Archaeologists have been working on the problem for centuries, and much of what they concluded early on was so wrong as to be humorous. For the better part of a century humans were thought to be descended from knuckle-dragging Neanderthals. We weren't, of course, and in any event Neanderthals weren't knuckle-draggers. They looked very much like us—but that's a part of a different enigma.

When I went to college in the 1960s, we thought the birth of modern humans occurred at twelve thousand years BP, and was surely explained in terms of brain size. Anatomically modern human beings, I was taught, did not actually appear until about that time. Our brains got bigger, we got smarter, and finally our brains reached a critical mass and we took over. The logic was impeccable. Any child could see the progression. End of story.

But when archaeologists pushed the existence of modern humans back many tens and then hundreds of thousands of years, the whole narrative linking brain size and human evolution began to come apart. Worst of all, to those still defending the old view, the human brain didn't suddenly get bigger at the end of the last ice age. Instead, at the precise moment of human ascendancy, when the human animal stepped up to rule the earth, its brain got *smaller*. Average cranial capacity shrank by 5 to 10 percent.

This was stunning. Wasn't our big brain the thing that made us smarter than the rest of the animal world, and therefore superior? Didn't we assume, in our science fiction stories and films, that as we continued to evolve about, our brains would expand until our descendants, somewhere down the generations, would have heads the size of basketballs? Wasn't cranial capacity the obvious and inarguable mechanism of advancement? Apparently not.

Scientists measured, re-measured, and re-re-measured fossil crania. They subjected their data to rigorous statistical analysis. They argued the question to a virtual standstill in the scientific literature. But still, the fact stood. The human animal, generally, was distinguished by its big brain, yet the moment the species embarked on the road to civilization was marked by a significant diminution of brain size.

Anthropology being what it is, conjecture grew to fill in the holes left by discredited facts. What was the link between brain shrinkage and the explosion of human influence? Not only was there no shortage of explanations, there were so many conflicting conjectures, so many mutually exclusive scenarios, that they added up to no explanation at all. The whole messy situation just hung there in the back of the anthropological mind, another reminder (if one was needed) of how little we really know about ourselves.

And finally there is yet another issue, equally puzzling, related and yet not related.

A science writer's livelihood is based on the assumption that people are interested in science. There is plenty of evidence for this. They watch the Discovery Channel. They buy books about science. They are fascinated by the drifting continents, the mysterious dark matter that more and more astronomers think holds together the universe, the stunningly beautiful lemurs of Madagascar.

People want to know, intellectually as well as practically, why arteries harden. They want to know what causes schizophrenia, why salamanders can grow new legs and we can't. Our interest in biology is intensified by our relentless self-absorption, our abiding conviction that we, and we alone, are at the very center of the universe. If human beings have a creed, it would have to be that nothing matters except me—and "me" was turning out to be an essentially biological concept.

So why, even at the height of the brain science revolution, did we spend less money on the combined disciplines of archaeology, sociology, psychology and neuroanatomy than we spent each year on, say, football?

◇

Fortunately, that wasn't my problem. For whatever reason, the human race existed. It was what it was, and it was nothing if not specialized. Everyone had their little niche, their own little piece of the machinery to run. One person did my taxes, another fixed my car, another filled my teeth. As a journalist, I was no less specialized. In fact, I was so specialized that I didn't actually do anything. I just watched the world of science and translated it for anyone who cared to watch it with me. I did what I did because I loved it. I loved the considered life, and even developed a certain fondness for the enigma. I loved to watch the great curling wave front of discovery. I loved to talk to the scientists. I loved to write stories that fascinated people, that lodged in their minds and wouldn't go away.

I loved it so much that I developed my own private game about it. I'd try to outguess the scientists, figure out where all this new information was going to take them. If that sounds arrogant it probably is, but I had an advantage because my work gave me a broad view of emerging science. Working scientists are so specialized that they often can't see much beyond the minutiae that shape their own lives and work.

Many scientists talk only to their lab mates. Neurobiologists who specialize in receptors mostly talk to other neurobiologists who specialize in receptors. They rarely, if ever, talk to anthropologists, and anthropologists don't hang out much with psychiatrists. As a science writer I was a veritable bumblebee, flitting from flower to flower, talking to everyone. It was surprising how often I could introduce scientists to useful new ideas that were just beyond the horizons of their own fields. One scientist told me—I cherish the moment—that science journalists are the modern incarnation of what used to be called the "general scientist," the fellow who knew a little bit about everything and who could therefore put things together: the synthesizer.

I took synthesis as my right and duty. I thought about it all the time because, unlike the average scientist, I had the luxury of doing so. I could lie in a hammock, sip iced tea, and ask more existential *why* questions. I didn't have to worry about getting another grant; I could just woolgather about such things as, for example, why the opium poppy and the tobacco plant manufacture chemicals that fit neatly into receptors in the human neuron and, in doing so, literally change our minds. I could play "What if . . . ?" and "You don't suppose . . ." and "What does *that* do?"

When I wasn't out covering some meeting of paleontologists or brain chemists, you'd probably find me with my feet on my desk, perusing journal articles or rooting through my mail looking for jewels. Who knew what I might find? Science could sometimes produce heart-stopping excitement. A spacecraft roaring into the sky, balanced on a blade of fire. A child cured of leukemia. An owl monkey which, by virtue of brain implants and computers, could levitate objects and control them just by thinking about them.

Stories about breakthroughs are irresistible to the press. Reporters go nuts over them. Unfortunately, that enthusiasm translates into a sensationalism that obscures the basic nature of science. Science is slow. Glacial, even. Putting a levitation gizmo into the brain of a monkey required the life's work of not just hundreds but thousands of people. Putting similar gizmos into the brains of quadriplegics was going to take still more.

Scientists are patient people. Very patient people. I've watched genetic engineers spend days at the bench rearranging things too small to see, only to dump their work into the hazardous waste bin, go out for beers, and then start over again the next day. Social scientists can perch in front of their computers, eyes boring into their screens, sorting and rearranging numbers with the intensity normally reserved for blood sports or high-stakes gambling. An archaeologist will kneel in a hot pit for hours, scraping at the soil of some country the average American couldn't point out on a globe. Good scientists develop attention spans that can freeze time. For a professionally scatterbrained creature like myself, to watch a scientist work is to realize that boredom is a form of pain. It stupefies the mind.

Yet that is the process, and in science process is all. The earth turns. Spring comes, followed by summer. School ends, and archaeologists everywhere leave their universities and museums and head for their digs in the ancient world. Throughout the hot months, they labor in their pits and take their photographs and finally, when summer ends, they pack their gear and go home. Over the winter they teach and write up their papers, which, in due time, are reviewed and edited and probably rewritten several times before finally being published in obscure journals that only other archaeologists will ever read. By the time the journals are delivered, the scientists will have gone on to other digs in other places; they might even have trouble recalling the details of the papers they wrote so long ago. In a certain sense, a scientific paper is itself a fossil.

But a scientific paper, once published, continues to live. The scientist's colleagues read it and argue over it. Routinely, someone in the university research office will make copies and distribute them to relevant campus mailboxes. In the fullness of time, one of these copies will work its way down the distribution chain to the public relations department. There, a research assistant may look at a picture and think, Aha! The media might like that!

A press release will be written, the draft passed around. The text will be vetted, altered, picked at, red-penciled, approved on seven different levels, and finally sent to the copy shop. The press releases, along with copies of the photographs, will go into envelopes and someone, maybe a work-study intern from the medieval languages department, will stick a pre-printed address label onto the envelopes and dump them into the outgoing mail bin.

And so the scientific process, this tedium and labor, this slow trickle of time and routine, produces, like the injured oyster, a singular pearl of compressed perception, intellectual beauty translated and packaged so that even a reporter can understand it at a glance, whether it concerns an exploding galaxy, a fossilized beast from the distant past, anything. In this case, it was a photograph.

◇

The photographer's lens looked straight down into a deep rectangular pit, the product no doubt of a long, tedious summer's work with dental picks and soft brushes. I could almost smell the dust and sweat. At the bottom of the pit, still partially embedded in clay, an old man's skeleton lay on its side, curled into a fetal position. His right arm was extended, hand open, as if grasping for something just beyond his reach. The gesture was so evocative that for a moment I thought I recognized it—knew what it meant, the way the heart knows things the intellect cannot. But then the feeling ebbed and vanished, leaving nothing. Any meaning, if meaning there was, was lost in the vast dark ocean of time that separated us.

Only after I'd studied the photograph for a few moments did I see a second skeleton in the grave—a small pile of what appeared to be more fragile bones. A child? I looked more closely. No, some kind of animal, couldn't tell what. But that was not remarkable. Archaeologists often found various animals in human graves. They were placed there in some rite, perhaps, or to supply food for the journey to the next world. A smudged news release attached to the photograph soon clarified that question: It was probably a dog; that, or a wolf cub.

Whatever it was, it seemed to be what the skeletal fingers were reaching for.

I read on. The dig was somewhere in the Jordan Valley, at a place called Ein Mallaha. The tomb had been sealed some twelve thousand years ago, at about the time the last ice age was ending. That meant the man had been buried at almost precisely the time when something, no one knew what, had reset human destiny—and in the process created the conditions that would one day produce a culture, technology, and mental outlook that characterized the most spectacular civilization the earth had ever seen.

Six hundred generations had passed between the old man's burial and the pop of the photographer's flash. Six hundred generations of birthing and dying, loving and fighting, building and tearing down, hoping and despairing, each successive life ending inevitably as the old man's had, all experience forever muted by the reclaiming earth.

After that, time and the chemistry of the grave did their work. The flesh melted and the bones, white at first, slowly turned a dark earthen brown; they alone would survive—just the bare bones, and the unspoken questions they represented.

I laid the photograph down, thinking to go on to another envelope, but something stopped me, and I picked it up again. What was I missing? I looked again, more closely, holding up the photo to the light of the window behind me. And then I saw it.

Although only a geological instant had passed since the body had been interred, a slip fault had already split the grave. Long forgotten earthquakes had cut a jagged line through soil and bone alike, severing the big bones of the leg and slicing through the spine just below the neck. The fault showed just enough motion to foretell the earth's intention, which was to carry the skeleton's head off in one direction and his rib cage in another.

Suddenly I saw the photograph in a different light. The fault, whatever else it might have been, spoke directly to the human dilemma. All the natural forces of the earth seemed to conspire against this new animal, intent on ripping heart and mind asunder.

I remember sitting there a long time.

Finally I leaned the photo up against the stack of papers that had accumulated on the left corner of my desk, the last stop on the way to the trash can. In the coming days and weeks, I would glance at it, *trying* to figure out what it was that bothered me, or pulled me, or . . . whatever it was. Eventually, in a month or two, the photograph went into a folder in the left drawer of my desk, the one reserved for mysteries.

◇

I shouldn't leave the impression that my entire life revolved around my job. Like most people, I lived in two worlds: the private one and the professional one. And in the fullness of time, just as I had begun to think I had mastered the knack for living, and also that I was beginning to get a feel for the science of the mind, my two worlds collided head on.

It was a winter morning in the late 1980s. My girlfriend and I were on the Pennsylvania Turnpike, on the way to Pittsburgh to visit her parents. A frigid mass of air lay across the Appalachian landscape, a reminder that the Pleistocene ice, while gone, would one day return. Our conversation had lapsed into the comfortable silence known best to lovers; now, as the Chevy followed the road over the frozen mountains, I was suddenly overwhelmed by the warmth of the car, the comfort of Lynn's presence, and her centrality to my existence.

Like so many achievement-oriented and otherwise articulate

males, I am often struck dumb by powerful emotions. But the inspiration that seized me at this moment was so strong and pure and heartfelt that it overcame inhibition and, somewhere between Breezewood and Somerset, I blurted out a proposal of marriage.

For a heartbeat or two Lynn continued to stare out the window, and I thought that perhaps I hadn't spoken after all—that the words, like so much of the romanticism in my life, had somehow been trapped inside my skull to echo meaninglessly until they faded and died.

But the sentiment had indeed been spoken, the question asked, and Lynn had hesitated only as she gathered the threads of her own inspired response. Then she looked across the car at me and smiled.

"Does this mean," she asked, "that I can have a puppy?"

She'd had her heart set on a puppy for a while now but I, a single parent whose children had just recently left the nest, cringed at the idea of my newly regained life being trashed by an infant of any species. A puppy was an engine of disorder. Puppies chewed up slippers, peed on the rug, barked at night, bit the mailman.

It wasn't that I disliked dogs. Dogs were okay, in a vague sort of way. But they had always been on the far periphery of my existence. Brownie, the dog of my childhood, had been left alone in the backyard to grow up as an incorrigible cat-killer and child-biter. Years later, as an adult in a crime-prone neighborhood, I'd kept a watchdog named Gypsy, but I had paid even less attention to her than to Brownie—she did her job and I did mine. So there were dogs around. I saw them in the laboratory and on the street. There were occasional dog stories in the newspaper, but of course I never read them.

Serious reporters laughed at people who covered frivolous news, and no news was more frivolous than dog news. Even reporters who did weddings and ribbon cuttings looked down their noses at journalists whose bylines regularly appeared on dog stories. I learned this when, as a cub reporter, I went to work for a paper that ran a dog-of-the-week feature. It consisted of a photograph and a short biography of some subscriber's dog, and as the junior reporter I had to write it. I hated it for the humiliation it signified, and moved on to better assignments as soon as I could.

And now, here I was, carried over some horrible psychic cliff by my compulsive romanticism. All I had asked the lady for was her hand. A puppy? Puppies grew up into dogs. Dogs shed fur. A dog in the house meant dog hair on the couch, dog hair on my slacks, dog hair in the refrigerator. Awww no, no, a thousand times no, no dog, no way.

But nature is an implacable force. Over the next weeks, Lynn patiently dismantled my arguments, one by one. An unsupervised puppy was kept in a crate, so it didn't chew up or pee on anything. You trained it, and it didn't bark at night or bite the mailman. You civilized it, and it became part of the family. What was more, some dogs didn't shed at all: certain kinds of terriers, including Scotties and Airedales. Poodles were another example.

Poodles?

Lynn had me backed into a corner, but even so I absolutely drew the line at poodles. Poodles were froufrou dogs, bred to loll on red satin pillows. I had a reputation to maintain as a hard-assed reporter. My God! What would happen if people found out I lived with a poodle? A poodle! No. I would not abide a poodle.

But Lynn herded me confidently toward her goal. Not all poodles were lap dogs. I was thinking of toy poodles and miniature poodles, corruptions of the original breed. The standard poodle, of which she spoke, was a real, collie-sized, waist-high dog. Producing a book from the library, she showed me a picture. Standard poodles had first been bred by fishermen in Germany, who had used them to swim out and set nets. They had tied colored rags in the dogs' wool so each fisherman could identify his dog at a distance. Later, poodles were hunting dogs who could both point and flush. A team of standard poodles had run the Iditarod, no less—finished, too. It was the French who poofed them up and replaced the fishermen's rags with ribbons, but that was an aberration. You could never tell about the French.

Lynn invoked the ghost of John Steinbeck and the big dog he took with him across the country in his famous book *Travels with Charley*. No literary wimp, John Steinbeck. He was one of my heroes. Lynn knew that. Steinbeck's Charley was none other than a standard poodle.

And so, in the fullness of time, Lynn and I stood in a Baltimore living room while several black poodle puppies, which resembled nothing so much as bear cubs, were set free. Most of them scampered and tumbled around the room, but one of them promptly made its way over to Lynn and sat down on her feet, as if to say, "I'll take this one." My part in this bonding ritual was to write out the check.

A few hours later, at home, the indoctrination began.

Lynn disappeared into the kitchen, leaving Charlie and me alone together for the first time. I sat on the couch and looked at him; he sat in the middle of the floor and stared right back, totally unabashed by the superior forebrain that was the hallmark of my kind.

I am here to stay, he said in that silent language that dogs use to communicate across the species barrier, *and the sooner you get used to that the better it will be for everyone.*

CHAPTER TWO

Very well. He would stay. But that didn't mean I had to waste time thinking about him. I had more important things on my mind—human things, things that were being done in neurosciences laboratories, things that had the potential to change our understanding of who we are.

By the 1980s, for example, it was clear to me that we were on the threshold of discovering whole new classes of drugs to treat mental illness. The invention of a broad-spectrum antidepressant was inevitable; Prozac, as it was ultimately named, was going to have more impact than most people would have dreamed.

At the time, most people really didn't understand that mental illness was a plague on the modern world. Depression, for example, was an immobilizing disease often confused with laziness, and it probably sapped more of our national treasure than the entire government budget. Schizophrenia cost at least as much. Scientists had begun to talk among themselves about other conditions, like extreme shyness, that might be diseases.

The government kept statistics but their accuracy was questionable. People thought of mental illness as shameful, the way they'd once thought of cancer as contagious. So they denied the illness existed. When a family member was stricken it was a stigma on the whole family, and so they kept it as quiet as they could. If direct confrontation of the disease became necessary, then the human animal behaved according to form: Blame the victim.

Scientists considered these attitudes medieval nonsense. The first detailed chemical maps of the brain told us that depression, for example, isn't caused by bad mothering or social injustice.

It was also misnamed. "Depression" isn't how one feels after getting fired or jilted or going bankrupt. Life has its ups and downs, sometimes horrible downs, but that is normal; the average, healthy person picks themself up and goes on.

Depression, real depression, clinical depression, reflects a breakdown in one of the brain's key mood control systems, probably involving the neurotransmitter serotonin. In fact, depression is probably not a single disease but a whole class of diseases, the same way cancer is turning out to be. Depression clearly has a genetic component but it can be triggered by a lot of things—even by certain viruses.

I do not mean to oversimplify. The brain is the most complicated organization of matter in the universe, and on top of that it is furiously metabolic—chemically speaking, it is a new organ every second. The chemical responses we call mood are tides of the mind, mediated by the flow of chemicals from one brain cell to another. Changes occur at lightning speed. The brain burns pure glucose and nothing else. As a chemical engine, it is built for speed. When we are working with our minds, really working (doing a math problem or reading history), we burn up as much energy as if we were jogging.

The evolutionary purpose of the brain, presumably, is to build models. It models the outer world, what we call "reality," in the inner world of the imagination. It then conducts thought experiments to play out various scenarios. What would happen if we went over the fence and into the field with yonder bull? What if I bought an ice cream cone for that pretty young woman in history class? How would I look in this coat, or that pair of shoes? Modeling is an extremely complex operation, invoking the machinery of perception, cognition, and emotion: The whole brain is involved. Together, the various parts of the brain study the model and decide what action to take.

Sophisticated though it is, the brain is not beyond comprehension, at least in theory.

The new neurobiology drove a stake through the heart of the nature-versus-nurture argument. Behavior involves both genetics and environment. This helped, at least in principle, to depoliticize psychology. It also gave us a useful materialistic way to look at ourselves. Accurate self-perception is the key to successful action, and successful action is what drives history.

So it was that, one step at a time, the mind was starting to make biological sense. The change wasn't instantaneous, like Einstein's famous formula that reordered the universe; rather, a glimmer here and a glimmer there started adding up to a new synthesis about the nature of human nature.

Understanding brain science well enough to make it coherent to my readers was plenty of work to give purpose and structure to my life. I immersed myself in it, reading scientific articles, press releases, whatever I could get my hands on. I attended scientific meetings and suffered through the slides and technical presentations. Then, after the formal programs were over, I would stalk the more interesting scientists in the bar, where they gathered to swap their current research and to speculate and brag. My job was to keep their glasses filled and my ears open.

◇

None of this had any connection whatsoever to puppies. To say that I accepted Charlie as being there did *not* mean I accepted him as something worth investing much mental energy in.

And yet this whole business, the marriage, the puppy—it was a slippery slope. Like it or not, I had become the master of . . . well, okay, co-owner, then . . . or semi-owner, or spousal associate, or something . . . of a fuzzy black bear-cub-looking animal who was nonchalantly making himself at home in my parlor. I resolved to simply ignore him, but that was an exercise in futility; he seemed to be everywhere I was.

We'd just bought our house and the backyard was choked with mulberry trees. I went at them with a chain saw, bringing them down and then chopping them up for firewood. Then I started stacking them.

I had only made a few trips across the yard when I realized I was not alone. Charlie was prancing along behind me, a puppy-sized branch in his jaws. That's when I noticed he was building a smaller, puppy-sized woodpile beside mine. That was also when I heard the clear, inescapable *click* of Lynn's camera.

There was something about a puppy that would not be ignored. When he came over and nuzzled my knee, it was impossible not to look up from my book and pet him. There was an odd, unexpected pleasure to be had from touching his woolly fur, a comfort of some sort. Calming. After a while I found myself doing it without thinking.

Thus a puppy changes one's life, not with dramatic moments but rather with a tide of small things. With Charlie to bark at intruders, nighttime silences were all the more secure. Good times became even better as Charlie, picking up the happiness, amplified it with his prancing, tail-wagging ecstasy. The world seemed new to us once again as Charlie explored it for the first time, encountering his first squirrel, his first snow, his first ocean beach.

If you have a puppy, he has to be walked, in the process of which you come upon other people, walking other dogs. The dogs have to sniff noses, genitals, and anuses, and the people have to swap gossip and, of course, dog stories. *Ooooh! A standard poodle!* Aunt Clara had a standard poodle. Spot, here, is a border collie; he has two ribbons toward an obedience title. Moonie is great, as malamutes go, but he's just not good with children. Cocker spaniels are *sooooo* sweet, but they're stupider than rocks.

Thus I came to notice, then acknowledge, and then finally be startled by, the prevalence in the human world of Charlie's kind. The world was awash in dogs—pampered dogs, stray dogs, lap dogs, sled dogs, guide dogs, herding dogs, circus dogs, police dogs, racing dogs, guard dogs. There were dogs on the street, dogs on television, dogs in the newspapers, dogs in the movies, dogs in songs. I could walk down Constitution Avenue alone and nobody would notice me, but if I had Charlie on a leash I couldn't get a hundred yards without someone stopping me and wanting to know what breed he was and whether they could pet him. Once, at a fair, two young men watched a long procession of girls ooh and ah over Charlie, then came and asked me if they could borrow him for a half hour.

Aside from attracting women, most dogs don't seem to have much in the way of actual function. Sure, there are service dogs and cannabis-sniffing dogs, but most dogs seem to lounge their way through life, sleeping in the sun, playing with balls, chasing Frisbees, eating, drinking, and then dumping their disgusting piles of excreta on sidewalks—forcing city dwellers, whether they own dogs or not, to develop the habit of walking with their eyes focused on the concrete immediately in front of them.

Dogs, dogs, dogs. Mayors and city councils wrangled interminably over regulations to control them, though no law seemed to have much impact. License laws were observed largely in the breach. Leash laws were a laugh. Dogs were the bane of police departments, forcing officers to expend inordinate amounts of time and energy on complaints about feral dogs, biting dogs, barking dogs . . . dogs, dogs, dogs, dogs, dogs, dogs, dogs. Dog-catchers are a necessary part of any government—though even the word itself, "dogcatcher," like most dog language, is ambiguous to the point of being wrong. Dogcatchers don't carry nets, and they don't chase or catch dogs. I know this because once, early in my career, I violated my no-dogs rule and did a story on a dogcatcher.

It was a fascinating experience to follow the guy around all day. Despite his lowly status and minuscule paycheck (he was the single lowest-paid full-time employee in populous Baltimore County), his true function was that of psychiatrist to the community. He counseled and reassured people whose sick or aging dogs had to be euthanized, taught children how to relate to their animals and to avoid being bitten by someone else's, tactfully explained the law to people whose neighbors had complained about recreational barking, and occasionally issued a citation. He was the designated person when there was any kind of crisis involving animals. He was a lubricant, of sorts, between the realities of modern city life and the deep, inchoate, utterly unreasonable urge to keep wolflike canines.

The dogcatcher—excuse me: "animal control officer"—described himself as a "dog person," and he owned a very nice animal. Even so, in the end, after a year's experience, what the dogcatcher learned from dogcatching was that there was no profit there, and the emotional storms were too powerful and murky to endure, especially when endurance earned you nothing but the disrespect of others. As we headed home in his truck that day, the dogcatcher confessed to me that his foremost desire in the world was to get another job. Any other job. Anywhere. Doing anything. Anything *else*, that was.

Naturally, the story I wrote wasn't about the dogs; it was about the dog people and the world they inhabited. A strange world indeed, and deeply contradictory.

Americans love dogs. They spend billions on dog food, veterinary care, toys, grooming supplies, rhinestone collars—you name it. They worry about their dogs as they would about human children. When pets die, their owners are disconsolate. Some bury their dead dogs in fancy cemeteries and even build monuments to them. A rich dog owner recently forked over several million dollars in a failed attempt to clone his dead pooch. Yet at the same time, the word "dog" is almost a universal pejorative; bad movies, unreliable cars, unattractive women are all dogs. The worst, most unbearable weather in summer comes during the "dog days." Dogface, dog meat, maybe even doggerel.

I didn't want to think about these contradictions, or what might underlie them. I tried to force the whole dog thing out of my mind, but it always crept back in again. Despite my resistance, Charlie seemed to be drawing me step by step into this new world—his world. That it seemed a nonsensical world made matters all the worse, because I don't believe in nonsense. Everything has a reason, and nonsense is something we just don't understand the sense of. If I think of nonsense as a mystery, then I can follow it—and, unfortunately, I am a sucker for a mystery.

I couldn't help but wonder what all these dogs were doing in our lives, but I resisted. I had plenty of mysteries involving a much more important animal, which is to say, us. Still, you can see how the same kind of curiosity that can make a science writer good can also make him vulnerable. Curiosity can lead to otherwise obscure realities that can open loopholes in one's carefully constructed model of the universe—loopholes that Charlie was adept at finding and wriggling through.

As for Charlie himself, he was totally unlike the earlier dogs in my life. For one thing, of course, I paid attention to him. He was Lynn's puppy, and I rather quickly discovered that "Love me, love my dog" was not just a catchy saying. It was a law of nature.

So Charlie would never be a generic dog. Under Lynn's civilizing hand he would soon be house-trained, and in the coming months he would learn to sit, stay, lie down, and heel. By the time he was six months old I could safely leave my sandwich on the coffee table; he would stare, but without permission he would eat nothing. When Lynn and I sat down at our computers to write, he knew it was time to lie quietly at our feet.

Steinbeck had called his Charley a "gentleman poodle," and the description applied to this Charlie as well. Purebred dogs generally embody recognizable behavior patterns—Darwin himself had been fascinated by this fact more than a century ago. Border collies, for example, have a compulsion to herd. Lacking sheep or cows, they will settle for children. Lacking children, they will herd chickens or ducks. Standard poodles have some herding instinct as well, but in them it is a minor characteristic. The dog books noted poodles for an assortment of characteristics, behaviors and attitudes which, when summed up in human terms, translate to "regal." Dignity is the natural order of poodledom. In this as in other respects, our Charlie was exactly as the dog book advertised: Even as a puppy, he carried himself with a certain self-contained dignity. I sometimes suspected that in another life he had been a particularly supercilious English butler.

Not that he was a milquetoast, by any means. In adulthood he would be seventy-five pounds of muscle and flashing fangs. He was gentle by nature but if circumstances required he could and did back off intruders, both animal and human, with a ferocity more popularly associated, say, with rottweilers—another gross mischaracterization, as the neighborhood rotty was a pussycat. But Charlie rarely found it necessary to actually fight. In almost any gathering of dogs, he immediately and without fanfare assumed the dominant role.

I have only known Charlie to sound retreat on one occasion. That was in Oregon, where he suddenly found himself in the presence of a visiting cougar. Exit, stage left. The poodle is brave, yes. But he is not stupid.

As I found myself enmeshed in my own maiden friendship with an individual of another species, I was struck again and again by the very fact of it. Charlie was basically a wolf, after all, a creature of the northland, and I was a tropical primate. Until recently, his kind had been predators of the most fearsome sort. My kind, on the other hand, derived from the trees of Africa. We were prey animals, living mostly on fruits and vegetables, and as such were the natural target of leopards, tigers, and snakes. As with other edible forms of animal life, our most keenly developed sense was fear. Forget that in recent times we have armed ourselves with spears and knives and become the meanest creatures to ever stalk the earth; that is a relatively new thing, and no matter how powerful we become, we retain a deep fear of animals with claws and fangs. Our fairy tales are populated with big bad wolves. The cats and snakes that ate our ancestors live on to this day in our nightmares. The fear itself, the undying, unquenchable fear, might be a large part of whatever made us so mean.

So what did it signify, then, this powerful but unlikely bond between such markedly different species? What was a wolf, of all things, doing in my parlor?

The oddness of it all nagged at me. Charlie, in his doggy way, touched something deep in my mind—something I couldn't articulate but that was there all the same. I itched to know, the way you do when you find yourself in possession of an answer but you don't know what the question was.

I had to keep reminding myself that the central mystery of life is humankind, period. It is the job of humans to put together the pieces of our own existence. We need to keep our Popean focus, no matter what. That was difficult enough without some alien animal like Charlie suddenly plopping right into the middle of it with a squeak toy. Charlie, the dog—dogs, dogdom in general—seemed to me like some extra piece of a jigsaw puzzle. Extraneous.

In terms of the human puzzle, there was simply no place for the dog at all or, if there was, it had to be on the periphery. The far periphery. But Charlie *wasn't* on the periphery, damn it, and when I tried to push him there he just crept back into the foreground. Once again, I'd find myself frittering away my time worrying about him. It was maddening. I had a bigger story going, much bigger, about a much more important animal. A larger, smarter, meaner creature that walked on two legs and was part beast, yes, but part angel as well.

◇

The thing is, Pope was right. The human needed to be understood first. Even in Pope's time, that had stood out as a philosophical truth. In my own time, the enigma had transcended philosophy, even art. Understanding ourselves wasn't just a matter of philosophy anymore, not since Hiroshima. It was now a matter of survival.

The bomb changed everything. For the first time, we had the ability not only to destroy one another but to destroy all of us at the same time. One miscalculation, one push of the button, one drunken Russian soldier with a firing key, one mad patriot American in a silo in South Dakota, one American president with a sudden blood clot in his left prefrontal lobe was all that was needed. Sure, there were safety procedures, but behind the procedures were a lot of very human people, and there is nothing whatsoever failsafe about the human animal or, for that matter, about anything the human animal builds.

When I was a child, my family lived for a time outside a Strategic Air Command dispersal base. The big, ponderous bombers took off over the town, struggling for altitude. When they passed over our house they were so low we could see the rivets in their skin. We knew what was inside: death. But not just death; hell's fire.

At school we were taught to duck and cover, though even we knew good and well that we were whistling past the graveyard. The joke developed that in case of a nuclear attack you should crawl under your desk, tuck your head between your legs, and kiss your ass good-bye. Mine was the first generation to come of age with the knowledge that the initial flash of a hydrogen bomb would burn your shadow into a brick wall while, at the same instant, gamma rays would poison all of your individual cells.

When I was in the second grade, it was said that humans could destroy the world in three hours. By the time I was in high school we had gotten better at it: With intercontinental ballistic missiles we could accomplish the task in fifteen minutes. By the late 1960s we had even found a way to raise the ante. To nuclear holocaust we had added environmental destruction. It wasn't clear which we were going to do first: Fry ourselves with hydrogen bombs or poison ourselves with our own waste. I wouldn't be at all surprised if historians looked back on us children of the cold war and observed that our legitimate fears often gave birth to outright phobias. Madness begets madness.

Whatever the historians of the future will decide, by 1970 it had become commonplace to say that the science of physics and chemistry had gotten too far ahead of the science (if science it was) of psychology. We thought of ourselves as logical and rational, but we also knew, thanks to Freud and Jung, that there was an unconscious, and that what floated beneath the surface often dramatically influenced how we used our conscious minds. This in itself was disorienting because, by definition, we didn't even know we were being influenced.

Somehow, we had to figure out what lurked in the depths of the human psyche, and how to exercise more control over it.

Otherwise, the only creature with a future would be the cockroach.

Around this time a third terror was added: The dream world of drugs that the flower children had been so eager to explore had turned on them, devastating not only the inner cities but the suburbs as well.

These three terrors—nuclear holocaust, environmental madness, and rampant drug addiction—made brain research a national priority. Neuroscience research budgets, which were almost nonexistent before, became larger. There were grants, now, to study the physical nature of the mind and, in particular, the causes and effects of addiction. It wasn't a lot of money, compared to other fields of research, but it was a significant increase and it made a difference. Drug addiction research was particularly hot, because drugs, after all, were molecules that affected the mind, which in itself was molecular in nature. The therapeutic uses for knowledge about these chemicals were obvious even to outsiders. The popularity of recreational drugs almost forced us to put the question of who we were in chemical terms.

But chemistry and psychology weren't the only fields to benefit. As an unintended consequence, the whole spectrum of human sciences was energized.

This was good, and this was bad. The public's understanding of psychology had often led to improvements—for example, in management practices. But it could also lead to some damning distortions. You could describe the history of civilization in terms of how each era defined the human mind—or, more correctly, misdefined it.

Darwin, a dog fancier, had observed that behavioral traits could be passed from generation to generation; with a savvy enough breeder, dogs could be deliberately engineered to exhibit certain behaviors. The same was true of other animals. This fragment of truth, half understood by amateurs, played directly into the false dichotomy of nature-nurture. Darwin's rich cousin Sir Francis Galton took it up to argue persuasively that it was time to undertake the scientifically controlled breeding of humans. We would be shirking our duty, he said, if we bred better dogs and horses but didn't extend the same courtesy to our fellow humans.

This seemed so logical that it took the world by storm. In the first part of the twentieth century, those who accepted that behavioral traits including intelligence could be inherited would produce eugenics. Germany carried the premise to its natural conclusion: A nation could grow powerful by not only encouraging the fittest to breed but also eliminating the unfit—and never mind that "fitness" was totally undefined.

As eugenics fell into disrepute, the pendulum swung hard in the other direction. By the 1960s, nurture became the explanation for all human difficulties. Social engineering was the great new hope—a hope that, like eugenics, would turn ugly. Though most Americans didn't understand the fact, this new definition of the mind as infinitely malleable had already led Joseph Stalin to administer a bloodbath greater even than Hitler's.

Now, in the darkness of the cold war, out of necessity, the physical nature of the brain was being approached once more. This time, everyone hoped, we would be much more judicious in drawing conclusions. But, given the lessons of history, there were plenty of skeptics; every major discovery provoked a clamor in the media. The far right saw brain scientists as amoral and the left thought they were cryptofascists. At the 1974 meeting of the American Association for the Advancement of Science, in Philadelphia, brain scientists were pelted with rotten eggs. Edward O. Wilson, who would later write the Pulitzer Prize–winning book *On Human Nature*, was attacked on stage while giving a talk.

Spectacular science and roiling controversy. Wherever human idiocy manifests itself, morticians and reporters are there to benefit.

◇

As I hung around with brain scientists, anthropologists, philosophers, and the like, I slowly absorbed their basic supposition about the human dilemma. Human angst, however complex in its expression, could be traced directly back to a singular event: the explosive growth of the human brain. This was so obvious that the scientists rarely even talked about it, but it shaped their thoughts and guided their experiments.

The primate brain began its steady expansion a long time ago, but beginning about a million years ago the pace of growth increased and proto-human primates raced ahead. Intelligence, otherwise defined as the ability to create a logical inner model of the outer world, was proving to have incredible utility. It upstaged tooth and claw, size and nastiness. This was a stunning moment in evolution. To model was to imagine, and imagination meant power. To imagine a new thing was the first step toward making the new thing happen.

Did we envy the saber-toothed tiger's big fangs? Then we imagined a substitute, and crafted spears. We didn't have fins, to move through water? We imagined ourselves up a hide-covered boat. We didn't have the ability to digest raw meat? We conjured up a fire. We saw it in the inside of our skulls, and then made it happen on the outside.

With the passage of time, the line between what we could imagine and what we could actually *do* grew more and more porous. The mind could observe the real world and, in a sense, bring it inside. It could cogitate on that world, and then take the result outside again and see what happened. Then it could bring the world back inside and cogitate some more. The endless loop of imagination and experimentation was more powerful than anything that had ever appeared on earth.

This was not precisely a difference in kind. The wolf, for instance, could clearly imagine eating the thing it chased. A small thing, but necessary to the survival of the wolf. But in humans the ability to imagine grew both in power and scale. Our imaginings roamed much further, escaping the bounds of our immediate ecology. Imagination led to success, and success encouraged more imagination. A bigger brain was so powerful that, at some critical point, it could only keep getting bigger. As it did, our spear points got sharper, our pottery more colorful, our needles finer. By the end of the last ice age we were on the threshold of possessing what, in the animal kingdom, was indistinguishable from magic.

But for every advantage there was a disadvantage. The cutting edge of the new mind was logic, and logic can only reach its maximum efficiency in the absence of strong emotion or physical imperatives. Marshall Rennels, the neuroanatomist who discovered how spinal fluids are pumped into the brain, was fond of telling me that some mental operations were mutually incompatible. If you don't think so, try to do even simple arithmetic with a full bladder. Basic needs take precedence, and basic emotional needs are no less compelling than physical ones.

In other words, to get the most out of our newfound smarts we had to also evolve the means to step back and detach ourselves from our own seething emotions. Detachment increased imagination.

But how could an animal like us evolve the ability to step back and be cool? The answers could be seen in the architecture of the brain. As the brain became larger, filters and partitions evolved to barricade off different parts so that they didn't interfere with one another. Emotions still ruled, most of the time, but in a crisis we could set them aside, grow cold, focus our minds, and act on the pure reality in front of us. At least, some of us could.

Achieving such cold detachment was and always will be difficult for humans. One need only look around, glance at the headlines, to see the problem. When we are seized by fear or desire, we lose our ability to evaluate reality. We don't see what is there, we see what we *want* to see, or what we think *ought* to be there, or what we are *afraid* might be there. The result is the miseries of life, from lost love to squandered finances to senseless war.

Those nightmares loom large, so large that we sometimes forget the strengths that do not make the headlines. Few of us lack the ability, at least on some rare occasions, to stop and rethink our situation in cold terms. Some of us do so frequently. Some of us can even do it on command, especially in our own fields of expertise. This is the human salvation.

Those individuals who weren't blinded by the emotions of the moment, who were most able to remain detached, were the ones who contributed most to the survival of the species. Cool heads could sometimes prevent disasters. When they couldn't, they were there to pick up the pieces and nurse the wounded. We might only have such wisdom at certain moments of our lives, but we were capable of it. That was the point. We were capable. Our evolutionary competition was not. So the ability to be cool and think was an evolutionary strength, imparted to us by those internal barriers and filters. We could partition our lives. It was a new advantage on the planet, and it brought our ancestors power.

But as always there was a dark side. Our minds, in order to grow, became increasingly estranged from our feelings. An uneasy partnership developed between the cognate self, on the one hand, and our emotional and instinctive forces on the other. We needed each other, the mind and the . . . the heart? The soul? Somebody had to be boss, and in this new world that would, increasingly, be the somebody with the smarts.

Or would it be the one with the truest emotions? Thinking was always risky, because it led to doing things differently. The heart, on the other hand, spoke the language of a billion years' experience on this planet.

The result of this conflict was the modern psyche, a battle-field between instinct and knowledge, emotion and thought. Increasingly we possessed the ability to control the world, but not ourselves. We could look outward, but it was very difficult to look inward. Inside, we boiled with Faustian conflict. We had become two separate creatures who did not understand and could not communicate with one another, a single animal divided against itself. We had won a great evolutionary victory, but the price had been eternal self-estrangement.

◇

In our archaeological attempts to untangle our mind's evolutionary history, we have been at a great disadvantage. The living brain is a goo the consistency of Jell-O, and in death it doesn't last long. Some human brains have been found pickled in acid bogs, but they only take us back a thousand years or so. With respect to earlier brain development, we can only hope to deduce what happened by contemplating the empty skulls of our forebears and filling them with our own inferences and speculations.

No matter how we approach it, the enigma keeps coming back to something that happened at the end of the last ice age . . . and that *something* changed everything. Before then, the human animal was certainly a successful beast, but it was still a beast among beasts. Men and women, while predators, had cause to fear predators themselves. Human populations grew, probably, but they never reached the numbers that would enable them to rule the earth. If they left a mark on their environment, that mark was subtle.

And then, twelve thousand years ago, the accumulated changes in the human brain somehow achieved criticality. Human populations exploded. Tool use increased exponentially. Agriculture did not appear instantly, but it became inevitable. For no known reason, the human animal transcended itself and, fully modern, walked out of the mists of the dying ice age—inheritor of the earth, master of all it surveyed.

Twelve thousand years. If there was a magical number in the science of the human species, that was it. Again and again, it drew me back to the picture of the old man and the puppy in the grave. That man had been there, a living part of it. If only those bones could talk.

CHAPTER THREE

That our minds and our hearts are at odds is not exactly news. We know that, but the knowledge isn't really useful to us. We know it in the way we know that the red giant star Antares is some 300 trillion miles away—all the while not having a clue as to what "300 trillion miles" really means. There is a vast difference between knowing and *knowing*, a difference that amounted to yet another iteration of the human enigma.

Charlie brought this home to me. He had a certain measure of intelligence, but not so much as to cause him much conflict. He had his feelings, and the certainty of them . . . and that was enough. He was a dog in full, and that meant full of the joy and life that always seemed just beyond the reach of everyday human beings. He knew about death, because he'd seen animals die, but it didn't preoccupy him. He had dreams—I could tell from his occasional somnolent snarls, yelps, and running motions. He could be fascinated, but I saw no awe. He seemed incapable of boredom.

He didn't have the equipment to comprehend the unutterable complexity and coldness of the universe.

He nevertheless insisted on running things, or trying to. I needed to focus, and he needed to be petted. I got a paw on my keyboard. I needed to decode a scientific paper, and he wanted to chase squirrels. What is so important, he seemed to ask, above a molecule we can't see on a cell we can't smell? . . . Why worry about such things when the squirrels have come down out of their trees and badly need to be chased up again?

He gave it no rest, even at night. I'd lie there trying to force an anthropological question into my pre-sleep hypnotic period, and Charlie'd come creeping in. *Who was he, and what was he doing there?*

So he was in my face and yet somehow elusive, like the dog in the old man's grave. That puppy was as anomalous in that pit as Charlie was in my own life. There was simply no reason for either to be where they were.

The more I watched people and their dogs, the less certain I was of any of this. At best, dogs play marginal parts in the great human scheme of things, yet they seem totally integrated. There was certainly nothing marginal in the rapport between Lynn and Charlie. Each got total response from the other. Watching closely, I could see that they were reading one another's slightest movements. The two animals, human and canid, sometimes seemed to be part of the same computer network. The bond was difficult to ignore. The dog was more than just "there," and his presence had visceral power.

In the photograph of the old man in the grave, which by now had been etched into my mind, I could see the old man's skeletal hand reaching out for the puppy. What was it about that gesture that touched me? Why were their corpses arranged that way, man and dog? Were they trying to reach across the millennia and tell us something? And if so, what? Anyway, the puppy in the grave might not even have been a puppy; it might have been a wolf cub. According to the accompanying article, it was impossible to tell the two apart when all you had was an immature bunch of bones. So why did I keep thinking of the animal as a puppy? Why did it seem to belong there?

In an orderly universe, everything has a place; there should be no anomalies. Journalists, like detectives and scientists, *have* to think that. They cannot afford to believe in coincidences. You have to take as your first article of faith that the universe somehow makes sense, in toto. Things connect because they have to. Albert Einstein himself refused to believe that God threw dice. In other words, if the universe doesn't seem to make sense, it is foolish to blame the universe. The fault is in yourself. You just aren't looking at your subject clearly enough, or from the correct perspective. That prime assumption is the bedrock of civilization.

So what would Einstein do if he were the one whose dreams were being invaded by a long-dead pile of bones? It came to me late one night. Of course: Einstein would say that the way to silence an intellectual ghost is to shine a light on it, learn about it. Knowledge is the silver bullet. There has to be at least some small amount of sense in it, whatever it is. Find out what the reality is, however marginal it might be. Things that make sense can't haunt you.

All right, then. I'd go to the library.

◇

It must be understood, to further my story, that libraries are holy places. In a world dominated by knowledge they are temples and, as temples should, they strike a chord deep in our hearts. Visitors to libraries, like visitors to great cathedrals, converse (if they dare to converse at all) in hushed voices. Our mothers taught us to behave that way, ostensibly to avoid disturbing the intellectual labors of others. But the subtext was clear. Lowered voices are the universal human symbol of awe, respect and no small amount of fear.

Walk into a big university's library and it is all there, man's relentless and compulsive study of history and politics, sociology and psychology, anthropology and religion, art and philosophy. Such a library contains our accumulated knowledge about who we are and where we come from and what we might be doing here, what we *could* be doing here, all arranged neatly, thousands upon thousands of titles, carefully coded and cross-referenced, interwoven by footnote and appendix, summing up whole lifetimes of intellectual labor, the fruits of that labor as gossamer as the motes of dust that hang in the shafts of sunlight emanating from the high windows. Yet in another sense, our knowledge is not gossamer at all. It has a substance. It is our cultural foundation, rock solid, unyielding, and enduring as the civilization itself. It is the written legend of man, the sum of our hopes, dreams, fears, and visions.

Of course, on this particular day I had arrived at the library to look up not man but dog.

By then I had left Baltimore and was teaching at Oregon State University, where, luckily for me, there is a veterinary school. I assumed that the library would include the last word on the dog, its origins, its domestication, and its strange place in the human scheme of things. Given that, I was surprised that my subject matter was so difficult to find. To get to the shelf that held the complete knowledge of the dog found in print, you had to get a map from the librarian. You went up an elevator, down a long hallway, hooked a left and a quick right . . . and then, if you hadn't gotten lost, there was a short run of shelves on one side of the aisle devoted, at least technically, to the creature of my interest.

I say "at least technically" because a quick scan of the titles revealed that most of the books about dogs were really about people who owned them and what they could do with them. By far the biggest category was of books involving dog pedigrees. Then there were books on dog training, from beginning dumb dog tricks to training dogs to hunt, to fight, and to sniff out explosives or drugs. Some of the more promising works included a few generalized remarks about the development of the dog; they all sounded the same, and had a "just so" tone to them.

I browsed both sides of the dog book shelves and found a small section on the domestication of wild animals. This seemed closer to the mark, but it only took a few minutes to learn that the books didn't have much to say about the dog in particular. They seemed to lump the domestication of the wolf in with the domestication of sheep, goats, horses, and other livestock. One size fit all.

Wolves got even shorter shrift—maybe four feet of shelf. I leafed through a few books. They all seemed to begin and end with the same lament: The wolf had been cruelly used and willfully misunderstood. It had been reviled as man's most fundamental enemy. It had been hunted and trapped and shot for sport. It had been stuffed and made into coats and muffs.

I picked some books from the wolf section and some from the domestication section, and added a veterinary handbook on the anatomy of the dog. According to their check-out stamps, the books I was most interested in hadn't been checked out for years, so I didn't feel guilty when I scooped them all into my canvas bags.

That, then, was my work for the next week. At home I stacked the books in my office and, as time permitted, went through them one by one. Most were superficial, showed some obvious misunderstanding of biology, or were otherwise unsuitable; those went back into the canvas bags. Then I got down to serious work.

◇

There seemed to be two ways of thinking about the domestication of the dog: the old and the new. The old version of the story said, basically, that early humans captured wolf cubs, raised them, tamed them, and eventually produced dogs; they did the same thing, more or less, with immature sheep, goats, and pigs. This seemed straightforward enough, and had been the last word on the subject for a hundred years and more.

But more recently that explanation had begun to show holes and improbabilities. For one thing, how did an animal like *Homo sapiens* even get the idea of enslaving animals? Early humans didn't see anything remotely like domestication in the world around them. They had nothing to emulate. They were also wanderers, and before they had beasts of burden they traveled light by necessity. Nor would it have been a simple matter to kidnap a wolf cub: To get to the cub, you would first have to go through mama wolf. If mama wolf was sick or dead, and the humans found themselves in possession of a cub, well . . . they probably thought it was delicious.

Besides, a tame wolf is not the same as a dog. As the environmental movement of the 1970s and 1980s romanticized the wolf, a lot of people tried raising them, with bad results. A wolf cub, raised with the constant companionship of humans, treated kindly and fed well, grew up to be . . . a wolf. It had little of the playfulness of the dog and no special sense of kinship with humans. It'd eat what it was fed, but it was standoffish, and the number of such experiments declined sharply after "tame" wolves attacked and seriously wounded the humans who'd thought themselves the masters. Half-wolf and half-dog combinations were also tried, and if the result seemed a little better, the half-wolf was still quite dangerous.

The environmental movement changed our perspective on a lot of things and, in the process, led to an era rich in discovery.

It did not, however, contribute much to our knowledge of the evolution of the dog. For one thing, the just-so story was tenacious. It was easily remembered, perfect for telling a child, and, anyway, people didn't really care very much. All that mattered to most people was the dog was there. Why didn't that suffice for me?

By the 1980s, most of the handful of experts on dog evolution had abandoned the capture-and-tame line; domestication was more complicated. A few good theories were beginning to pop up about the goat and the pig, but they didn't fit the dog. The dog was more elusive. I was beginning to understand that, by some unknown and mysterious principle, the dog was *always* more elusive.

It seemed to me that the answer was going to be something mindless, not a product of human intent but of environment . . . that, and chance. Wind and water and scorching sand and great frozen ice fields. Two very dissimilar animals, wandering through time, somehow deflected by some sort of ecological gravity and spinning into one another's orbit.

But that was philosophy and wool-gathering, not science. It couldn't be tested. If it was to be accepted, it had to be accepted on the strength of its logic, and my logic had more holes than a Wiffle Ball. What was the timetable? What were the molecular genetics of the change? What applied the force that drove the two together and why did the new animal become . . . a poodle?

Anyway, I was beginning to wonder whether the more pertinent question was why nobody seemed to care.

By this time I knew that dog evolution was among the most stagnant of scientific backwaters. For a hundred years and more, the matter of domesticated animals had not seemed particularly promising and had not attracted the brightest minds. Why would a promising young scientist go where the money most obviously was not? You would have to be stupid . . . stupid, or some kind of dreamer.

In any case, there wasn't much money for studying this kind of stuff, and the fact might be disappointing to scientists, but it wasn't entirely unreasonable. People were dying of cancer and other diseases. Society needed money for welfare, for roads, to maintain a military and a police force. How, then, did archaeologists talk the government into forking over big bucks to study dogs? Simply put, they didn't.

But the lack of money also went to a deeper truth. Like me, most of us are interested in people, not animals—and archaeologists are people like the rest of us. While excavating, they often come across the bones of household animals. In fact, the average excavation produces many more animal bones than human. The animal bones are naturally considered junk—archaeological static, nothing more. Scientists discard them with the other detritus.

I heard one story about a team in Southeast Asia, I think it was, that resolved to keep the animal bones. Who knew, they might be fodder for the next year's crop of graduate students. The archaeologists separated out the animal bones and threw them in boxes. Their hearts were in the right place but as space got cramped in the specimen tent, they hauled their animal bones out to the supplies storage area. The cook found them there, assumed they were garbage, and threw them away. Nothing is so difficult to change as a habit of mind.

In the little bit of significant or pertinent material I could find, there was one name I kept running across in the footnotes: Dr. Stanley Olsen. He seemed to be the acknowledged authority on dog evolution and had written a book entitled *The Origins of the Domestic Dog: The Fossil Record*, published in 1974. I gathered it was *the* book, so I set out to lay my hands on a copy. The university library didn't have it, but the librarian assured me that she could get one.

She called me two weeks later, exasperated. She'd looked everywhere she knew to look, and she couldn't find it. She could only conclude that the book didn't exist anymore, anywhere.

But it was out there, somewhere; it had to be. I trusted the librarian, but all the same I called around myself. I tried really improbable places, such as the U.S. Defense Department library and the National Agricultural Library, but I didn't do any better than the librarian had. With each day that went by this whole accursed quest was beginning to remind me of an investigative reporting job. Finally, not believing what the computerized catalog told me, I got someone at the Library of Congress on the phone. No luck, he said. They'd had a copy, of course, at one time, but . . .

Then came some mumbo jumbo about space and how the mission of the Library of Congress was to serve U.S. representatives and senators. Why would someone in Congress be interested in dogs?

Good question. It suggested an even more uncomfortable question: Why was I interested?

By this time I was intrigued not so much by what I'd discovered, which was precious little, but by the difficulty of discovering it. Why did archaeologists ignore the dog, which was directly related to human evolution, while spending their time and energy on dinosaurs, ancient clams, and Pre-Cambrian sponges? How could an animal be everywhere, and yet go almost completely unnoticed by the very people whose job it was to notice things?

My reportorial antennae started twitching. There was something wrong with this picture. I had the spooky feeling that there was something hidden in plain sight—that I was looking right at it and not seeing it.

◇

Again, being a reporter is a lot like being a detective. You do the little things and have faith that at some point the big things will fall into place. Always assuming you live long enough. So I plodded on.

Eventually I found an outfit at the University of Michigan that was pioneering the on-demand reproduction of rare books. I called them. We haggled, and I sent them a check. In due time my mailbox yielded up a very thin little volume of copied and bound pages. Olsen's book. Finally!

I tore open the package like it was a Christmas present. It was just what I'd wanted; the book was packed full of detail. There were comparison drawings of dog and wolf skulls, boxes of statistics, data, data, data. Unfortunately, none of the material made much sense to me. It was too technical. To really under-stand it, you'd need to have the background and context—a qual-ification limited, I'd wager, to a hundred people, worldwide.

I tried anyway. I read Olsen's book several times, and eventu-ally some parts almost made sense on their own. Some passages I could figure out, sort of, with the aid of a technical dictionary and a lot of rereading. I understood that the dog was clearly de-scended from the gray wolf, and that the wolf had its origins in an ur-carnivore that lived some fifty million years ago. In its present form, the gray wolf had been around for at least fifteen million years. Humankind, by comparison, was a Johnny-come-lately.

I didn't feel comfortable, though, even with what I thought I understood. As a science writer I'd learned to distrust my own reading of scientific literature. I have seen too many fellow sci-ence writers get into trouble by misinterpreting something, or putting the emphasis in the wrong place, or failing to get the larger point. Scientists, when they write, write for the people who know the terrain, and that definitely didn't include me. My habit was to view scientific literature as a means to help me frame questions. Then I could bring those questions to the sci-entist in person, do some flattering and maybe some begging, and get the story in English.

Stanley Olsen was at the University of Arizona in Tucson, or at least he had been when he published his book. I looked him up, and yes! He was still there, alive and working.

At the moment of this particular discovery I was sitting in a dreary second-floor office at Oregon State University. It was midwinter in the Pacific Northwest. Classes had just broken, and students in slickers were making their way across campus, emerging from the foggy drizzle and then, a few moments later, disappearing into it again. Water accumulated on the battlements above me and fell onto the copper roof of an entryway below. The steady *ping, ping, ping* of those drops was so much a part of my existence that I often didn't even hear it. In Oregon, they say, you don't tan, you rust.

There was a sun beyond those cloud banks, though. I remembered seeing it once, though that seemed a lifetime ago.

Tucson, eh? I picked up the phone.

A few days later, I was walking down the main street of the University of Arizona, flanked by palm trees, basking in the almost too-warm sunshine.

At the university's natural history museum, a woman at the reception desk directed me to the top floor. That turned out to be the stage area, and I immediately got lost in the backstage of the scientific mind. I threaded my way through shields, spears, prehistoric animal skeletons, partly assembled displays, and old packing crates that smelled of far-off lands. I wandered into a canyon cut beneath two cliffs of books, then down what seemed to be a through path but that dead-ended in a small room stacked high with Pacific Northwest Indian artifacts. I finally resorted to shouting for help. Dr. Olsen responded, and his voice guided me through the maze and into a cubicle he'd fenced off with half-wall partitions near a bank of open windows. It was bright in his makeshift office, with a view of palm trees.

Olsen was a squat, muscular man who belied the stereotype of professor or scientist. His bare arms were covered with tattoos which, I would discover in due time, testified to his days in the merchant marine during World War II. His face was wrinkled and weatherbeaten and his desk was as exotically cluttered as the rest of the museum workspace. He stood up to greet me, putting what appeared to be a mammoth tooth on top of his papers so they wouldn't be scattered by the warm breeze that came in through the windows. In a few moments I had my tape recorder running.

Olsen started studying paleontology in 1945. Ultimately, he spent twelve years at the museum of comparative zoology at Harvard. He was among the first to start thinking in modern terms about the environment as a mold. That led to the question of interactions between animals and humans at the dawn of the Holocene.

The world's top zoologists travel through Harvard, either as faculty or frequent visitors. As a young scientist, Olsen had the best of the best at his disposal and so he made use of them. He went from scientist to scientist, asking for their thoughts on the association of animals and premodern people. He was shocked not only by how little they knew, but how little they cared.

"I had to make friends with them, wheedle the information out of them," he told me. "People didn't have the background and they were divided by discipline. Generally, archaeologists didn't know much about zoology, and focused entirely on human skeletons. Zoologists didn't know much about archaeology, and focused only on the animals. Nobody was putting the two together."

He could have been discouraged, but he saw the situation in another light: A whole area of study was there for the taking. He and his friend and fellow student Paul Palmerly talked about it in late-night discussions, enthusiastic about the opportunity to break truly new ground. All they had to do, really, was to apply archaeological thinking to environmental issues—and the environment of early humans was heavily influenced by the other animals around them.

As a rule, every beginning zoologist specializes in some animal; this is the only way to get a dissertation approved. Olsen figured he'd go for something that had been domesticated—the horse, the pig, the rabbit, something like that. On the list he made, the animal that stuck out was the dog.

What creature, Olsen reasoned, was found in closer proximity to the human species than the dog? What creature was closer to the human heart? What creature was likely to have been more important to human evolution and development? The more he thought about it, the more the dog seemed like a gold mine.

That had been decades ago; by the time I spoke with him, Olsen was an older and wiser man.

As he thought about his own long-ago innocence, Olsen turned his chair around toward the windows and stared into the middle distance. His voice took on a wry tone.

He thought there'd be a lot of interest in research on dog origins. After all, humans loved dogs, right? But that love, apparently, didn't extend to the people who studied them. Grants were hard to get, and they didn't get any easier even after Olsen had established himself as a founder of zooarchaeology. If he'd had any sense, he said, he'd have switched fields when he'd had the chance. But by that time the dog already had him hooked.

As he sat in his breezy office, Olsen reminisced about a life spent traveling from site to site on tramp steamers and hitching rides on trucks and ox carts. For years he and Palmerly slept in culverts and under the stars, looking for fossil dogs that, he hoped, would lead him to the origins of *Canis familiaris*.

The two researchers framed their strategy in what they knew about the ecology and climatology of the last ice age, when a significant proportion of the planet's water was trapped in the glaciers. The air in the middle latitudes dried up, while in the north, just beneath the shadow of the glaciers, green plains and forests supported mammoths, giant deer, and great herds of caribou. Carnivores like the lion, the saber-toothed tiger, the gray wolf, and that newcomer to the meat-eating world, *Homo sapiens,* followed the herds. That zone, then, was the place to look for dog fossils.

In Dr. Olsen's reasoning, there had probably always been an association of some sort between wolves and early humans. After all, they occupied the same geography and both species ran in packs, a mode of life somewhat unusual for predators. Meat-eaters tend to need a lot of territory to keep them in protein, so they usually evolve into solitary animals. From hawks to tigers, most species hunt more or less alone.

Was Olsen suggesting, I asked, that therefore these two species of pack carnivore had some deep and inchoate affinity for one another? Dr. Olsen turned away from the window and gazed at me for a long moment. Then he said, "Speculation."

What we know, he said—and he was very precise about it— is that there was a geographical proximity. Wolves and humans associated with one another, in some fashion. *Association* was the scientific word, he said rather sternly; *affinity* was a subjective matter, an issue of feelings. It was true that the mammalian brain evolved to govern by feelings, and that feelings were what guided all mammalian life. But love, fear, yearning . . . such things didn't fossilize, and as a scientist Olsen had to stick with what he knew for sure. Otherwise he would get lost in maybes. What Olsen knew for sure was that human bones and wolf bones were commonly found in the vicinity of one another at sites far older than modern humans.

He listed some of the sites on his fingers. At a dig near Box-grove, England, archaeologists excavating 400,000-year-old pre-human artifacts came across a number of wolf bones. A similar association was found at Zhoukoudian, in northern China, dating to about 300,000 years ago. But the most dramatic association was found in Lazaret Cave, near Nice in the south of France. There, some 150,000 years ago, early humans partitioned off the cave into what appear to have been separate living quarters and the entranceways to all the larger compartments were guarded by the skulls of wolves.

I asked the obvious question: What did that signify? By all estimates I knew, wolves and man had not at that point developed a close relationship. But did the findings at Lazaret Cave indicate the beginnings of one? Did such a precise arrangement of the skulls signify the development of wolf as totem? And if the pre-human animal was developing some fascination with the wolf, was the wolf also developing some fascination with the man?

Olsen refused to have an opinion. It would have been pure speculation, he said.

But the association, if nothing else, was solid.

"There were lots of places, I discovered, where dog bones were found in the process of archaeological digs. All over the world, in Iraq, wherever. But what came out in the research was two words: *dog remains.* That was it. They didn't tell you what kinds of dogs they were, long-legged, short-legged, a mastiff, whatever. Just *dog bones.* Most institutions didn't have any dog skeletons, so you couldn't even make comparisons."

It was both frustrating and unbelievable to Olsen. After all, these great museums had the bones of humans and most other animals, right down to bats and shrews. But the most familiar other animal of all was conspicuous by its absence. Olsen's work, like my own wanderings, had quickly come to be defined not by bones, but by the vacuum where those bones should have been.

Ultimately Olsen had to find his own modern dog skeletons and make his own measurements. What he found, after meticulously comparing bones, was that the dog had a shorter muzzle than the wolf. Always. The essence of "dogness," therefore, was a foreshortened muzzle. The transition between wolf and dog should be accompanied, at least hypothetically, by a rapid shortening of the canid nose.

Now *there* was something a scientist could work with. Wolf skulls fossilized well, and could be dug up and measured. So the quest for the short-nosed wolf became Olsen's guiding star. In the decades to come, he painstakingly collected canid skulls (both wolf and dog) and visited the few museums that collected them. Each skull was measured and charted, length of snout compared with size of head.

"Compared to wolves," he explained, "dogs will characteristically show a degree of difference in the proportions of their skull. Their dentition becomes weaker. Smaller teeth, shorter face. Because dogs don't have to do all the fighting that wolves do, they don't need the same battery of teeth.

"You do find short-faced wolves in the Russian collection and in the Alaskan collection, and they seem to turn up associated with human cultures—almost always, if not always, at mammoth kill sites. That's neat, because that means they were killed by a mammoth thrashing around, one who was able to kill a few dogs before it died . . . if they *were* dogs. My conclusion is that they'd been tamed to a degree that all of their skulls were affected. We call them 'tame wolves.'"

Over the decades, Olsen managed to push the date for the dog back to six thousand years before the present, then seven, and finally eight.

"And that," he said with a finality, "is as far as I've been able to go. There are those who say it goes farther, and they might be right, but they're guessing. Eight thousand years. That's what we know for sure."

Beyond that, he said, there are some foreshortened skulls in Alaska that might date back twelve thousand years, to judge by stratification—except that they were found in river gravel. River gravel gets churned up frequently, so depth doesn't necessarily correlate with age.

I asked the obvious question: "Carbon dating?"

He smiled wanly. "Do you know," he asked, "how much carbon dating costs?"

◇

Olsen had been right about zooarchaeology in general, though. The new generation of archaeologists didn't have much more interest in the dog than their predecessors had, but they did become increasingly interested in the other animals that shared the ancient world with humans. Like Olsen, they had the sense that the animal world would somehow, somewhere, yield a clue as to what transformed humans 12,000 years ago.

"The next generation became much more rigorous," Olsen said. "I started teaching students who were interested in doing more with the faunal material from sites. I started teaching classes. That's what I'm doing now. I have thirty-five students right here in this university who are interested in having this background . . . What do you do with the fauna? How do you know it's this and not that? What does this indicate as far as the culture? Why did the humans collect these animals and ignore others?"

At the height of the cold war, Olsen discovered that the institution with the most fossil material on dogs was on the other side of the bamboo curtain—in Beijing. Getting there was tricky, not to mention dangerous and illegal. Still, he persisted. He traveled third class across China, through Mongolia and Tibet, looking for dog fossils.

"It was exceedingly difficult," he remembered. His Scandinavian features earned him suspicions and cold stares from the people he had to depend on.

"You had all the bureaucracy and all that, but in the end the only way you got cooperation was you had to earn their trust. It had to be personal. It took most of my life to make the contacts I have in China, and I'm seventy-five."

Most of Olsen's research papers were published in small journals, and his book, as I had discovered, was so out of print as to be a fossil itself. He was fascinated by the fact I'd managed to get a photocopied version, and he wrote down the name and address of the company that had done it for me.

As for his lifetime of dog work, he'd finally and reluctantly written it off as a labor of love. He wasn't sure, looking back, exactly why he'd persisted. He'd seldom got any grant money, and when he did it wasn't enough.

Finally, I asked the obvious question. Did Olsen like dogs?

"Of course," he said. "People like dogs. Dogs are animals that everybody likes, for no reason, and I think dogs recognized early on that humans are built-in friends.

"I always treated my dogs as if they were members of my family, another child. Absolutely. My last dog . . . it was half malamute, half German shepherd. It had epilepsy, so I had to feed it three times a day three separate pills, nine pills a day. It lived to be fourteen. I was a captive during that time, you might say, because the dog wouldn't let anybody else but me do this.

"I was spending a lot of time in Russia at the time, doing zoology in Leningrad, looking at dogs. Once I had to cancel a trip to Russia—and it was hard to get permission back then, and I actually had the funds. But I couldn't get anyone I trusted to take care of my dog, so I had to cancel the trip."

His voice grew misty and distant. "Anubis was the dog's name. After the Egyptian god, the keeper of the dead. I called her Nubie. She was just a great dog, the best dog I ever had. In fact I haven't had the desire to get another dog since I lost her. She was just like my brother. My sister, I guess, since she was female.

"I truly like most dogs. I don't like most people. One difference is that you can trust a dog. Dog comes to you when you've come home, you've been gone for a while, it's tickled to death to see you. People act like that, there's something they're going to ask you for, mostly. A dog's honest.

"Nubie," he said softly, remembering.

Outside, the breeze swelled, tossing the palm trees.

"She died three years ago, and I miss her."

He sat there, staring across campus, as I packed my equipment. I was at the door before I realized I had forgotten to ask an obvious question. I stopped and turned back to him.

"What's your current project, Dr. Olsen?"

"Goats," he said. "I'm working on a grant to do fieldwork on goats."

"Goats?" I repeated, freezing at the door. "But you've been working on dogs for thirty years. Forty. You're the world's leading expert on the paleontology of dogs. Goats?"

He grimaced. "I can't get money for work on dogs. There's no interest in dogs. I'm tired of struggling with it. Nobody cares about dogs."

CHAPTER FOUR

All in all it had not been a successful trip. The Tucson sunshine had been nice, but by the time we flew into the massive Oregon cloudbanks en route to Eugene, I was glum. The dog was everywhere in human culture and had even invaded human language. Dogs were a multi-billion-dollar business. Yet the world's leading authority on the origins of the dog couldn't get a grant? Was nobody even remotely curious about where these creatures came from and what they were doing here? It was downright depressing. Even Charlie's ecstatic, tail-wagging welcome didn't do much to change the funk the trip had left me in.

Scientists generally think of journalists as sloppy thinkers, but we have our methods. Our speculations are a bit like scientific hypotheses—not biases, necessarily, just places to start. We try to ground our speculations in fact, the way detectives do. But our greatest strength is our ability to ask the outlandish question.

From the journalistic point of view, scientists often seem like very timid thinkers.

I suspect there is some utility in both perspectives, though in the long run, scientists are a lot less likely to make asses of themselves. With respect to dogs, however, there was something about the picture science had painted for us that was woefully inadequate.

We have an adage in journalism, and now I clung to it: *"Even when you learn nothing, that was still something you'd learned."*

I kept remembering those 150,000-year-old wolf skulls in Lazaret Cave, each skull placed next to an entrance to a room, as if to guard it. The scientists were correct: Given the vast stretches of time that had passed, the arrangement might have been coincidental; the skulls might have been shifted to where they are by natural forces of some kind. I had trouble imagining that, however. People are, after all, great arrangers of objects. Putting a wolf skull at the entrance to your cave apartment seemed like such a *human* thing to do. With a skull guarding your door, you might sleep better at night. People thought that way—at least some modern humans did. It was hard to imagine that our almost-human ancestors didn't have a similar turn of mind.

I was also having trouble accepting that man and dog didn't team up until eight thousand years ago, which is as far back as Olsen had gotten. Granted, the fossil evidence would take you no farther . . . still, I wasn't a scientist and wasn't required, as Olsen was, to leave it at that. The whole thing made my teeth itch. It didn't make evolutionary sense to me. Eight thousand years marked no significant ecological or geological boundary— certainly nothing so powerful as to create a new animal overnight.

I had only two hard facts to work with. One was that while dogs were everywhere one looked, humans gave them no serious notice—and, what's more, didn't see anything odd about this arrangement. It was as if we were deliberately ignoring dogs, and *that* is the kind of thing that catches the attention of psychiatrists. And, of course, science journalists.

The second hard fact was that the dog had descended from the wolf.

I had attempted to start with the dog and work backward, and I'd failed. Okay; I'd try it the other way, starting with the wolf and working forward to the dog. Find out how the wolf fit into the environment that became the womb of the human race.

I'd seen a wild wolf once. I was about sixteen then, hiking in the Manzano Mountains south of Albuquerque. I'd just come to a clearing when a gray wolf emerged from some brush on my left. It stopped for a moment when it saw me, then dashed across the clearing and disappeared. The whole encounter probably didn't take five seconds.

The thrill was tempered, however, with pity. My wolf was a big animal, but gaunt and scraggly. It had a distinctive limp and its gray hair seemed thin. I could see its ribs and there was some kind of scab or encrustation on its side. It looked like a straggler from a vanished time and, of course, it was. Even so, there was something magic and mysterious about it.

◇

In the days before DNA studies confirmed it, you could say with some certainty that the wolf and the dog were the same species, at least in the classic sense that they could interbreed. Not normally, and maybe not by preference, but they'd do it. The union would then produce viable cub-pups.

The fact that they shared the genus name *Canis* didn't mean there was any mistaking, say, a wolf for a poodle or a poodle for a Pekingese. But it did mean that whatever made the dog a dog almost certainly had its antecedents in the wolf. Therefore, if you knew enough about the wolf, and put that up against what you knew about the human, the relationship ought to become much clearer. That was my thinking, anyway.

By this time I had begun supplementing the slim pickings of the library with books I purchased myself. There were only a few published books on wolf behavior, and I bought them all. Over the coming months, as the Oregon rain came down and the fog swirled through the fir trees, I occasionally pulled a wolf book down and leafed through it.

As I'd observed in the library, the books all seemed to begin and end with the now familiar complaint about the human vendetta against the wolf. The very idea of the wolf, the human concept of wolfness, had been seized upon and remanufactured— wolves had been twisted and stretched, damned and praised, demonized and romanticized, transformed in whatever way might best serve the parochial beliefs of each successive time, place, and cultural schema.

Wolves were obviously a highly emotional subject for humans. They connected, somehow, to something deep in the human underbrain. Perhaps that's why I could so readily remember the one I'd seen so long ago in the Manzanos.

They were fun to read about, too.

The trouble with reading to the exclusion of most other activities was that, well, eventually you ended up in the doctor's office getting lecture 873 about how the body needs exercise. In my case, I was unfortunate enough to have Lynn along, and everywhere Lynn goes, she carries a notebook. She dutifully wrote down the doctor's directions. Back home, after the requisite amount of whining, I pulled on my rain gear and headed for the door.

Take the dog with you, Lynn called after me.

So it was that, with Charlie as my guide, I proceeded to discover the rainforest.

◇

There is something wistfully primordial about the rainforests of the Oregon Coast Range. The mountains themselves are brand-new, as geology goes. They were created as the westward-moving continent collided with a volcanic island chain, proba-bly something like Hawaii. The Coast Range is the crumpled remains of those islands, created under the sea and then shoved up to be sculpted, these last fifteen million years or so, by water from the sky.

The water came from where all water ultimately comes from, which is the ocean. In Oregon, the water cycle is unusually straightforward. The winter weather pattern over the northern Pacific creates waves of moisture-laden air that wash against the land as incessantly as the waves of the sea itself. The wet air, cooling as it rises over the low Coast Range, precipitates out in a thousand kinds of rain, ranging from a sort of settling fog, through drizzle and light rain, and finally the occasional frog-choker. Someone had told me when I took the job at the state university that it only rained once a year in Oregon, and this was mostly true. The rain started in September and ended, if you were lucky, in May.

Outsiders know mostly the Oregon summers, when the clouds vanish and the air takes on the crystalline quality of Santa Fe or Taos. But the Oregon rains define the place. According to the late Ken Kesey, who wrote *Sometimes a Great Notion* and occasionally taught at the University of Oregon, the gloom ulti-mately shapes the minds of Oregonians. It made the settlers who came from New England even more dour than they were to begin with. As history unfolded, it then worked its reverse magic on the periodic tide of newcomers, including postwar southern-ers fleeing Reconstruction, Okies running from drought and dust, and house-rich Californians hoping to capitalize on Oregon's cheap living. All of them were shaped, eventually, by the damp gloom of Oregon's climate.

But if the ecology of the region creates sour people—I'm not making this up, Oregonians brag about it—that fact exists in sharp contrast to the scenery. The rains produce what seems like a shockingly lush landscape. The mountains are green beyond green as the vegetation strives to sop up every bit of solar energy that penetrates the fog and to make the very most of the blue-skied summers. And the forests teem with striking and exotic life forms, from humongous beetles to the aptly named banana slug, which is often referred to as a "crawling dog turd."

I probably wouldn't have noticed nearly as much if Charlie hadn't brought his discoveries to my attention by coming to a point and holding it until I looked where his nose was aimed.

As the months passed, and we walked together in the foggy forest, he showed me a strange little snake that had a fake head on the tip of its tail, and a string of territory-defining bobcat pawprints along with their signature of scrapes in the muddy clay. I was surprised by how many salamanders and the like lived in the trickling little streams. I also discovered something about Charlie. While he would put almost anything in his mouth, including coyote droppings, he drew the line at the banana slug.

Behind the beauty, though, life is hard in the rainforest, incredibly so. The harshness of the environment, in fact, is the reason for all the unusual plants and animals. They've had to develop extreme mechanisms to survive.

It all goes back to the water and the rock. The lava that had composed the defunct island chain was of a type that weathered into clayey mud that served best to glom onto your boots. In the summer the mud dries and cracks like a Dust Bowl lake bottom and in the winter it absorbs the water and transmits it downward, dissolving and carrying with it what few nutrients are available. As a result, the northwestern rainforest is a place of silent herbaceous desperation, an environment that pits plant against plant and forces evolution to accelerate, producing a bewildering variety of flora especially adapted to extract nutrients from miserly soil or steal them from other plants.

The beautiful Douglas fir trees, for example, are plentiful for the simple reason that they, almost alone among trees, are adapted to survive a climate that swings between nine-month monsoons and three-month summer droughts. Like the wheat that grows in Oklahoma and Kansas, the Douglas fir has a tap-root that goes all the way down to the water table.

As Charlie and I explored the forests, I was particularly struck by the strange lichens that hung from the white oaks and, in the winter, seemed to give the trees a sickly gray-green foliage. One variety of this stuff looked to me like a staghorn fern. One day, I pulled off a sample and took it to the university's botany department, where a woman in a lab coat recognized it instantly as *Lobaria pulmonaria*.

She told me it was a particularly strange product of evolution. Most lichens consist of two symbiotic life forms, a fungus and a blue-green alga, but *Lobaria pulmonaria* has a third partner, cyanobacteria. All three had branched off from some primitive predecessor; then, over millions of years, the harsh environment fused them again into a mishmash that—like the piece I'd brought to her lab—appears to be a single entity.

The community of cells that makes up the tissue of *Lobaria pulmonaria* comes close to being a perfectly closed system. Each partner thrives on the byproducts of the others. The alga soaks up the sun and excretes sugar. Then the cyanobacterium eats the sugar and excretes a variety of nitrogen compounds. The fungus eats the output of both other partners and provides, among other things, a sheltering outer skin. From any perspective, *Lobaria pulmonaria* is a lot of things—including an object lesson in evolutionary biology.

Symbiosis is a wonderful and fascinating force in the natural world, but it is not very obvious. In the generations following Darwin's great synthesis, people had been more interested in the way species split apart—in how one species divided, with the passing millennia, into two and so on, until we got the biological cacophony that covers the surface of the earth today. That view of evolution is valid enough, but inadequate. A century later, having developed the instruments and the insight to understand life at a deeper level, we discovered that schism is only half the evolutionary story. The other half is symbiosis. Things break apart. Things come together.

As a child, I was taught that symbiosis is fairly rare—a curiosity for children's books. The standard example was the pilot fish, which swims in front of sharks and acts as a sort of guide for its mentally deficient partner. The pilot fish eats bits and pieces of whatever the shark eats and, for its part, the shark declines to eat the pilot fish. One of the more fascinating wrinkles of this is that the symbiosis of the shark and the pilot fish, unlike that of the lichen, has a behavioral component. Using the example of *Lobaria pulmonaria*, one can see that the bodies of two (or more) lifeforms can be symbiotic without sharing a body. This is a symbiosis of behavior, of mind.

The shark and the pilot fish were such a sterling example of symbiosis that I was very disappointed when, as an adult, I discovered that the whole thing was nonsense. Pilot fish aren't "pilots" at all; they are parasites, pure and simple. The sharks don't benefit from the association, and they certainly don't *like* the pilot fish. I'd lost my favorite example of the mysterious process of symbiosis.

But by then we were finding plenty of other examples of behavioral symbiosis. Certain "cleaner fish," for example, inhabit corals and eat the parasites off the skin and gills of big fish like groupers. They only come out, though, when the big fish exhibits certain behaviors that seem to promise that the big fish won't eat the cleaners. It is more complicated than the pilot fish story, but the result is the same.

So nature is red of tooth and claw, yes, but if it suits her whim she can also be cuddly and cooperative. The great Darwinian engine pulls things apart and then slams them back together again with wild abandon, as if to see what will stick and what won't.

As scientists figured out how and where to look, they found

examples of symbiosis everywhere they turned. Most surprisingly, a symbiotic fusion event was found to lie at the very center of animal metabolism.

When compared with the cells of less organized creatures, like sponges and alga colonies, those of vertebrates are especially efficient. The secret of that animal energy turned out to be tiny organlike structures called mitochondria, highly adapted metabolic refineries that inhabit all animal cells. They turn glucose, the biological equivalent of crude oil, into adenotriphosphate, or ATP, which is the gasoline of the cell. But mitochondria, as critical as they are, turn out not to be merely parts of the cell. They are separate life forms.

That was a big, breaking story in the '60s and '70s. At some point, probably a billion years ago, the ancestral mitochondrion, most likely a bacterium, invaded a cell. Like many viruses and very small bacteria, at first it was just a visitor. It happened to be a welcome visitor, because it had the capacity to turn glucose into ATP, the fuel of the cell, in a more efficient manner, presumably, than the cell's own refineries. As time passed, and the inevitable mutations damaged the cell's natural but less efficient power-producing machinery . . . it didn't matter. The mitochondria stepped in and made up the difference. Over vast stretches of time, the cells lost more and more of their ability to survive on their own. The mitochondria, in the meantime, lost the ability to do much of anything *besides* make energy: All their other needs were met by the host cell. At some point in the remote past, when the sea was still a fermenting soup of life, animal cells and mitochondria fused forever. If one ever dies or mutates, the other is a goner as well.

It tells you a lot about life and evolution to think about how the mitochondria moved in and made themselves at home, thus creating a more perfect metabolism. Symbiosis is turning out to be a common story. Human beings may be as much a product of accretion as we are of mutation and natural selection.

The story of the mitochondrion repeated itself in plants, with an invasion by some ancient cell that subsequently evolved into the chloroplast, which captures energy from the sun and manufactures the sugars that plants need in order to live.

Such were the ruminations provoked by my discovery of the *Lobaria pulmonaria*—and of a growing list of other downright weird flora and fauna I found in the Oregon rainforest as I walked along with Charlie.

◇

One day Lynn and I were hiking through the fog-shrouded mature timber when we heard a strange noise from far away. *Eeep-eeep-eeep! Eeep-eeep-eeep!* We both froze. Quickly the *eeep*ing got louder and louder. The thing, whatever it was, was coming right at us!

At that point Charlie danced out of the fog, wagging his tail all the way down to his rib cage, the very picture of poodle pride. He stopped in front of Lynn, displaying the dinner-plate sized *eeep*ing creature.

Take that thing back where you found it! she commanded.

Charlie stood there for a moment, tail slowing down and then dropping in a "What did I do wrong?" gesture. He laid the thing at her feet and it immediately stopped *eeep*ing. Charlie looked at Lynn with his head slightly cocked and his ears flared. It was his "Don't you love me?" expression.

Lynn and I stared at what he'd dropped. It looked like a black guinea pig with a long pink nose and, on closer examination, no eyes. Or, at least, none that we could see. It wasn't exactly ugly, but you wouldn't want to keep one.

The thing, meanwhile, was running around in circles snuffling at the ground, looking for who knew what.

Lynn stood up and met Charlie's stare. "No, you may not keep him."

He stood there, pleading with his eyes.

Her hands went to her hips and her voice went up an octave and now it had a cutting edge to it. "Pick that thing up and take it back where you found it."

Charlie looked at Lynn for a moment, digesting the finality of her judgment, then turned his attention back to the creature, which in this time had traveled maybe four feet. Dutifully, but with resentment emanating from his entire body, he went over to the animal and picked it up. It immediately began *eeep*ing again.

Charlie walked away, the same way he'd come, until the fog began to swallow him. Then he stopped and looked around, his "Follow me" signal. So we did: Climbing over moss-covered fallen trees, threading through stands of witch hazel, detouring around blackberry thickets until, in a small amphitheater defined by old fir and white oak, Charlie stopped. With a resentful look at Lynn he dropped the creature, which immediately disappeared under the thick carpet of leaves.

It was a mole! The damned thing was a mole! I'd just never seen one nearly that size.

Lynn was at Charlie's side almost before the mole disappeared, praising him, petting him, kissing him—ugh—on the nose. Before long, he was his usual, happy, bouncing self.

Love me, love my dog. So it is, and so it always will be.

◇

Minor disagreements like the mole affair were transient, anyway. You couldn't hold a grudge in a place like that. On our long walks, as Charlie and I made our way through the cloud banks and fern fronds, I saw beauty everywhere.

Beauty tends to make human beings thoughtful. The same does not apply to dogs, however, and the same forest that helped me chill out made Charlie want to *do* something . . . and then something else . . . and then something else.

We were a bizarre pair. As I ambled through the enchanted fog, moisture dripping from my wide-brimmed hat, Charlie leaped ahead, plunging through the various emplacements of downed trees and brush, leaping over streams. I walked and he ran, up and down, back and forth, nose to the ground and tail waving in the air. Often all I could see of him was that black, pompommed flag of a tail.

The whole idea of "taking the dog with me" reeked of human vanity. The truth was, he took me. I lumbered along like a flagship, clomping and snorting, disturbing the vegetation and sending the bobcats, foxes, coyotes, lizards, frogs, rabbits, and whatever scurrying for cover. Charlie played the part of a screening destroyer. He took point, then right flank, then left flank, then point again—anywhere but the rear. Sometimes he seemed to defy physics and run in two directions at once, going everywhere in a hurry, nose to ground and tail pompom waving, up the trail and back and forth and around and over, yip-yipping with each delicious new discovery.

At first I discounted everything he did. He was burning off doggy energy: That was enough of an explanation for me. After a while, though, I could see that his enthusiasm wasn't exactly random. I was the anchor of his explorations, but if he wanted to see anything he had to get out of the perimeter of my disturbance. He kept me in mind, though, and when he found something, he'd often stop to show me. I'd catch up with him and he'd be standing there, immobile, staring at something, but what? I'd stand there and study the area he was pointing at. Nothing. Nada.

Then I'd take a step and—

—ka-*WHOOMP!*

The land erupted in grouse.

There is little on earth quite as heartstopping as three or four ruffed grouse launching themselves into the air from around your feet. They are sudden, they are loud, they are big, they are everywhere, and they will freeze your brain. Later on, even after I knew what they were and was kind of expecting them, they *still* made my heart jump. Yet I never saw them ahead of time, no matter how precisely Charlie pointed them out or however patiently and diligently he sought to show me how to detect them. I must have been a great disappointment to him.

I wasn't a complete doofus, though. I had at some point, I'm not sure when, figured out what he meant when he froze like that, focusing his nose straight ahead and sort of bristling with intensity. That was what hunters call a *point.* Sometimes he even bent one front leg in the classic pointer pose, but generally he expected me to be smart enough to figure that when he went deadly still *this was not a drill.* There was something there.

Looking back, I realize that at some point on those walks Charlie concluded that, despite my dim understanding of the natural world, I was trainable. At the time, I was oblivious to his ambitions. To me it was all about . . . well, me. I was doing what the doctor ordered. I'd walk, and I'd admire the beauty of the forest or at least make a good show of doing so.

The truth was, though, that the transition from work to walk wasn't all that easy. Deep in my primate mind, I was stuck in whatever problem I had left unsolved. The mental gears still whirred, the psychic transmission downshifted, the forebrain weighed and balanced, the mental billiard balls slammed against the inside of my skull. At the time I was writing about philosophers, and they'd lodge in my mind like so many mental burrs. Every one had a deadly opponent. David Hume had Bishop Berkeley. Voltaire had Rousseau. Francis Galton and William James. Foucault, Derrida, Lacan. Postmodernism. Illusions of reality. Reflections of illusions of reality. Echoes of reflections of illusions of reality. The meaning of it all.

Philosophy was a tar pit, and I was stuck in it.

Charlie labored under no such impedimenta. Reality held endless fascination for him as it did for me, but for him there was nothing ghostly or philosophical about it. Charlie's reality was the day, the moment, the glorious scent-carrying fog. Reality was the rabbit out there—he knew it was out there, because he had caught a whiff of it when the wind shifted. (Whiff of rabbit always and eternally meant there was, in fact, a rabbit, and no postmodern shilly-shallying.) Or maybe it wasn't a scent that tipped him off, but some more complex facet of the sensation-rich forest. Or the clue might be a negative one. Maybe, for example, the stillness that was too still. Charlie recognized the fact that nothing was going on for the remarkable thing it was, and he knew that if he froze, and joined the absolute stillness . . . ah, yes, then he would momentarily locate the fox.

And then, of course, there was the lout who came tromping along behind him, wheezing and sneezing and tripping over branches, generally upsetting the neighborhood and destroying the moment. No doubt about *his* existence, either. But then again, nature balanced out. One had to concede that the lout was pretty adept when it came to opening a can of dog food.

There was a strange thing, though. Despite the intellectual dampers that governed my own emotional experiences, some of the joy that was the dog managed to transfer itself to me. I don't know if it was osmosis or what, but Charlie lifted my awareness of the forest and, more important, of my own animal roots. He radiated something and I was warmed by it, but couldn't quite put my finger on what exactly it was. It was enough, though, to make me wonder: If I was so damned intelligent, and if my intelligence made me master of this land I walked, and conferred to me actual ownership of this creature, Charlie, why did that same intelligence deny me what was so available to Charlie, which was the ecstasy of the moment?

Okay, these thoughts were muddled. I grant you that. But

they comprised my first inkling that Charlie held the key to something that moved beneath the surface. What, I didn't know.

Soon, Lynn no longer needed to remind me to take the dog when I headed outside. With increasing frequency, in fact, it was the dog's idea to go for a walk in the first place. He'd get a certain look. He'd hang around, broadcasting on some doggy frequency. I'd get the urge to push back from the computer screen and . . . yeah, sure, some fresh air would be great. I needed to decompress. It was easier to decompress with Charlie along.

Why was that? Why, why, why?

And there I went again, back into my habitual cycle. Instead of decompressing, I analyzed my inability to decompress. And so while I easily found beauty in the forest, Charlie found something deeper, which was joy.

But the differences between us were not immutable. If I was alone, I found the beauty, but if I was with Charlie some of his joy communicated itself to me. The difference was dramatic.

So I asked the obvious question: What, exactly, was it that moved from Charlie to me? Was it a pheromone, some chemical that changed my mind and lightened my spirit without me being aware? No, not likely. Scientists had looked hard for pheromone receptors in the human nose, and had failed to find them. They couldn't even find the tiny dimpled structure where other animals, including Charlie, kept their pheromone sensors. If we'd ever had them, and we must have, they had evolved away.

Yet there was certainly an effect. I could feel . . . something. The effect wasn't limited to me, either. There were reports in the literature that dogs could lower blood pressure, for instance, or calm depressed mental patients or cheer up the lonely elderly. Nobody had the foggiest idea how dogs did such things, but they did. So dogs had some kind of unexplained powers.

I didn't believe in ghosts or that sort of hokum, but biological action at a distance was a known phenomenon. For confirmation I didn't have to look any further than the opposite sex. Merely by appearing in my presence, a woman could alter my state of mind. Again, I didn't know the mechanism but it did make sense—mother nature had been working on it for millions of years, for very practical reasons. I knew better than to deny it existed.

But dogs? *Dogs?*

And then I'd catch myself intellectualizing again. Why not just relax and enjoy it, I scolded myself. So I'd try my best to get back in touch with whatever the dog had opened up in me. Five minutes later I'd catch myself theorizing about how it worked. I couldn't not.

Why had evolution given the dog something it hadn't given me? And how was it that he got inside my mind and made me . . . well, different, more aware of my natural surroundings, when he was around? Why was I susceptible to his dog nature, so different from my own?

I was at least certain of one thing: The human mind is a puzzle box. It is a thing without substance that somehow emanates from a three-pound glop of gray goo. Nobody knows what it is, but we know it never stops churning. Never. That is part of the human condition.

And Charlie? By all accounts, he was a lesser creature. Yet that somehow made him ever so much more . . . more . . . more . . .

More what?

◇

That kind of question, transposed into scientific lexicography, is a matter of hardware—or, as some scientists prefer, "wetware." Knowing how animals' brains differ from one another is the work of comparative neuroanatomy. Scientists study modern brains and their predecessors—the brains of primates and mammals— hoping to figure out what the brain is by documenting how it evolved, how the circuitry came together over time, how nature tweaked the system to make one brain metamorphose into another.

This brings me to Paul MacLean. Were it not for him, I probably wouldn't be asking these kinds of questions in the first place or, at least, would be asking them with considerably less precision.

To be sure, Paul MacLean was never a household name, not even at the pinnacle of his intellectual reign in the sixties and seventies. Studying brain science wasn't—and still isn't—likely to get you on the cover of *People* magazine, but back then, in my own household, where gossip about brain scientists put food on the table, the world's top-gun neuroanatomist was an item of everyday conversation. Sitting around the dinner table you might have heard a sentence start with "As Paul MacLean would say . . ." Or a daughter, expressing her frustration, might react to a fatherly edict with, "That's not right, Dad. You're thinking with your lizard brain!"

Paul MacLean was one of those people who were "of their times." In another era he might not have been so influential beyond his chosen field, but those decades were special times.

My generation sometimes looks back on the '50s and '60s as a time that was almost magical. Those were our salad days, and we tend to forget that there were worms in the salad. Scorpions, even. Marijuana, for whatever reason, heralded an era of drug use run amok, and as for free love . . . well, it was a myth right up there with the free lunch. In large part we behaved as we did because those were frightening times, and drugs and sex become especially appealing when the world seems about to end.

For us, the "good old days" were also the days when Nikita Khrushchev could pound his shoe on the table and declare that he would destroy us all—and we never questioned that he was capable. The historical ice was so thin that one small geopolitical misstep could have set off a chain of reactions that would lead to chain reactions after which, to again quote Khrushchev, the living would envy the dead. (For younger readers, that's where the rock group the Grateful Dead got its name.)

To remember that time with any honesty is to remember the depth of our fatalism. As diplomats played nuclear brinksmanship and their proxies fought dirty wars in third-world jungles, Dr. Strangelove became a cult figure. An episode of Rod Serling's TV program *The Twilight Zone* dropped the idea of airline hijacking into the public mind, and terrorists went for it. Serling, for his part, was defensive. "I can't be held responsible for every nutso that crawls out of the woodwork," he was supposed to have said. I felt kind of sorry for him. One really good episode ruined his career and his life and earned him an unenviable place among history's bumblers.

But the appearance of nutsos was hardly Serling's fault. They were showing up everywhere, often with death on their minds. Charles Whitman climbed a tower at the University of Texas and shot everyone in sight. Thirteen died and many others were wounded before Whitman himself was shot and killed. Thus opened the age of senseless murder, of anger and guns, and guns and bombs: madness, all madness, under the shadow of the mushroom cloud. People of acknowledged wisdom and intellect wondered whether the schizophrenics in the asylum weren't the only normal people left. What did it mean, anyway, to be "normal" in a crazy world? Yes, it was an absurd idea, which completely perverted the nature and tragedy of mental illness. Still, it fit the times.

The human psyche had always found its most deadly enemy in the mirror, but the imperative "Know thyself" had been of real interest primarily to adolescents, poets, and philosophers. Now, when we lived on the edge of the nuclear abyss, the old questions gained a new and wider currency. What was the source of the insanity that seemed to lurk behind the newspaper headlines? Did the mysterious gray circuitry of the human brain carry some ancient program or programs that would inevitably bring our species' brief experiment with civilization to a tragic end? Did we make the world mad, or was it the other way around?

Given those circumstances, psychological research seemed critical to the security of the nation. Several experiments hinted that what had happened in Nazi Germany could well happen here. Was the Third Reich built on a mental perversion? Was a Hitler created from the bottom up, instead of the top down? The fear of generalized madness led to a federal initiative to search out the dragons of the mind, discover the causes of craziness and addiction, and in the process reveal the nature of human nature. Granted, the bureaucrats could be pompous, but they had the right idea.

This was the effort that, as one thing led to another, shaped my career as a journalist. Finally, one day, it would lead to my fixation on the old man and the grave and, by long extension, on the reporter and his dog. Meanwhile, it funded scientists like the neuroanatomist Paul MacLean.

By the time I met him, MacLean had already made his mark in comparative anatomy and somehow convinced Congress to bankroll what amounted to his own private laboratory of brain evolution in Poolesville, Maryland, prime real estate just north of the Washington beltway.

MacLean was a scientist, but he was more than that. He was a phenomenon, and the phenomenon was bigger than the man. His work wasn't just about him. It was about us all, and the historical juncture that we, the human race, had come to.

How do I explain it? How do I segue between the dog bounding ecstatically through the rainforest and MacLean's coolly mechanistic vision of the human dilemma? The jump might seem at first to transcend logic, but then whoever said biology was logical?

And history, especially the history of which MacLean was a part, wasn't logical at all.

◇

If you look at history from the viewpoint of brain science, human events are simply a special case of biology. That is to say, the brain produces behaviors, which in turn produce history. Acts of love and hate, fidelity and betrayal, truth and mendacity, altruism and mass murder all emanate from our minds.

So it stands to reason that neurobiology, like history, weaves a tapestry of contradiction, thick with paradoxes and backtwists of plot. Nothing is ever quite as it seems—not the man, not the puppy, not time itself. The lives of individuals and species diverge and then loop back on themselves to form symbiotic relationships and finally fuse into a new creature, reaching unity again.

A lichen, a single thing, is really three. A hive of bees or a den of ants, which appears to comprise many individuals, is—in the most important sense—only one. Human beings are apes plus . . . something. Or is it minus something, as the neoromantics believed? In which case, our much-touted intellect is our curse. Each insight gained in the laboratory somehow serves to reveal the fundamentally alien nature of the reality that lurks behind it. And history, like the convolutions of the brain, makes for some strange juxtapositions.

And so the story of Charlie and me owed something to the old man in the grave, and the old man in the grave was somehow connected to the dog—assuming that the animal buried with him *was* a dog. Through the old man, then, the dog was somehow connected to all the men and women who share the world with all the dogs that sit on satin pillows and doze in backyards and slink through city alleyways—to the whole unfolding tale of *Homo sapiens* and *Canis familiaris*, the two animals in the world whom we think we know best but who, when we aren't watching closely, pull us through a looking glass and plop us down in the most surreal of times and places. Which brings us again to Paul MacLean's laboratory.

The first time I met him was in either 1976 or 1977. I wanted to do a profile. After much wrangling with a very protective legion of secretaries, I landed an eight A.M. appointment. I drove around the Beltway and headed up north through a bucolic landscape.

Well, a green landscape, maybe—but not so bucolic. For some reason, the country north of Washington, D.C., had been favored by all those acronym agencies that don't exist, at least not on paper. But extant or not, they have somehow managed to spawn dozens if not hundreds of brooding enclaves, and the sweeping meadows and cornfields I passed were punctuated with razor-wire fortresses. There'd be a farmer plowing his field, right alongside a fourteen-foot chain-link fence guarded on the inside by pacing Dobermans and armed men. Beyond those would be an emplacement of low buildings, bristling, likely as not, with antennas.

I was of course fascinated by these installations, if for no other reason than I was a journalist and I wasn't allowed inside. Journalists are creeped out by secrets, even when they are legitimate secrets. So I made mental note of what I saw as I drove, but it didn't strike me as particularly unusual. This was the cold war landscape, that was all. We were used to such things in those days.

Like many reporters I have a fetish about being early, and when I arrived at MacLean's laboratory the parking lot was empty and the door was still locked. Killing time, I walked over to a long window that stretched across maybe fifty feet of the building's face and found myself staring into a dry-land terrarium. It seemed empty at first, but then I spotted a small lizard that blended almost perfectly into the environment. Seeing one, I then saw another, then another.

I stood and watched. The lizards were just sitting there, sort of bobbing their heads. I watched them for a while and then sensed a presence behind me.

"Watch the head-bobs," MacLean said. "They're specific to the species and the temperature. If you know the temperature and count the head-bob rate, you can probably figure out the species. If you know the species and you count the bobs, you can calculate the temperature."

Thus began my education in the comparative anatomy of the brain, a set of concepts elegant in their simplicity and profound in their importance.

Over the next few hours MacLean explained to me how the brain evolved in three separate and distinct bursts, each modifying and improving on the one before. The reptilian brain, which has since become known as the R-complex, came first. The "mammalian brain" came second and the "primate brain" came last.

Because nature dislikes throwing things away, the new brains didn't obliterate the older ones, they just grew atop them. The reptilian brain could still be seen and dissected in modern times, which was why MacLean was keeping those lizards. They showed him what was at the bottom of the contemporary human brain, without the obscuring layers.

Reptiles and the like are preprogrammed creatures, who live their lives without having much say-so about their futures. My favorite example is the bullfrog, a delicacy known not only to the French but also to those of us who grew up in western Oklahoma. The bullfrog will sit on the bank of a pond and, when some insect comes flying through its visual field, it will unroll its lightning-fast sticky tongue and snatch the insect out of the air. The action is automatic: When something—anything—flies through the frog's visual field, the tongue fires out and snags it. This is true even when the thing dangling in front of it is a bare hook, and the guy with the pole is in clear sight. That's how I came to eat so many frog legs as a child. If you haven't had the pleasure, I'm here to tell you they are superb.

The hard-wired brain probably wasn't much of a drawback

in the beginning, when all creatures were equally programmed. But evolution is in part a game of one-upsmanship, so at some point several hundred million years ago, one of those creatures (we don't know which one) developed a secret weapon: choice.

The creature did this by budding out a little polyp of new brain tissue, connected to the reptilian brain but not really part of it. This little bit of brain was basically a complicated set of switches, interrupting and augmenting one of the reptilian brain's earlier preprogrammed switches. The animal with the extra tissue was no longer predestined to do whatever it was programmed to do. Oh, it may well have *wanted* to do that, even *yearned* to do it, but it wasn't *compelled* to do it. Thus was emotion born, as an override.

At this moment in deep time, emotion was a modulating device. It probably overrode the deeper programming only on rare occasions, in crises. Even so, emotion gave the animal that had it some flexibility which, in the evolutionary scheme of things, was profound. Now there was a creature that could consider its situation *in the moment* and, if it made sense, refuse to follow its own inborn programming. This tiny modicum of choice bestowed so much advantage on the animal's progeny that they were much more likely to survive—and carry on the gene that occasionally caused the reptilian brain to throw out more buds of emotional circuitry.

Behavioral plasticity became the new evolutionary driver. Pretty soon, the old reptilian brain was budding out all over the place, and those buds were growing, butting into each other, and fusing into a second brain that would eventually far outweigh the original. It was nothing less than a second biological computer, and it spoke the strange new language of feelings. Enter the highly successful line of creatures that today we call mammals.

The third brain, what would be called the primate brain, developed in much the same way, beginning with buds off the mammalian brain. This tissue was different yet: It was as cold as the reptile brain, but it was highly programmable. It could learn from the past, and could do so in abstraction. It could observe and see into the future better than any creature that had ever lived. It could build models of the universe and test them against the outside world, and then change them to incorporate whatever was learned. Finally, the brain had language-handling capability but unlike, say, the brains of most birds, it didn't come equipped with an inborn or narrow language range. Rather, it soaked up language from its environment. The result, depending on experience, would one day become an animal that could speak and understand English, Spanish, Mandarin . . . even mathematics.

Nothing is ever free, of course. The inevitable side effect of these evolutionary improvements was that, for the big-brained primates, the inner world took on a larger and more tangible importance. The human would end up building models of the universe and, absorbed in those models, would often forget where the inner world stopped and the exterior one began. A brain that held other races inferior, for example, saw a world full of examples proving it correct. As scientists like to say, we humans have a tendency to change the universe to match our theories.

So it was that Paul MacLean was the first to define the human dilemma as growing directly from the fact that we had three brains in one—a "triune brain," as he called it. We weren't individuals, we were committees—and, like all committees, we were given to inner uncertainty, dispute, and even feuding. We were the only creature in nature capable of ganging up on itself. Much later, reading Freud, I would come to understand that the dirty-minded old Victorian, whatever his faults, had gotten a glimpse of that problem.

MacLean was no Freudian. He was an anatomist, pure and simple, and he viewed the triune brain from the outside, not the inside. What his dissection labs showed him was that the human brain was full of fossil wiring—that many of the brain's circuits may have originated in the Silurian or the Jurassic or the Eocene. But they are still there, embedded in the human skull

I'm simplifying, of course. Nature was no neatnik. Stuff got smeared around, adapted for different purposes. Scales had a certain function in dinosaurs, but the feathers that evolved from them had quite different uses. Modern reptiles had a bit of higher cortex, and mammals had quite a lot. Brain evolution was a graduated process. But the magic of threes was reflected throughout biopsychology.

I remember sitting at a round table in MacLean's office as he explained all this, drawing diagrams of the triune brain on a legal pad. Once he was convinced I had the outline of what he was saying, he told me to step back, mentally, and consider that nature had sewn a real clinker into this design.

Because each layer of new brain budded out from the underlying tissue, the various parts of the upper brains didn't communicate directly with one another. They had to take detouring paths through the lower brains.

Vision, for example, happens in the occipital region in the very back of the brain. But seeing and comprehending are two different things and, for the one to become the other, the visual information has to get from the very back of the cranium to the forebrain. It can't go there directly, though. The visual information highway first leads down through the emotional brain and into the reptilian brain, then up again to the forebrain.

This means information doesn't just travel through the brain the way a telegraph message travels along a wire. At every step it is processed, then processed again, and processed again. That means that by the time vision gets from the back of the brain to the forebrain, where it can be understood, it has already picked up an aura that includes a lot of reptilian programming and emotional spin. That is why our vision, in all meanings of the word, is so tangled up in our habits and emotions. Forebrain or no forebrain, emotion precedes logic.

In other words, everybody in the cranial boardroom has a vote; logic, being the junior member of the committee, doesn't even get to see the issues or hear the questions until the other members have marked them up, interpreted them, and possibly changed them beyond recognition.

There was more, much more. Before I left that day, MacLean would lead me through his bestiary, room after room of lizards, marsupials, nonprimate mammals, and primates. Many of their brains had been surgically altered, so that their behavior expressed deeper brains. A monkey, its higher brains burned away, acted like a reptile.

Brains are like Russian nesting dolls, MacLean told me. Inside one animal, there's another, and within that one still another. This is true even in humans. Visit a facility for seriously brain-damaged patients, and what do you see? You see people rocking back and forth. Everything above their reptilian brain has been damaged by trauma or disease, all the filters removed, so humans do just what lizards do. They bob.

The whole idea of the triune brain redefined the human dilemma, and did so in ways that matched what we could witness in the real world. Yes, three minds are probably better than one . . . but, as history attests, they also might not be. I kept remembering that old canard about the animal that was built by a committee. I'm speaking, of course, of the camel.

◇

This was all in the days before MRIs and PETT scanners. As those and other instruments pushed the frontier ever further into the human psyche, human behavior began to make more and more sense—if "sense" is the proper word. Clinical depression could be traced to imbalances in the serotonin system. Sociopathology and schizophrenia began to yield their anatomical secrets. By the turn of the century, even the misery of adolescence could be visualized on computer screens (in adolescence, it turns out, the circuitry that links the forebrain to the emotional system is still incomplete, making it excruciatingly difficult for the adolescent to resist temptation). As the anatomy became ever more clear, some began to argue that MacLean was wrong, sort of. One scientist compared the brain to an ant den of brains. The triune brain became really three congresses of brains, each a squabbling cauldron of imperatives and desires, each pulling in its own direction.

But the triune brain still served as a splendid model for our inner conflicts as well as for comparing, say, the brain of a human to the brain of a dog. Me and Charlie, to be specific. I had three brains and he had, basically, two and what . . . a tenth? He wasn't stupid, but geometry was simply not a functional option for him. I was computational, he was emotional. I was vision and he was smell. I was forever confused and he rarely knew doubt.

There was something complementary there, between me and the dog. I couldn't put my analytical finger on it, but I felt it. There was a similarity, or maybe it was a significant difference, or some combination of the two. It felt like the connection between us spanned immense reaches of time. There were moments, sitting before the fire and listening to the rain beat on the roof, when I could almost grasp its meaning. But then it would skitter out of my conscious mind, like so much quicksilver.

Some questions are like that—like ghosts. They haunt you until you quit denying they are there and then you go out and do something about them. Hire an exorcist, see a shrink, whatever. Human beings have a thing about questions. To Charlie, questions are either answerable or they are not. I saw the slippery terrain between those two outcomes, and it is inhabited by dangerous creatures. The dog question was an itch inside my head, like psychological poison ivy.

This all happened over a very extended period of time. The rains stopped and summer came and went and the rains came back again. Even a full professor could keep library books for only one year, and eventually someone called and asked me to bring the wolf books back. I did, but that didn't end my obsession because now I had plenty of books of my own. Another year passed.

At some point, I'm not sure exactly when, the dog began to edge its way further and further into my precious sleep-hypnotic period. I'd try to focus on postmodern interpretations of language, say, but before I knew it there was the damned dog again, prancing through my mind, invading my creative space, this last and most private bastion of my life.

CHAPTER FIVE

I tell my students that if they want to succeed as writers they need to develop an iron discipline of mind. They have to focus, focus, focus—keep their fanny in the chair and their eyes on the screen. The mind will try to pull away, to go do something else. Sharpen pencils, water the plants, format your hard drive, mop the bathroom.

I once knew a writer who, upon sitting down at the computer, was often seized by a powerful urge to clean her oven. On one occasion, having succumbed to the urge, she had an epiphany. It was a sign. She *hated* cleaning the oven, hated being down on her knees scraping out gook, hated the smell of the cleaner. So if even cleaning the oven was preferable to writing . . . why was she torturing herself with writing? Ambition? Masochism? This was madness.

With that, she quit writing. I couldn't criticize the logic.

I myself was pretty good at keeping nose to grindstone, but the dog question not only continued to itch, it began to seem like pure recreation. Far more satisfying than sharpening pencils or cleaning the oven. So, with a certain amount of sheepish guilt, I went back to the library, finally, and once again checked out all those wolf books, took them back, and put them on my office shelf.

The wolf now became my primary intellectual diversion. I would commit the requisite number of hours to my regular work, then would go walking in the fog with Charlie, and then, settled into an evening in front of the fire, start reading about *Canis lupus*.

Since I'd first checked out the wolf books, a couple more had been published, mostly aimed at popular audiences. I leafed through them and was shocked at the degree to which postmodern romanticism had crept into the subject. Postmodernism was a new-age philosophy, and as such tended to value feelings above knowledge. While I wasn't looking, the wolf had been elevated to a mysterious, almost godlike position. It had become a totem.

I had the impression that, if nothing else, the renewed interest in wolves had led to a few more token grants and, as a result, some limited science. Or was that my own maturing understanding? Maybe it was just that I knew the dog better, now, and was more convinced than ever that his existence represented some secret I had been denied.

Thus I immersed myself ever deeper in the wolf, or at least in the printed wolf. I examined its formidable digestion system, considered at length its strange olfactory world, studied its remarkable reproductive rituals. I read accounts of the wolf by ancient hunters and herders and by modern scientists. I created, in my own head, a simulacrum of the wolf. I decided to visit the Portland zoo to see the wolf in the flesh, but it was a disappointment; they didn't measure up to the book wolf. The zoo had three wolves. They just stood there in the murky drizzle, immobile and miserable-looking. Eventually my patience collapsed and I went on to the monkey house.

In some ways books are better than reality, at least if they're good books. The wolf books I read that winter changed me somehow, gave depth and texture to my understanding of how different we humans are from other animals. In coming years, that appreciation would flower until, somewhere along the line, I realized that I probably knew more about the wolf than the wolf did about itself. I could say that without arrogance because my knowledge, human knowledge—knowledge derived from the primate brain—was quite different from . . . what would you call it? Wolf knowledge? MacLean would have called it mammalian knowledge. The knowledge of feeling, the knowledge borne of the genes, which in human terms isn't really knowledge at all.

Primate knowledge is principally the knowledge of information, of data points connected with theoretical constructs. Abstractions, symbols, extrapolations, hypotheses confirmed by experiment. In the purest sense the primate forebrain itself does not involve feeling, though it can certainly evoke feeling—as when, perhaps, we learn we have a fatal disease. A wolf would never anticipate death, so would not know how to fear it. A wolf is alive until it is dead.

I sat by the fire, considering the wolf, trying with my big forebrain to *be* a wolf, as much as that might be possible. With the raindrops and the flickering of the white oak logs, I could feel the problem begin to yield.

◇

The mind of the wolf is desire. Its knowledge is the knowledge of bone and flesh, imparted by vast stretches of time and perfected by the relentless grinding of ecological Carborundum. The wolf simply isn't like us. It does not possess our need to understand everything. All the wolf needs to understand is in its long legs, its big feet, its fur, its stomach, its anal glands, its sexual organs, its tongue, its nose, its teeth, its massive, crushing jaws, the deep yearnings of its instinct.

The wolf embodies the three best-known forces of evolution: competition, cooperation, and time. Its story is one of complexity and irony. The wolf, as it turns out, is but half the tale. The other half is its principal prey, the hoofed animals. The wolf did not evolve, it co-evolved, and the dynamic of that evolution was a long, slow, syncopated waltz of hunger, terror, blood, death, and rebirth.

Follow the bloodlines of either the wolf or the ungulates back far enough and they fuse in an omnivorous animal that inhabited the Eocene, some fifty million years ago. It could eat either plants or animals—fruits, say, and insects—but it wasn't particularly good at gathering, catching, or digesting either one. This made it inefficient, and Nature hates inefficiency. The result was that the environment tended to favor those offspring that were better suited to digesting either plants or protein.

What began as minor variations quickly grew large and defining. The vegetable eaters lost their ability to eat meat and, to a large degree, the meat eaters lost their ability to subsist on plant material. The former would give rise to deer, elk, moose, caribou, and the other hoofed animals. The meat eaters developed the teeth, jaws, and digestive system we associate with the carnivores, including the big cats and the wolf.

The evolutionary relationship, then, was circular. The carnivores preyed on their cousins the herbivores. The slower of the herbivores were the most likely to be eaten, so the survivors, by definition the swiftest of the lot, reproduced in kind. Generation by generation, they ran faster, so the ancestral wolves had to run faster as well. This evolutionary one-upmanship led to extreme change.

This change was expressed most visibly in the differential evolution of the bones of the foot and leg, which grew longer and more efficient. Horses came to run on three toes, then on one, the nail of which became a hoof; the caribou, the deer, and most of the other prey animals evolved to run on two hoofed toes. The result was some very fast animals. The caribou, the preferred prey of the wolf, can typically run forty miles an hour.

The ancestral wolves, in hot pursuit of the ungulates, started down the same path of differential foot evolution as their prey. At some point in the distant past they rose up on their toes and ran with their heels elevated. The fifth digit of their front feet, the one corresponding to the human thumb, eventually became a vestigial bump halfway up the limb. The fifth digit of the back foot disappeared entirely. At the same time, the bones of the foot became longer and longer. A dog's elbow is up so high, we think of it as a shoulder.

But the evolutionary pressures on a predator are different from those on the prey. The predator needs flexibility and dexterity. The wolf simply cannot match the ungulate's length of leg and still perform fluidly, as a predator must. As a result, the top speed of the average well-conditioned wolf is probably not much above twenty-five miles per hour, and that can't be sustained for long. In any marathon between a healthy wolf and a healthy caribou, elk, deer, or moose, the wolf invariably ends up hungry.

The ungulate, on the other hand, has a big disadvantage in its size. The same bulked-up muscles that make it a marathon runner also make it heavy, and its inertia makes it a slow starter. This means that, depending on the condition of the wolf and the condition of the caribou, there is a certain specific radius inside which the advantage tilts to the wolf. If the wolf begins its charge from within that radius, it can reach the caribou before the caribou gets up to speed.

So the wolf, like many other predators of large herbivores, adopted the tactic of the ambush and the stalk, stealthily maneuvering in close and then charging with all its might. Over the millennia, it evolved into a coiled spring of a sprinter, capable of reaching its maximum speed in seconds as it bounds toward its prey in leaps of up to sixteen feet.

The distance within which a predator can reach its prey before the prey can hit full speed is called the spook radius. Its length differs from species to species, of course, which makes it mathematically complex. The spook radius has to take into account the sprint speed of the predator and how long it takes the prey animal to overcome inertia and surpass that speed. A physicist could figure it out, but the striking thing is that each individual predator and each individual animal of prey knows instantly and innately where the radius is as it applies specifically to them.

The existence of the spook radius was surely noted by observant human hunters long before the nature-nurture question arose to bedevil us. I personally saw it for the first time in antelopes on the high plains. As I came into an antelope's view, its head would go up and it'd study me for a moment, then return to its grazing. It'd graze on but keep an eye on me as I walked toward it and then, when I reached its spook radius—bang, the antelope was bouncing over the next hill.

The precise spook radius of a particular animal obviously depends on its weight, inertia, muscle, and design, as well as on the metabolic cost of the contest. Other issues are health and weather conditions. Timing was critical—very much as in those middle-school word problems in which Train A leaves the station at a certain time and at a certain speed, and then, later, Train B leaves, moving slightly faster. When, if at all, will Train B overtake Train A?

There are other factors, as well. A healthy antelope can always outrun its predators, but if it bolts every time it sees one it will quickly exhaust itself—at which time it would lose its advantage and become easy prey. Likewise, if a predator makes a habit of opening its charge from outside the radius, when it has no hope of a kill, then it will soon become too exhausted to hunt and will starve to death. In this way, evolution selected for animals with a good sense of the spook radius.

The spook radius is an example of a hard-wired psychological response to a physical fact. It is not intellectual. It is a feeling, a hunch, an instinct, an uneasiness. It is a boundary of the mind, etched there by generations of blood and gore. You can see it in documentaries shot on the African veldt: The lion pads by a herd of prey animals while the animals just stand there, warily watching but not running. A lion is dangerous only if it approaches the spook radius. Those who understand where the line is drawn, live to reproduce. Those who do not, do not.

And so it went—nature's way. The predators won the battles but the prey won the wars. As the eons passed, slow or ailing prey were pulled down by fast wolves, while slow or sick wolves went hungry. Along the way the carnivore gene pool spun off line after line of successful killers. The civets, hyenas, cats, and weasels split off some forty-five million years ago; raccoons and bears, thirty million years ago. By perhaps fifteen million years ago, when the more or less modern wolf developed, the continents of Africa, North America, and Eurasia were contiguous. Wolves hunted the entire supercontinent.

The Pleistocene ice, when it came, changed the climate of the entire earth. A significant proportion of the planet's water was trapped in glaciers as tall as mountain ranges, and weather patterns rearranged themselves into a globe-girdling series of climate bands. On the earth's surface, the prevailing winds blew down off the ice; the low temperatures tended to precipitate out humidity in the north. This created high-latitude forests and alpine meadows. By the time the air got to the middle latitudes, it was dry. Great dunes of wind-driven dust formed around the globe at about the latitude of Louisiana. Wolves and the ungulates they followed were naturally drawn away from this desert.

There was only one direction in which they could escape: north, into the climatological shadow of the ice.

◇

All this, the evolution of the predators and the prey and their place in the environment, has been well worked out by scientists. In this effort, paleontologists who specialized in the carnivores enjoyed a special advantage. The essence of these animals—their jawbones and teeth—was durable and tended to be well represented in the fossil record.

There was nothing subtle about the basic dental array of the predator. Assemblies of jawbones and teeth could be read like a book, a bloody saga that traced the development of the wolf from the Eocene into the present. Wolf teeth included chisel-like incisors and dagger-sharp canines (the latter of which would reach their evolutionary extreme in the saber-toothed tiger). Behind the wolf's canine teeth were three cutting premolars and two grinding molars. The hindmost molar, situated between the big muscle attachments of the jaw, had the most leverage. At some point early in the evolutionary story the hindmost premolars began to develop into carnassials, "flesh teeth." The top and bottom carnassials meet in a scissorslike conjunction sharp enough to slice through moose tendon. Subtle but distinct changes and variations in teeth and jaws marked not only the development of the wolf but also the points at which the line of the wolf split from that of the other carnivores.

Fossilized jaws and teeth, along with other, rarer, skeletal parts, tell us what long-dead animals ate and how they lived out their lives; this in turn, provides clues about the ecologies that shaped and sustained them. Given the jaw of a proto-wolf, for example, one can safely conclude some key things about its metabolism. Where there were sharp canines and heavy carnassials, there must also have been a digestive system capable of absorbing large quantities of protein—and an animal whose arteries were practically immune to the high cholesterol content of its diet. The jawbone of a predator also implies the existence of prey, perhaps ruminants, with their multi-chambered stomachs containing bacteria that could break down otherwise indigestible vegetable matter. These things, observable in the present, must have evolved, stepwise, with the bones recovered from the stone.

In the late twentieth century there was a scientific controversy over whether evolution proceeded by tiny steps or in periodic leaps and jumps. As often happens on such occasions, both sides ultimately turned out to be correct. Sometimes it was slow, other times it was fast. The wolves, though, were classic examples of long and gradual development—classic Darwinian creatures. The changes in their teeth and jaws were small and incremental; as the jaws changed, the teeth changed to match, growing larger or smaller or disappearing altogether. The result is what, for a wolf, is a remarkably well-designed mouth. The average wolf is blessed with an occlusion so perfect that the teeth tend to clean themselves.

To appreciate this one only needs to consider what happened when evolution makes a sudden leap, as it did in the case of the human. Teeth and jaws might have evolved in lockstep when change was slow and steady, as in the wolf, but the jawbones and teeth turned out to not be equally plastic, genetically. Given enough evolutionary pressure, jawbones could evolve faster than teeth. When our ancestors were caught up in the evolutionary cyclone that changed them into humans in a geological instant, the shrinkage of the jawbone outpaced the ability of the teeth to keep up. The resulting mouth is not pretty to behold: a small jaw containing too many oversized, jammed-together teeth, which are notoriously susceptible to tooth decay and gum disease. Rotten teeth have been the source of much human pain; infections beginning in the teeth and gums were partly responsible for our ancestors' short life spans. Today this quirk of differential evolution between tooth and jaw constitutes the gods' gift to the dentist.

As paleontologists study the teeth and jaws of a long-dead animal, they seek to envision what that animal was in life. They read those fragments of deep time much as I read the books they then proceed to write. The scientific mind (ultimately aided by computers) clothed the bones in flesh and then, having done that, strains to imagine the whole animal in life, in action, since life in the final analysis is more than mandible and dentine. Life is motion, which is to say behavior—and it is life, and curiosity about life, that drives scientists to reconstruct the past in the first place.

If teeth were the turtles of evolution, brains were apparently the rabbits. They were far more susceptible to mutation. Simply put, the mind evolved faster than the body.

This story has only recently been understood. An animal might have many thousands of genes in each cell but, in most cells, the majority of those genes are turned off. Most organs function with just a few genes operating. The switching mostly takes place during gestation. By birth the switches are set, and set permanently. Kidney is kidney and heart is heart, forever.

The brain, however, is a thing apart. It is so complicated that it needs to activate more than half the animal's gene content. This means a huge number of genes are hard at work, cranking out proteins, enzymes, and other products to make possible what's been called the "three-pound universe."

Active genes, though, are the ones most involved in evolution. If a cosmic ray damages a gene that has been turned off, probably nothing will happen. But the brain churns with metabolic activity, and mutations were more likely to affect the offspring's behavior. As a result, the brain is potentially the most rapidly evolving tissue in the bodies not only of humans but also of wolves and frogs. That's how the human brain evolved from lemon-sized to grapefruit-sized in less than 3 million years, while the rest of the body stayed more or less recognizable.

Darwin was the first scientist to notice with what dazzling speed the brain could evolve. I say he was the first *scientist* to do so because people who worked with animals had figured that out long before the advent of written language. By the time Darwin came along, there had been generations of people who, for example, made their living breeding dogs to perform various inborn behaviors.

Darwin lived in a time and a place where flocks of sheep still roamed the countryside in herds, shepherded in large part by dogs. What's more, different breeds of these dogs had different behavioral specialties. Those specialties broke down to two groups. There were herding dogs and there were guard dogs, and their behaviors were quite distinct.

Guard dogs were big, ferocious-looking beasts which, in the language of shepherds, thought they were sheep. They preferred the company of sheep to that of humans or other dogs, and were quick to intervene and protect their "fellow sheep" when a threat appeared. Many of them, bred to protect their herd from wolves, also hated other dogs. Even today, at dog shows, breeds like Great Pyrenees, Saint Bernards, and komondors generally have to be kept away from the more social dogs. When there is contact, conflicts are often quick and savage, and are usually won by the larger and fiercer, guard-dog breeds. In modern times such conflicts might well be followed by that most terrifying predator of all, the attorney at law.

Herding dogs were also highly specialized by breed. Some moved the sheep by running at them. Others showed their teeth. Still others used a wolflike pose combined with a stare, a behavior known universally as "giving eye." At least one, the briard, frightened sheep into moving by simply presenting its large and imposing profile.

In the cities, breeds like the rat terrier evolved specifically to fit the whims of wharf gamblers, who made bets on whose dog would bring back the most dead rats within a specified time period. In the country, foxes and bears were hunted by packs of hounds bred specifically to chase their prey up a tree or into some kind of corner.

One can't think this through very far until another, nondog question sneaks into the mind. As specific dogs had certain specific behaviors, humans had specific behaviors as well. Human nature. We were born, we now knew, to process language and care for our offspring. Were we also born to breed dogs?

This was a Russian doll question, and I immediately tucked it aside to ponder another day.

In any event, Darwin-era breeders might never have heard of the genome but they were pretty good rough-and-dirty genetic engineers. They knew that *like* breeds *like*, and yet can also produce variation. That variation includes specific behavioral as well as purely physical traits. When carriers of specific behaviors are recognized and isolated, they can produce . . . well, with luck and perseverance, whatever a breeder wants.

In Darwin's time, a new wild card was introduced into the game: the development and refinement of the long gun. Crude weapons like the blunderbuss and the musket had been around for some centuries, of course, but the industrializing years after Darwin published *Origin of Species* saw a quantum leap in the accuracy and convenience of weaponry. At the same time the repeating rifle made marksmanship less important, since if the first shot missed, the shooter still had a second. The revolution was completed as mass production lowered prices, putting long guns within the means of what was called the "gentle class."

All this forever changed the gentleman's sport of hunting. Medieval rituals like riding to hounds in pursuit of a fox would hang on for a century and more, but the spear, the bow and arrow, and the crossbow were instantly outclassed. With a scattergun it was even possible to kill birds in flight—a power so remarkable as to fascinate the rich and the near rich. Darwin himself was a passionate bird hunter who loved nothing better than to roam the English countryside with a dog and a shotgun.

Suddenly, where such gentlemen had once needed dogs that would chase and tree game, they now needed dogs that would point, flush, and retrieve. Breeders understood the law of supply and demand and they quickly got down to the business of producing what would sell.

Darwin inevitably found himself drawn to this revolution in the dog breeders' art. He befriended breeders, watched them work, and helped them field-train their dogs. He was there as they developed the breeds we know today as pointers and retrievers. Some dogs pointed with a foot up, some pointed by freezing, and some went ahead to flush the birds without command. All these dogs had "soft mouths," which meant that they would retrieve dead and wounded creatures without chewing them up. Each one was an example of behavioral evolution.

Darwin also noted that each dog was a specific individual with a distinct personality. Yet each personality fit somewhere into the spectrum of the breed. A border collie would classically have a very low boredom threshold and what we now think of as a type A personality. A golden retriever, whatever its individual strengths and weaknesses, was generally a laid-back character who loved everybody and would rather play than eat. A terrier, of whatever variety, would be stubborn as a post and eager to kill something . . . exactly *what* it killed didn't really matter.

A hundred years later scientists would come to understand that complex inbred behaviors could be the direct result of not just a single hard-wired program but a chain of them. My own favorite example is offered by the cougar. The cougar, despite its undeserved reputation for general mayhem, is actually a very specialized animal. Given a choice, it hunts deer, and it does so in a very patterned way. It leaps onto the deer's back, turns its head sideways, and uses its teeth to sever the spinal cord at a certain place in the deer's neck. Each act is governed by genes.

The occasional cougar, however, is born missing one of the necessary programs in the cascade. It might, for example, jump onto the deer's back, turn its head sideways . . . and then freeze, not knowing what to do next. In the wild, such animals will starve, but in captivity they teach us volumes about the complexity of inherited behavior chains.

Some such behaviors, like the cougar's chained kill reaction, are strictly a matter of genetics. But most behaviors are more or less malleable. Though the best gun dog might be born to its task, it still has to be trained from puppyhood.

Early dog breeders quickly recognized that behavior was both nature and nurture. Given this obvious fact, the political fight over whether nature or nurture holds sway over the human animal seems almost bizarre. But a fight it was, a fight that raged over the intellectual landscape and spilled over into politics and then across the battlefields of World War II. The nature-nurture controversy dominated politics for 150 years and is still with us today.

Scientists, or at least the deep thinkers among them, shunned that controversy. They understood the assumption behind it—that humans, even if they had evolved, were different from all the other animals. They were, as David Hume had asserted, part angel and part devil. The idea that humans might be, instead, three pounds of closely packed and highly metabolic neural networks was hardly something you could sell in Joe's Bar.

So there developed two perceptions of human psychology. To the average person, to be human was to be spiritual. To the scientist, to be human was a result of a collision between nature and nurture. By the time Paul MacLean and his contemporaries began to study brain evolution, insiders never ever bothered to ask whether behavior was governed by nature or nurture. They knew the answer was yes.

MacLean once suggested to me that I think of behavior, and by extension of consciousness, as the interface between genes and environment. What we think of as "self," the conscious "I," cannot conceivably exist anywhere except where the two forces meet. It is, in the words of another scientist, a "transitional phenomenon that occurs between two differing states, external and internal."

Candace Pert, codiscoverer of the opiate receptor, put it this way: Do we have conscious choice? Of course we have conscious choice. Nature built us to make choices, and we do . . . within whatever perimeters Nature allows.

The mind also allows us to know certain things. Like the wolf, we know the state of our own bodies—are we hungry, tired, angry, passionate? Is beauty a thing we are born knowing, at least in part? Does a kitten, at birth, have some deep insight into the mouse? Are we compelled, as insects and birds are, to perform a mating ritual—in our case with gifts of flowers and food? Certainly, wherever the skulls of carnivores and herbivores are found, we can be sure that the brains they once encased had an inborn understanding of the spook radius.

Scientists, in other words, see no real separation between the study of jawbones and the study of behavioral evolution. The inner life of a mammal, centered as it is on emotional computation, has to include pleasure and pain. Even a few bones will allow us to peer, at least fleetingly, into the minds of long-dead animals. You can be pretty certain, for example, that the proto-wolf, given its teeth and jaws, would not view a bucket of oats as desirable. It would far rather eat the horse.

Chapter Six

That is the essence of a wolf: heavy jaws and sharp teeth, the tools of hunger. Other animals also have impressive jaws and teeth; the cougar comes to mind, but the cougar's hunger is focused primarily on deer. The wolf's hunger is much broader and perhaps more relentless; it hunts a wider variety of animals across a spectrum of environmental niches. Its kill programs are commensurately more flexible, often expressing themselves in tendencies instead of in programmatic reactions. Attacking wolves, for example, tend to circle a herd of prey animals, or even an individual animal, before the attack. Maintaining this circle, they tend to dash in to rip, slash, and tear. But if their preferred method of operation fails, the pack won't hesitate to try something else. Wolves are like humans in this way: The nature of wolves includes improvisation.

Note the plural: not "wolf," but "wolves." One can consider a wolf's jaw, or talk about an individual wolf, but that is a human conceit. The thing that most defines the species, beyond the immediate matters of killing, is its gregarious nature. Wolves are pack animals. Unlike cougars or leopards, they seek the company of their own kind. Wolves are born with a social sense—a sense of rightness and well-being that depends on their acceptance into the pack. The lone wolf is an aberration, and not one nature seems to prefer. Rudyard Kipling said it best in his poem "The Law of the Jungle":

> Now this is the Law of the Jungle—as old and as true as the sky;
> And the Wolf that shall keep it may prosper, but the Wolf that shall break it must die.
> As the creeper that girdles the tree-trunk the Law runneth forward and back—
> For the strength of the Pack is the Wolf, and the strength of the Wolf is the Pack.

Social behavior, an inborn propensity to congregate, is an old story in zoology, with roots deep in the circuitry of the brain. Sociality is not like love or friendship; it's seen in creatures lacking the brain circuitry to produce those emotions. Social behavior appears in schooling fishes and in insects and, as I write this, a team of scientists is claiming to have documented its existence in microbes.

We know from fossilized footprints that certain herbivorous species of dinosaurs traveled in herds and, like modern elephants, traveled with their young enjoying a protected position in the center of the group. Other animals, like the modern musk ox, stand shoulder to shoulder, facing outward, to mount a common defense against an approaching carnivore.

For predators like the wolf, the evolution of the social impulse also related to the inexorable mathematics of appetite, metabolism, and stomach capacity. A lion or a wolf pack can only consume so much protein at once; then, satiated, it will quit hunting. This protects the surviving prey animals. If those prey animals are superstitious—and I know scientists who contend that the animal brain is at least crudely capable of superstition—there is almost something sacrificial about the equation. Let the lion have Horace, and the rest of us can live for another two or three days.

My favorite illustration of the "let-them-have-Horace" school of biology is the periodic cicada of the central and eastern United States. Adult cicadas are big, meaty, and totally helpless; in the years they hatch they are a bonanza to insect-eating birds. I have seen robins and blue jays staggering across the lawn in what can only be described as a state of food intoxication. They run out of appetite before they run out of insects. The cicadas simply overwhelm the capacity of the birds to consume.

The cicada's adaptation was a lockstep, multiyear periodicity. If cicadas came every year, bird populations would adjust upward to take advantage of the dependable hatches. But birds are powerfully and probably inescapably adapted to an annual scheme of survival—spring migration; nesting; summertime maturation of the young, followed perhaps by migration. Because cicadas reproduce on a longer cycle, no bird could evolve a breeding or migration pattern to take full advantage of the available cicada protein.

The cicada has gone even one better, building a flexibility into its periodicity. The cicada clock is apparently very susceptible to mutation, so a few cicadas crawl out each summer. If they are quickly eaten, well . . . bad timing, Horace. If they survive and reproduce, then a new variant cicada emerges with its own, different cycle. So the cicada has it covered both ways: Even in the unlikely event that a bird or some other predator manages to adapt to one cicada cycle, the cicada can quickly change its hatch cycles to compensate. In this fashion the cicada has one-upped the bird, at least temporarily winning the ancient competition between predator and prey.

The congregation of migratory prey animals, such as reindeer, accomplishes much the same thing. Caribou normally spread out over the landscape, but during migration, when they are at their most vulnerable, they band together. As summer and winter fade into fall and spring, as many as 200,000 caribou may come together, literally covering the landscape. That is in modern times; in the Pleistocene, caribou herds were much bigger.

As these great herds crossed the territories of wolf packs and human bands, the mortality rate was numerically high but proportionately small. The predators could gorge themselves to the limit, like robins pigging out on cicadas, but when the caribou were gone, they were gone. Not until the arrival of fairly modern humans, with their ability to make multiple kills and to store meat by drying or smoking it, did the tactic show a weakness.

The downside of congregation is the pressure it puts on the ecology. A herd of several thousand grazing animals would destroy its own pasture if it didn't keep on the move. The risk of a herbivore eating itself out of its ecological niche is compounded for predators, who necessarily exist in numbers that are small by comparison with those of prey animals. Solitary predators tread most lightly on the land, which is undoubtedly why animals like cougars and bears generally come together only to mate. In lean times even pack predators like wolves are forced to break up, each animal going its separate way to forage-hunt for mice, voles, rabbits, and other small animals.

On the other side of the equation, pack behavior allows wolves to set up ambushes and launch coordinated attacks on large prey animals. The efficiency gain, real enough even when the prey animal is relatively small, becomes dramatic when the pack corners a really large creature, like a moose.

Wolf experts relish telling stories about confrontations between wolves and moose. A full-grown moose (at least now that the giant animals like mastodons are gone) is the most powerful animal a wolf might reasonably contemplate for dinner. A moose can tip the scale at almost a ton of muscle, sinew, horn, hoof, and notoriously foul temper. It probably qualifies not only as the largest herbivore in the northern hemisphere but also as the most dangerous.

It is unimaginable that a single wolf could take a moose, but a pack of six, in a coordinated attack . . . now *that* is another matter.

The tactics most commonly employed by a wolf pack attacking a moose have a military precision. One wolf typically lunges in, seizes the animal by the nose, and hangs on for dear life while the moose thrashes its head frantically trying to dislodge it. It swings the wolf around in the air, pounds it into the ground, attempts to smash it with its hooves. While the moose is so occupied, the other wolves dash in under the rear hooves to slash at belly and flanks. Blood loss, and not a single mortal wound, ultimately does the trick and the moose almost inevitably goes down.

In this kind of attack, success or failure hinges on the willingness of that first wolf to leap in and grab the moose's nose. Such a maneuver involves considerable risk. Call it courage. The willingness of the wolf to take that risk is linked directly to its trust of its fellows and, hence, its membership in the pack.

The human mind, which loves nothing more than to frighten itself, typically endows predators with a ferocity quite out of line with reality. Predators are actually delicate and temperamental mechanisms. To catch and kill prey, especially large prey, requires that the killer be in top physical and psychological condition. The sprint demands prodigious amounts of energy and the kill requires perfect timing. Animals fly through the air. Hooves and horns flash as the prey fights for its life. A single mistake can produce a serious injury to the predator. That's why a predator as theoretically dangerous as a cougar will flee from a pack of dogs. It could easily fight off the dogs, but it would emerge a wounded victor. A solitary predator might well starve to death before it healed well enough to forage again for its own food.

The wolf can afford to take risks that a solitary animal cannot. If the wolf that grabs the nose of the moose happens to drag itself away with two or three crushed ribs, it won't starve; its packmates will feed and nurse it until it recovers.

Wolves have no hands, but they can still carry. A wolf will consume a stomachful of meat, take it to a wounded or sick packmate, and regurgitate it. It sounds disgusting to us humans, but it works for the wolf. As a result of such comradeship, wolves frequently survive broken bones, concussions, and other injuries that would lead to starvation in a cougar.

So pack behavior not only contributes to the ability to kill by means of coordinated attack, it increases the odds that individual wolves will live to fight again. This, in evolutionary terms, boosted the acceptable courage level as well. If early people thought of the wolf as brave, that was not without a basis in reality. Courage is an emotional quality, and the wolf's mammalian brain is fully capable of feeling it. If you analyze the trade-offs, courage is a quality that can develop only in a pack animal.

Not that inherited behaviors totally rule an animal's life. They don't. They tend to focus most strongly on moments related to the survival and reproduction of DNA, such as mate selection and the kill. That leaves plenty of room for learned behaviors and the development of individual character. An animal as flexibly intelligent as the wolf can, if the occasion demands, override much of its specific programming—and, anyway, most of canid life (like most of human life) is lived in the programmatically blank moments between sex and heroic acts of combat. The wolf fills this time foraging, playing, solidifying relationships with its packmates, and generally behaving opportunistically.

Charlie, adapted as he was to human civilization, could perform remarkable feats of counterintuitive behavior. If he set out
to follow some programmed behavior, like chasing a rabbit,
Lynn's command could stop him and bring him back. When I
saw this happen, with Charlie or any other working dog, I was
struck by wonder: When humans override their deepest desires,
it is called "willpower."

Charlie's ancestor, the wolf, had all the dog's nascent qualities. Within the capacity of its brain, the wolf learned from its
experience and modeled the world accordingly. Confronted with
a new situation, it applied what it knew from the past or followed the lead of an older, more savvy wolf.

That is another quality of pack carnivores. In a social group
of intelligent individuals, experience equals wisdom. The
younger animals have a propensity not only to follow the older
ones but to turn their adventures into lessons. This leads to a
secondary tendency of the younger members of the pack to support their older packmates, who therefore tend to live longer
than they might on their own. This effectively extends the useful life of their acquired knowledge. For the young this translates,
in evolutionary terms, to an extended adolescence, occupied by
learning. An infant caribou can keep up with the herd within
twenty-four to forty-eight hours of its birth, but a wolf cub will
probably not be allowed to take part in an attack on a moose before it is two years old.

A pack of wolves, in short, is more than a herd. It is an extended family, a gang, a platoon, a team, a tribe, a band. There is
not only cooperation but mutual respect, trust, and obligation.
This fact is critical and, in the study of the wolf, highly illuminating.

From the wolf's point of view, social life is just the way the
world is. Humans, and especially scientists, demand more: They
want to trace out the evolutionary mechanisms. Unfortunately,

behavioral genetics is devilishly difficult to understand, especially for early scientists. It was counterintuitive from the get-go. Besides, there is no such thing as a fossil of a pack.

Add the fact that humans insist on viewing the wolf as a singular animal. Both sets of my own grandparents had in their living rooms a classic Victorian reproduction of the singular wolf, perched on a snowy hill and baying at the moon. If that famous painting was based on an actual wolf, which I rather doubt, we can say one thing for sure about its state of mind: It was one very unhappy wolf. Wolves sing in choruses.

The myth of the lone wolf illustrates the whole conundrum faced by the humans who hunted the same ground. The wolf was in many ways like humans, but in many ways it was the opposite. The wolf was both kindred and alien, and it was both these things at once. This made it difficult to think about wolves with any clarity. So many inconsistencies made for latent images, fantasies, and guesswork—guesswork that often blended into politics and, like the lone wolf painting, would become downright laughable as we learned more. All the same we tried, and tried again. It was somehow terribly important to us that we understand the wolf.

◇

The real problem in understanding the wolf, then, is not the wolf at all. It is the human mind, that organ of abstraction, doomed by its extreme self-awareness to get tangled up in its own ideas and trip over its own suppositions. Extended logic is a mode of thinking that is new to the earth—one of nature's occasional wild-card experiments, nothing more and nothing less. And, as prototypes often do, it contains a couple of glitches.

The most obvious bug in the architecture of the human mind is that all roads lead to the lizard brain. The intellectual formations of the brain can only communicate with one another via impulses that travel through the emotional and reptilian brains, both of which have to kibitz. Thus the original impulses tend to get garbaged up by ancient fears and wants. This brings us back to the now well-known difficulty of separating what we humans know from what we *want* to know, what we see from what we *expect* to see.

My favorite philosopher, Baruch Spinoza, spent his life grinding eyeglass lenses, so that humans might see more clearly. His vocation naturally had a profound influence on his hobby of philosophy, and he thought a lot about that other kind of myopia, the inner myopia. One of his conclusions was that our lives are lived in spirals of learning—we revisit our experiences. We deal with our mother, for example, when we are infants, and then we put the matter to rest. Or we think we do. Then in adolescence, as we seek to break away, we run into the same problem in its Mr. Hyde persona. Warfare between mother and offspring usually results in an uneasy truce, but it's not one that will hold. We have to deal with the mother problem yet again— all is circular, like Spinoza's lens blanks—when we become parents ourselves, and the original relationship is reversed. Even our mother's death doesn't stop us from coming around, again and again, to rethink who she was and what she did, both to us and for us. The same is true of other important subjects, so that as we progress up the spiral of existence we spend our lives dealing at ever higher levels with a limited number of powerful issues. All our best stories, in other words, are the old ones, told anew, with improved insight.

Spinoza's spiral of learning generalizes beautifully. I noticed, thanks to Spinoza, that a writer's professional life works the same way. We learn grammar, but don't fully appreciate it. We learn transitions well enough to do them, and we move on. We learn clarity . . . and on and on and on. Eventually, we find ourselves coming around to view grammar again with a new wisdom, born of experience. Grammar, to the journeyman, becomes plastic. To a master, it rates a deeper look yet, as we realize that the words on paper work the way they do because of the deep language-processing circuitry of the mind. Then we learn to say one thing while appearing to say another, to play the melody and harmony at the same time.

Intellectual life is no different, generally, and so as I contemplated the dog, and read extensively about scientists who contemplated (or avoided contemplating) it, I kept coming back to that *something* that had happened to us twelve thousand years ago. We had inherited great power, but with it came great angst. The two were inseparable. Sometimes the angst drove us, sometimes the power. Different sides of the same human coin.

The ability to intellectualize has its decided advantages, of course, which it's difficult to overstate. We live in our inner worlds, yet our fates are often determined by outside reality. If that reality can be determined, then the abstract can be made unambiguous and the resulting clarity can be of incalculable value. The fall of an apple from a tree, or the roll of a ball down an incline, are events that can be controlled and repeated—quantified, and reduced first to language, then logic, then numbers. As Newton grasped, the motions of the real world lend themselves to the application of mathematics. When something is true mathematically, it tends to be true physically. When something is true physically, a corresponding mathematics can always be found.

Well, okay, not always. Not, certainly, when legend attached itself to scientific questions, as astrology and Catholicism once attached to astronomy. Galileo must have had some reflections on that, as he was led into the inquisitorial torture chamber. Yet in hindsight, the Renaissance struggle over astronomy, the sun-centered solar system, the gravitationally determined orbits of the planets—all this conflict was actually over fairly quickly and with little bloodshed (at least by the horrible standard of the time). If only our newfound knowledge of the anatomy of the mind could be accepted so easily.

It won't be, though. As a historian of science once pointed

out to me, astronomy was relatively easy to objectify—that is, to separate out from wants and expectations. This was in large part because astronomical objects did not really matter, at least in an everyday way, so the human doing the objectifying did not have an immediate stake in the outcome. The stars were there before we came, and would be there long after we were gone, and our wishes and conjectures ultimately had meaning only within our own psyches. Copernicus, Galileo, and the rest didn't really change anything that mattered critically to the serf behind the plow.

The distance of the stars, and their forever abstract nature, allowed physics to mature into the first true science. Others followed in a significant and revealing order: physical chemistry, geology, biochemistry, biology, and finally the psychological sciences. The birth of each new science was a stronger and more invasive blow to the human ego than the one before it. Chemistry brought the idea that the world we thought we knew was really determined by particles and processes we couldn't hope to actually see. Creationists are still reacting to what they see as geology's most preposterous conclusion, that the earth existed for billions of years before humans showed up and during most of that time life was right there on the scene, as it is today, evolving. In physiology, the discovery that there was no spiritual vital principle in the nervous system was, for generations, a heresy. And so it went.

Biology was in some ways simpler to contemplate than physics, since we saw it all around us, but it was damnably difficult to objectify. It was tough for scientists to design controlled experiments for animals and their mysterious metabolisms, and it was almost impossible to reduce them to mathematics. Worse, animals are alive, as man and woman are alive, and so they fell within the fog of human mythology about itself and its own transcendence. Objectification of animals, and most especially of the human animal, ran directly counter to the human instinct—and scientists inevitably proved to be as human as the alchemists and wizards who had come before them.

This inherent murkiness of the life sciences has confounded biology from the beginning. Charles Darwin's work won acclaim around the world, only to have the romantic moralism of the Victorian age immediately imposed on it. The evolution of humans, as a result, was soon widely perceived as the heaven-guided ascent of man from his beastly past to his more respectable present. Monkeys and apes were conceptualized as imperfect humans. Herbivores were seen to be gentle, while predators were vicious, except when they were being depicted by romantic painters and writers as symbols of the naturally heroic. The lion was still king of beasts while the wolf, traditionally cast as the bad guy in the fables of European shepherds—can you blame them?—came in for a lion's share of bad press. Only in the minds of the late Victorian intellectuals did wolves become objects of our romantic imagination.

As scientists of the twentieth century struggled to free themselves from such thinking, they labeled it "anthropomorphism." It became a scientific sin to ascribe human motives, emotions, or perceptions to animals and protohumans. They were animals, metabolic extensions of their ecological niches. That, and nothing more. It was even said that animals could not feel pain. One talked about animals in terms of energy cycles, food chains, and environmental systems. If that mind-set seems harsh in light of today's knowledge and sensibilities, it bore rich fruit. It was part and parcel of the legitimization of biology, the foundation of the sciences of biochemistry and molecular genetics, and the appearance of modern medicine.

But as the pendulum swung from romance to realism, the new extreme turned out to have its own excesses. Brain science discovered that animals, particularly mammals, were well equipped with the circuitry to feel, and to do so every bit as deeply as humans. In fact, to judge by what could be learned from neural circuitry, they could probably feel even more deeply than humans. This immensely complicated the problem, since humans have long considered feeling love, fidelity, and courage to be the highest human quality.

Investigating life that closely resembled the investigator was a real hairball. Geologists and astronomers didn't have to deal with that much emotional static. It took biologists a century to even *begin* to address it. They finally tried to solve the problem by considering (correctly) that the animal was the product of an ecology, and that understanding the animal meant first understanding the ecologies.

Unfortunately, if ecologies could in fact be profitably quantified, that quantification tended to obscure the issues—the animals and their lives—that originally interested us. Science and beauty might indeed be two facets of the same thing, but they were nigh impossible to bring together.

So it was that scientific thinking—disembodied thinking—though it created a new world with many advantages, also led to disregard for the natural world. In the middle and late twentieth century, the scientist who claimed animals had feelings might pay for his indiscretion with his career. The intellectual impulse that had led to factories and the consumption of natural resources on a gigantic scale simply had no place for nature. As a result, rivers turned brown and poisonous, skies grew yellow, and there was a burgeoning sense that the natural world was dying. This gestalt, as it crystallized in the sixties and seventies, led to a new round of romanticism about nature.

The wolf, meanwhile, had shifted in the human perspective. The Victorian artist might think the wolf was a heroic symbol, but well into the twentieth century it was considered a marauding killer. It still howled in the forests of Europe and America, posing a direct threat to farmers, herders, even perhaps in some circumstances, humans. Russian literature was rich with lore about packs of wolves chasing sleds through the taiga. That was one of the essential Russian horror stories.

A century later wolves had all but vanished from the temperate climates, killed out by bounty hunters and eradication programs, and were rapidly disappearing even in the northlands. In Alaska, helicopter pilots made a living taking hunters out to kill wolves from the air with machine guns.

As the wolves disappeared, the memory of their depredations dwindled with the passing of each generation of farmers and herders. Environmentalists dismissed any threat the wolf had posed to humans as legend. It simply didn't happen. And there was no doubt that the wolf was in danger of extinction. Suddenly the big bad wolf was a protected animal, and the helicopter pilots packed up their guns and hired out to people with cameras.

Whatever the facts, there was something about the wolf that would not be ignored. As the environmental movement progressed from fresh new breeze to howling cyclone, the wolf was at or near its center, recast now as the naturalistic personification of the last cowboy—the lone, angry, romantically unbound holdout against the parking lot, the hamburger stand, and the strip mall.

Over the years, as I kept trying to make sense of the dog, scientific interest grew in the wolf, the pack, its evolution, and its ways. The dog was still not worth studying but the wolf, ah, the wolf—*that* was a different matter. Suddenly there were young biologists of the first rank whose fondest desire was to study the social lives of wolves, and there was at least some public money to finance their efforts.

The passion of the wolf researcher for the wolf reflected an attitudinal sea change that was affecting all of science. As a journalist I could see it almost everywhere: Climatologists were embroiled in controversy over global climate change and the harm being done to the ozone layer; biologists spread the alarm about the decimation of the rain forests; oncologists signed on as advocates against a growing list of possible carcinogens; and the word "environmentalist" ceased to distinguish between the science and the movement by the same name. The animal rights movement invaded veterinary science and gathered partisans in physics labs, hospitals, and university philosophy departments. As part of this change the very idea of objectivity fell at least temporarily into disfavor.

◇

A profound cultural shift was occurring. The reductionism that had destroyed Victorian romanticism was receding, and romanticism once more bubbled forth, now in the guise of postmodernism. Science, and the exactness it implied, was suddenly much less interesting to writers, sociologists, and politicians than were irony and ambiguity. Everybody quoted Derrida, Foucault, and Lacan, though few actually read them—I knew, because I had, and they were unreadable. The acronym "dwem" for "dead white European male," began to appear, and at social functions of the proper sort nobody would dare talk reverently about Shakespeare. It was far more fashionable to focus on the fundamental ambiguity between rationality and passion, truth and emotion, the idealized past and the implacably pragmatic present, the way things were and the way they ought to be.

Nowhere was this dichotomy more explicit than in the study of the wolf. Ancient, pre-agricultural peoples had apparently loved and even worshipped it, but as our ancestors began herding and farming, they learned to hate it. The wolf, to a farmer or herder, was the epitome of evil. Now, in the blink of an eye, we city dwellers loved it. The pendulum had switched positions without ever swinging through zero or offering an instant of neutrality. It was as though the human mind contained the wolf in some deep, value-laden place, and while it could exist there as either good or evil, there was no neural circuitry for moderation. The human imagination seemed to have no place for the actual wolf.

As I studied the literature of the wolf, I was oddly protected from the emotional fog. I really didn't care about the wolf one way or the other—or not, at least, with any great passion. What I really cared about was the problem in front of me, which happened to be the dog. This meant I could achieve a certain distance from the wolf. As a result I was fascinated in a detached sort of way as virtually every student of the species came to struggle with how to handle the real wolf vs. the romanticized wolf. Each one, from the scientist L. David Mech to the writer Barry Lopez, criticized those who had romanticized the wolf, implying that they would not stoop to such a thing. The wolf, they said, does not exist to fit our preconceptions. It is a real creature of the real earth, they said, and as such it was a mixed bag of good and evil, beautiful and ugly, heroic and repugnant. They would speak of the real wolf. This they promised.

And then each of them, in turn, and in stages, page by page, broke that promise again and again until it was forgotten entirely and the wolf, the objectified wolf, metamorphosed once again into wolf as totem.

I shouldn't be too harsh. In fact, some reality did creep in around the edges. For one thing, the wolf too had changed. Unless descriptions from earlier centuries were to be entirely discounted, the wolf of old was a much larger animal and much, much more aggressive. This made sense, considering the selection pressure exerted on the wolf with the introduction of cheap and accurate firearms. When more and more humans could afford guns, the wolf, which had been defined as the archenemy of the most powerful species ever to stalk the earth, paid dearly. It was not difficult to imagine that long guns and bounties had led to the gradual disappearance of the large wolf and the intrepid wolf, placing a premium on shyness and secretive habit. The modern wolf, in addition to knowing the exact mathematics of the spook radius, also seemed to understand innately that it was not a good idea to associate with human beings.

These forces converged to make the wolf even more mysterious. To my surprise, I discovered that in many gatherings of experts and advocates I was the only one who had ever seen an actual wolf in the wild, albeit I'd done so for only for a few seconds. What did we have, aside from fairy tales, legends, and campfire stories, to tell us what the wolf actually was?

The nature of the wolf was therefore a fair question for the imagination and I, as any reader might, built my own scenario. Though I had never witnessed a pack of free-ranging wolves on the hunt, that was the scene that formed most readily in my mind. That was partly because the hunt had been so well described, by Lopez and Mech and others, but also because the hunt was surely when the wolf was seen at its most wolfish. So what I had was a literary composite, produced from science and near-science but shaped and filtered through my own mind, informed in part by the black, wolflike animal in my own parlor.

I only needed to close my eyes, and I was there. In my case, "there" was a snowy landscape at the edge of a great mountain range. The snow was clean, white, and mostly unbroken.

The human mind is a vivid cinematographer. I could see it all before me, on the silver screen of knowledge enhanced by imagination. There is a crust on top of the snow but it isn't thick enough to support a ninety-pound wolf, even with its big, padded feet. So the lighter, alpha wolf, a female in this case, breaks the trail. The others follow in her footsteps.

I count seven of them. Directly behind the alpha wolf is her mate, followed by a single pup surviving from last summer's litter. Behind the pup is an older wolf with a pronounced limp and hair that is grayer and thinner than the others; perhaps this is a former alpha wolf. Behind the old wolf come a male and a female from the litter the year before. Another male, this one related in some long forgotten way to the alpha wolf, follows closely behind. Last comes the omega wolf, the scapegoat wolf, probably an in-law or a stray wolf that was accepted into the pack last summer. He trails some twenty yards behind the rest.

They are, as wolves always are when they have not just gorged themselves, hungry. In legend and myth the wolf is pure appetite; in this particular instance, the stories are not wrong. The wolf is always hunting; no vole is too small to stop and devour, no skunk too stinky, no porcupine too bothersome. But this day, in my vision, there is larger game in the offing—game for which the wolf is destiny.

Suddenly the wolves stop, nostrils aquiver with the scent of caribou. After only a moment's hesitation, the column changes direction and moves with more enthusiasm. They follow the scent, a smell they associate with eating. Their mouths drip saliva. In a few minutes they stop again, as they top a small rise. An old female caribou is visible in the distance, grazing along a line of willows. Prey.

The caribou's eyes are not as good as the wolves', and she is upwind. The wolves have the advantage. The pack closes up for what can only be described as a strategy meeting, noses together. Nobody knows how they communicate, exactly, but an information exchange clearly takes place. Understandings are reached and assignments made. Wolf packs are capable of executing surprisingly complicated hunting maneuvers, including ambushes.

The elderly wolf and the pup will not take part in the kill. They veer off, heading toward a rendezvous point.

The omega wolf takes the male yearling and heads off in another direction. They are to cut off the caribou in case she bolts. The snow, in any case, will slow her more than it slows the wolves.

A few minutes later, as the main body of wolves approach the prey, she indeed does try to flee. But before she reaches speed, the yearling, followed by the omega wolf, hurtles down from a small rise and is upon her. The yearling tears a huge piece of flesh from her shoulder, and as she wheels to face him the omega wolf dodges her hoofs to open a long wound on the opposite side of her belly.

The caribou tries to run again, but the snow is red with arterial blood and she is soon at bay. The wolves circle her now, a programmatic movement that keeps her off guard. One by one, they seize opportunities to streak in and open another bleeding wound. It is a death of a thousand rips and tears. As the caribou begins to go into shock, she lurches and stumbles but catches herself and stays on her feet.

The intensity of the moment tapers off. While several of the wolves keep the caribou active and her blood flowing, two of their packmates lie in the snow, resting and watching. Another goes off to fetch the old wolf and the pup. In other circumstances, the wolves would carry food to the dependent wolves in their stomachs, regurgitating it for them to eat as they do for pups. But in this case it is more efficient to bring them to the kill.

In a half hour the big ungulate goes down with a grunt and the wolves move in. As she thrashes in the snow they tear at her underbelly. Her kicking feet become entangled in her own intestines.

The wolves begin to feed before she is even dead, ripping at her liver, gorging themselves on huge strips of flesh from her haunches. Her last twitch is anticlimactic. Presently two ravens appear to share in the bounty; they hop sideways toward the carcass, keeping a wary eye on the wolves. The old wolf and the pup reappear, along with the wolf sent to fetch them. Other scavengers wait, out of range, for the wolves to eat their fill. In hours there will be nothing left but bones and the contents of the stomach.

◇

This hunt with its variations, repeated infinitely in the north-land, captures what seems to the human mind to be the two sides of the wolf. The relationship between the wolves is so hu-man it gives the heart pause; the other aspect, the bestial one, is so beastly as to turn the stomach.

From our newfound understanding of the triune brain and its evolution, we know that we are not committing the sin of anthropomorphizing when we observe that wolves are protec-tive of their young and old, or that they strategize and engage in complex teamwork to achieve their ends—or that, with their alpha and omega wolves, they engage in the same hero worship and scapegoating as do humans. To observe the pack's tender but clearly intelligent treatment of their cubs inevitably re-minds us of the human family. The wolf skull does not contain the circuitry that allows it to do mathematics, but the circuitries of love, of respect, of anger—those, we now know, are all there.

Are a wolf's impulses so analogous to human emotions that we can legitimately use those words? Scientific modernism of the mid twentieth century would have said they were probably not and that, in any event, we had no way of knowing. To com-pare the wolf's feelings to our own had about it the fetid scent of romantic anthropomorphism. It was better not to clutter our conceptualization of animals with such emotion-loaded descrip-tions. But the neuroscience revolution of the seventies and the eighties changed this logic; we discovered ways of knowing what animals feel—or, if not exactly *knowing*, then at least making highly educated guesses. And if we had once erred in thinking animals were too like us, we had erred a second time when we denied that any likeness existed.

I am, at bottom, a product of the Enlightenment; as I reach for the words to express what to me are still uneasy concepts, I recall an interview I had, in the early 1980s, with Candace Pert. Dr.

Pert, who had earned a place in scientific history in 1973 as co-discoverer of the opiate receptor in the brain, was by then a senior researcher at the National Institutes of Health. By this time in her life she had personally disassembled and studied thousands, if not tens of thousands, of brains: human, cat, rat, and mouse.

I forget what the interview was supposed to be about. At the time, the neuroscience revolution was yielding a breakthrough a month, and Candace Pert was involved in many of them. Whatever the subject that had brought me to her laboratory, my curiosity was satisfied and my notebook was full. Still, I hesitated to leave. During the interview my eyes had been repeatedly drawn to a large, four-color print on the wall—a blown-up photo of a slice of rat brain, its active morphine receptor sites labeled with radioactive tracers. Suddenly, in the letdown that follows a focused interview, an off-topic question formed.

What, in all her years of research, was the most striking thing she had learned? If she could say only one thing about all those brains of all those different species, what would that one thing be?

Dr. Pert was clearly taken aback by the question. The interview had been technical, and now I had shifted dimensions on her. She paused for what seemed a long time.

Now, many years later, as I struggle to describe the legitimacy of ascribing human qualities to the wolf, her words echo in my mind. *I think*, she said of the brains she had seen, dog and cat, human and rat, . . . *I think I would have to say that the most striking thing was how alike they all are.*

As one studied animals in general, and the wolf in particular, and was carried from the facts to the meaning that lies behind them, one simply could not maintain the sharp conceptual lines that classical science had aimed to draw. If we were to feel our way forward, in some honest search for truth, we had to find a new path—we had to pick our way, somehow, between the saccharine truisms of new-age hype and the old, cherished intellectual illusion that we can somehow remain cool, detached, and objective.

Putatively objective, reasonable fact, applied to the behavior of the wolf in the light of modern science, revealed it to be a sophisticated social creature guided, in its relationships with its fellows by a set of emotions we humans have all ourselves felt to one degree or another. That this creature, which is not human, which in fact is the epitome of brutishness, can provide so many human parallels . . . well, that's uncomfortable. It challenges our secure perception of ourselves as unique.

True, in some ways we are unique. In our ability to do mathematics, for example. But in our hearts, in our ability to feel emotions, the answer is clearly *no*. The circuitry of emotion, passed down and shaped by the forces of nature, is not subject to human patent or copyright. Other animals possess emotions, and tested their limits far before our own kind arrived on the scene. That we share emotions with the wolf does not exactly make the wolf human, or the human a wolf, but it does make us similar in some deeply important respects. To deny our similarity is simply to avoid the truth.

Charlie had led me into some dicey territory. I didn't reject the idea of objectivity—couldn't. Even if it was admittedly beyond the human capacity to achieve a state of objective perfection, objectivity still had its demonstrated uses. Without objectivity, there would be no science, no technology, no civilization. It was undeniably a good idea, as we thought about our world, to try to remain cool and objective. At the same time, if it was a tricky and mysterious truth we were after, we'd better be aware that objectivity, the coin of our realm, has a flip side as well. To put the matter differently, if I am to be truly objective to *any* useful degree, I have to also be aware of my feelings—if for no other reason, then so I can factor them out.

This much, at least, I had learned from the canid kind. While humans may be unique in some respects, we can't afford to set ourselves apart from the other animals. If we do, we'll never understand ourselves, or what happened to make us what we are.

◇

I cast and recast what I knew, looking for a clue. The wolf, when not engaged in the act of killing, is gentle, playful, considerate and protective of its packmates. It defers to age and experience and learns quickly, not only from its own mistakes but from the mistakes of others. It has a sense of what is right and what is wrong and it strives with its essential wolfness to remain in tune with the world.

Let's just call these things what they are. A resolve to remain in tune with the world is called "ethics." There is a perfectly good word for an act of deference, performed by a young wolf to an old one, and that word is "respect." I am a parent, and while I never regurgitated my food to feed my young, I think I can understand what a parent wolf feels when he or she feeds its cubs. And as I read about the bond between the mating pair in a wolf pack, and consider the obvious grief that the one suffers on the loss of the other, the concise and objective word that comes to mind is "love."

If we can speak of wolf cooperation and wolf love, then we can also ascend to the other level, and speak of the society of wolves. A wolf may be born only a wolf, but a wolf pack develops a group savvy for which we have another fine, utilitarian word: culture. This much is not my own thinking: The experts seem to agree that one wolf pack is recognizably different from other wolf packs. A pack's culture appears to evolve over time, and seems to have the ability to accommodate not only for changing circumstances but also for the changing personalities of new generations of citizen wolves.

Every time we say they are like us, we must also say they are not. Wolves forever remain wolves, not humans in wolf's clothing. They are unlike us because they are wolves and we are not.

Wolves and poodles, for reasons that I do not pretend to understand, love to roll on odoriferous, rotten carcasses, collecting in their coats what they apparently think is the lovely smell. Wolves and dogs regurgitate their food for the dining pleasure of their companions. The human stomach lurches at the very thought.

Nor do we rest easy with the realities of the wolf kill—realities that most romantic portraits of the wolf either ignore entirely or show through a lens smeared with Vaseline, the way old-time *Playboy* photographers used to shoot the girl of the month. Humans are killers, undeniably, but we prefer that the actual act be done offstage and by the quickest and most humane means. Even those of us who still hunt embrace the sporting ethic of the clean kill. While a wolf might casually drag out and begin to eat the liver of an animal that is still alive, the human imagination simply cannot tolerate the visible suffering of a victim. "Victim," in fact, may be a concept that is confined to the human species, along with the concept of the coup de grâce. Nowhere in nature, as far as I am aware, does it cross the species line.

Sometimes, as I found myself struggling in this morass of issues, I suffered panic attacks. I was a reporter, not a philosopher. All I was trying to do was figure out the lowly dog—which I had absolutely no business doing in the first place.

Yet I sensed that in these differences and similarities I'd find a clue as to what happened to my own ancestors . . . to the old man in the grave and, yes, I supposed, the puppy too. How did it get so complicated?

Humans dream. Do wolves dream? I know Charlie does, or at least his nocturnal kicking and woofing seem to indicate so. But I see no evidence that Charlie has that other kind of dream, the waking dream that so characterizes humans, the kind of dream we call a vision.

Though wolves communicate, they do not have language; as a result, their cultural evolution is limited by the length of their memory and the persistence of their habit. They do not draw pictures on rocks, or make tools, or bury their dead, or ask the gods to intercede in their behalf.

But when all those differences and similarities are totaled up, one defining juxtaposition remains. Wolves are of a piece with the subglacial environment in which they live. Put simply, they belong there. Over millions of years, the wolf and its ungulate prey were honed by one another until they constituted a finely tuned ecological machine that flowed across the landscape like the wind, capable of sustaining and perpetuating itself for what might seem like forever. Generation followed generation, living and dying but never really changing themselves or altering their environment. They were there; as time had meaning to human beings or gray wolves they had always been there, and they belonged there.

Humans did not.

◇

Meanwhile, science was not standing still and neither was the accepted date for the appearance of the first dog. Olsen still refused to push it back any further than eight thousand years ago, but other experts were beginning to credit evidence that would put the first dogs earlier. There were fragments of tooth and jaw that, to many, seemed more doggy than wolfish, and that significantly predated Olsen's fossil. Mitochondrial DNA studies were too new yet to convince everyone; graphs and charts just didn't have the verisimilitude of a fossil you could hold in your hand. Still, they were gaining credibility and pushing Olsen's date back. Scientists were starting to talk about the dog appearing about twelve thousand years ago—the magic number.

Most of the scientists I spoke with shrugged off the correspondence of dates. Coincidences happen and, anyway, the final answer was not yet in. Nor would that answer arrive in our lifetimes, if ever.

That was not acceptable to me. Reporters, like detectives, are constitutionally suspicious of coincidence—especially if the coincidence in question is stunning in its implications. And what could be more stunning than the idea that modern humans appeared at the same time as the first dogs? It implied that they were created in the same environmental cauldron and *that* meant . . . well, something.

The other fact that dropped into the equation was the persistent matter of cranial capacity. At precisely this geological moment, some twelve thousand years ago, the human lost nearly 10 percent of its brain mass and, in the process, became the animal destined to build civilizations, pyramids, and spacecraft. And as that new, smaller-brained but somehow smarter animal walked out of the swirling fog of time, it was not alone. It was accompanied by, of all things, a mutant wolf.

This wolf was also different from its forebears, having lost 20 percent of its brain mass at the same time it won a place in the human sphere. On the basis of neuron count, it was dumber. But that would not prevent it from becoming the second most successful animal nature had ever had the inspiration to create.

I didn't know what this all meant, but it was very exciting to think about. If it did ultimately turn out to be coincidence I'd be the fool, but the risk seemed worth taking. I felt I was finally circling an answer or, if not exactly an answer, then some valuable clue.

No one had yet floated what I considered a compelling theory for how the human had changed so drastically around twelve thousand years ago, and I didn't have one either. It was easier to contemplate the dog. It would ultimately be proved that only a few genes separated the dog from the wolf, but whatever those genes were, the alteration was dramatic and complete. The dog, from that moment on, was not simply a specialized wolf. Had that been so—had the modern dog simply been a wolf of a different kind—then, when released on its own, it would have slowly and inevitably regressed back to its wolfish state. That doesn't happen.

The dachshund, the saluki, the Saint Bernard, the poodle, the German shepherd—allow them to stray and to interbreed at their own whim, and after a while you get some sort of root animal, all right, but it wouldn't be a wolf. It'd be a dingo, of the sort that populated the Australian outback, an animal nobody would ever mistake for a wolf.

It wasn't all that difficult to understand why the dog became so successful; you only needed to look to its companion. The dog didn't miss its lost brain mass because it had access to the far bigger (even if somewhat diminished) brain of the human.

My mind went back to the old man in the grave. Only now, I usually found myself thinking not of "the old man in the grave" but of "the old man and the puppy." Nor did I any longer assume the puppy had been buried there as some kind of a food item. My working assumption was that it was a companion— that, or some sort of guide.

I admit, I saw the danger there. *Post hoc ergo propter hoc* is a logical fallacy, as my undergraduate philosophy professor had said. Just because things coincide doesn't mean one causes the other. The stock market went up, and then I caught a cold: This didn't mean the stock market rise caused my cold. Likewise, the simultaneous emergence of the modern human and the dog might have been a complete coincidence.

But did I believe that? Not for an instant.

Chapter Seven

Anthropological enigmas take a long time to solve, assuming they are solvable. So while I felt I had made an important correlation—wolf and human both lost brain mass at the same time—it didn't lead to a revelatory conclusion. I was still stuck on the dog, and had been for a number of years. I could no longer remember exactly how I got myself into this maze, and I was beginning to have trouble imagining how I would ever get myself out.

Meanwhile, there was Charlie to remind me at least daily of my plight. *I'm here*, he seemed to say, *I'm doing my job; why aren't you doing yours? Or maybe we should just chuck it all and go chase a squirrel.*

Why not, indeed?

From Charlie's point of view I was the omega wolf. Lynn was Charlie's true god and master, and the glory I basked in was of the reflected sort. All the same, while canids may have their social orders they are not particularly snooty about them. There was room for Charlie and me to be pals. He obeyed my commands, at least when he sensed it was in his interest to do so, and I learned to let him be my guide on our walks. Once I turned the scouting over to him, I saw a lot more.

Thanks to him I saw the rabbit and her newborns over in the thicket of scotch broom. I saw the decaying remains of a six-point buck on the farthest edge of the property. I saw the immature raccoon who had taken to sleeping in the high crotch of an apple tree. Charlie supervised my labors in the garden and undertook to protect me from the gophers with such enthusiasm that he left the yard cratered with potholes deep enough to swallow the back tire of my John Deere riding mower.

He even tried to enlist me in his feuds. He was clearly exasperated that I would do nothing about the gophers—yeah, right, just get out my nuclear weapons! And then there were those damned pheasants!

Charlie despised pheasants. They were territorial, and so was he. They didn't like to fly, but Charlie was rarely so happy as when he could frighten one into the air, sending it on a noisy, irritable, caw-cucking glide downhill and into the cover of the swale. I thought the pheasants were beautiful and I wished them no harm, but each time we flushed one my own heart soared with excitement along with Charlie's.

Our house was built into the side of a moderately steep hill, overlooking the aforementioned swale that expanded in the distance into a little valley. The deck, jutting out from the hillside, sat high above this and offered a good view. Equally important in the land of rain, it was protected by deep, overhanging eaves. That made it a fine place to sit and think, even in winter rainy season. When summer came, the clouds vanished and the air turned as dry as it had once been wet. Then our little valley took on the almost surrealistic clarity I remembered from my childhood years in New Mexico. On such days the sunsets were spectacular, and it became my habit to watch them from the deck. Charlie loved that deck as much as I did; when I sat down, it usually wasn't long until he came and sat beside me.

Charlie's presence changed experiences, even the experience of sitting there doing nothing. I would look at the valley and think my own thoughts, often to do with an issue involving the university, say; or I might brood about my writing.

Charlie knew nothing of my work or the occasional crisis it raised, and even if he had he wouldn't have cared. I tried to explain to him where his dog food was coming from. He seemed to listen politely, as he did to anything I said, but it didn't stick. Dog food? He was blithely unconcerned. That was a human problem, and he had the utmost confidence in my ability to solve it. His was not to worry about it. The food would be there in his bowl when the time came.

But he knew when I was in a funk, and *that*—his human wallowing in a funk—was something he cared very much about. So he'd show up next to my deck chair and sit down so that I could reach out my right hand and touch his neck. It was calming to feel his wool. He'd sit there, I'd occasionally stroke him, and he'd watch the valley.

He was good at it, too—at watching the valley, I mean. Human eyes are better in many ways than canid eyes, but dogs are better at detecting movement. This has something to do, I'd read, with the way their brains go on red alert when patterns change in their visual cortex.

There was nothing particularly remarkable about that—it was all physiology, how one brain cell connected to the next. I was more struck by his uncanny ability to communicate his observations to me. As he was born to be a human companion, so I seemed to have been born with the ability to understand his body language. A slight twitch of his ears and I almost instantly spotted the quail, moving uphill to roost in the big fir on the ridge. A flaring of his nostrils and a tensing of his body called my attention to the clump of underbrush where the deer had stopped to scan the landscape before emerging. In a moment they would head skittishly toward the bucket of apples they knew from experience that Lynn had left for them. A few minutes later, the appearance of a pheasant cock would elicit a low, angry growl, squelched only by my command.

What it boiled down to was that Charlie saw things long before I did. Then he called my attention to what he saw, and I'd see it more clearly than he could. We made a pretty good team, the dog and the man.

As I thought about the pair of us, sitting on the deck, I recalled a story I once did about pre-Columbian Indians in what is now South Dakota. Archaeologists there had unearthed an ancient massacre site that well predated the arrival of white men. This caught my eye, and my editor's, because it contradicted the then-current notion that Native Americans were peaceful until Columbus and his followers brought violence to the new world.

Not so in this case. According to the archaeologist I talked to, the site of the massacre had been an Indian village on a narrow, triangular peninsula of prairie that jutted into the Missouri River. That was a highly defensible position, protected on two sides by steep river banks. On the third side, at the base of the peninsula, the residents had built a tall log barricade. Outside that was a deep dry moat.

The discovery of the village, long since covered by prairie grass, had caused a lot of excitement. It was not, after all, the kind of living arrangement one would have expected of a peaceful culture.

A bit of preliminary poking around revealed that the Indians who'd once lived there had had good reason to worry about their fellow man. In fact, they apparently hadn't worried enough. At some point well before Columbus sailed from Europe, invaders had stormed the settlement, burned the log barricade, slaughtered the villagers, and dumped their dismembered bodies into the moat. As the dust blew and the rains came and went, the moat was partially filled in and the bones covered. Now that they were being exhumed, the extent of the massacre became apparent. The bones represented men, women, and children, and there was no doubt about what had befallen them. There were still arrowheads in some of the bones, and the dismembered skeletons showed the distinctive marks of stone hatchets.

Anything so contradictory of conventional wisdom was news, so it wasn't long before I found myself following two archaeology graduate students to the site, along a high-grass plain near the river. The grad students cautioned me about the area's huge rattlesnakes, but reassured me that they were easy to spot because their movements made the grass heads sway. You couldn't miss them—and believe me, I didn't. The rattlers were all over.

The scenery was, of course, dramatic. The Missouri River flowed through willow and cottonwood, and back from the floodplain stood a line of sentinel bluffs. At one point the archaeologists paused to let the panting reporter take a rest and, fulfilling their role as tour guides, they pointed out those bluffs. The Indians, they told me, used to sit at the tips of the promontories, watching for game—the earliest European explorers had remarked on the practice, which continued into the modern era. From up there you could see practically forever, and the game moved along the river.

As they sat and watched, the men made arrowheads and other stone implements . . . well, not exactly true. Working stone takes concentration, so the men worked and their dogs, sitting beside them, watched the valley. When something moved, down there, the dog would alert the hunter, who would then lay aside his stonework and decide what to do.

I was struck by that story, so before I went home I made it my business to investigate. Just as the scientists had said, the promontories offered striking views of the river. And if you went to the right place, looked down at your feet, and scratched the soil with the tip of your toe, sure enough, you'd be standing on a little hillock of flint scraps, broken arrowhead blanks, and assorted other implements that had either fractured improperly or in some other way failed to pass muster.

Now, many years later, sitting beside Charlie on our deck overlooking the valley, I gained a deeper and more personal appreciation of the pairing of hunter and dog—and of how important that animal had been to Neolithic humans.

Modern humans, of course, hunt different game with more abstract implements (though, like our ancestors, we break a lot of things before we are finished). But the old Jungian feelings are still there. Certainly Charlie and I derived great pleasure from sitting together on the promontory. Instead of chipping flint, I mulled over the events of the day, tried to integrate something interesting I had read, or attempted to untangle whatever mess that was my current project. I was, in effect, somewhere else. Charlie kept watch. When there was something to notice in the sweep of valley below, he let me know.

Charlie was proving to be quite a remarkable animal, functioning both as an extension of myself and an amplifier of nature. He lent me his nose and ears, on one level, and on another he lent me his joy. He showed me, by example, how to know myself. He opened my mind to the world around me and intensified all I saw, and because of him I saw things that I otherwise might never have noticed. Some of those things, like the approaching deer, I saw as soon as he showed them to me. But other revelations were more subtle, and I needed to be guided.

As all this percolated ever deeper into my brain, I wondered yet again just exactly who these four-legged creatures are, and what they are doing here? Where did they come from? And what is the source of the power they have over us?

And power is one thing they certainly had.

◇

When Lynn proposed a puppy as her marriage price, I had no inkling what I was getting into. Blithely innocent, I assumed that *having a puppy* was the equivalent of having a good reproduction of a Picasso painting on your living room wall. But no, having a dog is not enough; you apparently have to *do* things with it. You have to teach it to come, to sit, to heel—stuff I hadn't anticipated, but all the same . . . it wasn't a big deal. Or so I told myself at first.

In hindsight, and given that Lynn was both a true dog person and also a social creature, what happened was perfectly predictable. I'd understood that the dog had to be trained, but I'd thought that "training the dog" had to do mostly with teaching him to go outside to do his business. But that kind of stuff was simply an opener; next came obedience school. He had to earn his "good citizen" title. So one night a week, for six or eight weeks, I was a bachelor again, knocking around the house like a clapper in a bell while the lady went out on a date with the dog.

When Charlie finally earned the imprimatur of good citizen, and the three of us had time to celebrate, my education also got pushed forward another notch or two. The "good citizen" title was not the end of the process. Oh, no. It was only the beginning, the first step toward an obedience title—and from there, who knew? The stars!

I'd understood when I married her that Lynn is ambitious. She is a writer, after all, and writers generally make up for their lack of good sense with an excess of ambition. But . . . dogs? Could dogs be a tool of one's ambition?

I struggled to stay above the madness, but psychologically a puppy burns very bright, illuminating everything around it. I wasn't allowed to simply disappear. I had a standing invitation, brushing on obligation, to attend doggy class along with the rest of the family. I found excuses, of course, but eventually I ran out of them and found myself sitting on the sidelines watching the lessons.

By and large, this was about as dull as it sounds. Convincing a puppy it should sit perkily at its owner's side while other dogs were doing something interesting involved an infinity of coaxing and correction, sharp words, and dog cookies. The instructor lectured about various training approaches—and there are dozens, though they immediately got mixed up in my mind. The owners put their dogs through their paces, one human-dog pair heeling around the floor under the glare of the instructor while the others stood quietly awaiting their turn.

"Stood quietly" might be a bit of an exaggeration. In a beginning dog class, there is rarely a moment when such quiet actually occurs. Usually at least one dog is up and pulling at his leash, and rare was the evening that was not punctuated by two dogs going at one another with growls, snarls, and flashing fangs. The first time this happened, I was halfway off my seat before the owners pulled the dogs apart, but later I learned to be less alarmed. Dog "fights" are rarely that; despite the deadly-looking lunges and the bloodcurdling noises, the dogs are just playing dominance games. Both dogs innately know the rules, and in the rare instances when blood is drawn, it is most surely an accident.

And then, occasionally, something would happen that would seem to say more about the humans than the dogs. One evening, for example, a class of prideful obedience dog owners were practicing their "stays" in an old horse barn. It was a difficult venue, since the place smelled of horse dung (doggy perfume!). A bunch of furniture, including an old refrigerator, had been pushed up against a far wall, adding to the funky atmosphere. It was normally difficult to get beginning dogs to perform under such circumstances, but on this particular evening the animals and their owners were outdoing themselves. Sit. Down. Heel. Stay.

Finally came the moment when every dog was at a beautiful

stay in front of its owner. You could feel the pride in the air. The instructor stood in the ring and surveyed the circle around her with a baleful eye, obviously uncomfortable with the self-satisfaction she saw in her students. Then, in a fit of inspiration, she marched over to the abandoned refrigerator, flung the door open, and yelled, "Ice cream!"

Every dog in the barn broke its stay.

Generally, though, watching doggie class was right up there with watching second-graders practice soccer. I went for the sake of peace in the family. Besides, even when I didn't go I'd have to listen to a breathless blow-by-blow account when Lynn got home.

In time, though, all this work paid off and Charlie was deemed ready to go into the obedience competition ring. Whenever I couldn't avoid it, I'd spend an afternoon watching from the bleachers as various dogs performed (or more likely, failed to perform) under the commands of their owners.

All this happened in a rectangular ring marked with knock-down fences. There was a rigid set of procedures, enforced by stern-faced judges—high drama, as far as the dog owners were concerned, though from the bleachers it often looked more like low comedy.

The "downs" were a special problem. The last thing a red-blooded canid wants to do when there is a bunch of people and other dogs around is lie down and do nothing. To lie down under such circumstances is to be submissive and, worse in a dog's mind, bored. I could almost see the steam coming out of Charlie's ears as he lay there and the minutes passed and *absolutely nothing happened*.

I don't know exactly how the dog felt, of course, but as I was sitting in the stands watching the dogs lie there, it felt borrr-ring . . . and boredom, as any psychiatrist would tell you, is a form of pain. Five minutes doesn't sound like long, but try it: Sit and watch the second hand of your watch go around the circle five times. Better yet, spend five minutes observing the stapler on your desk. You'll get the gestalt of what it's like to watch a bunch of dogs in a down.

In actuality the boredom was often broken because most of the dogs just couldn't take it. In advanced competition the dogs are expected to lie there while their owners leave the area. I mean . . . what's a poor dog to think? How long is he supposed to stay down? Did it matter, when the human master wasn't looking? When a tree falls in a forest . . . ?

I could see the dogs pondering it. Can dogs ponder? Yes, of course they can, and if you look closely you can see them do it. There is a hesitation, a defocusing of the eyes, coupled (I assumed) with a focusing of the mind. The dog is definitely pondering, which, if you are a dog, is damned hard work.

Finally one dog would do the bored-dog thing, which is to scratch. Since it is awkward to scratch while in a down position, the dog would sit up to do it. The judge would raise her pad and write something. From the stands, the spectators couldn't see the word she wrote, but they knew what it was: *disqualified*.

If one dog could break its stay, and not get hit by lightning, well . . . you could just see the rest consider the implications. By and by a second dog would stand and stretch. The judge's pad would come up, and the pencil would write. *Disqualified*.

And then, the poodle being one of the most irrepressible of animals, Charlie would lose it. He'd leap up and start running around the ring. Once. Twice. Three times. Beautiful form, that poodle. When he ran flat out, he looked like a greyhound in shape and form, long legs stretching forward and back in the air, then coming together to hit the ground and leap once again through the air like a coiled spring.

At about this time, Lynn and the others would be escorted back into the ring. Lynn would look at the racing poodle and slowly put her hands over her eyes. There was a word for it, I learned. Charlie had been overcome by the "zoomies."

Disqualified.

◇

So there were the dogs, and then there were the dog people. Lynn and her friends called themselves "dog moms." It was an appropriate phrase, since some 90 to 95 percent of the participants were women. Oh, there was a male or two involved, but most of the men I saw at these dog matches were sitting along with me in the stands. I wondered whether this was significant. We "dog dads" (yes, I wince) talked about the phenomenon we'd been caught up in, and we agreed there was surely some deep meaning. If only we knew what it was.

We did understand that dogging is about more than dogs. Dog owners stick together. When a critical number of dog owners is reached, they automatically seem to coalesce into a mixed pack of humans and canids. They train together, they go to competitions together, they go to dinner together. Sometimes I was snatched off my preferred perch on the far periphery: Maybe the club met at our house, or I was recruited to schlep equipment. Whatever the occasion, it was always educational.

I learned early on that many of the clichés about dogs and their owners are true. The edict "love me, love my dog," for example, is a fundamental fact of nature, right up there with Newton's Big Three. Another truism is that people look like their dogs, at least far more often than statistics would predict. But what matters is the deeper relationship, the link between dog and human that goes to the core of the human's personality.

You could see in such relationships that *something*—that too-vague word again—passed between the human and the dog that allowed the dog to understand how its human looked at the world. The psyche of the dog automatically snapped into place. The result was that the dog augmented and telegraphed the human, acting out in ways the human would like to act but would never, ever, be allowed to.

The way the flow of energy and information passed between dog and human was deeply psychological. To learn to read the dual dog-human consciousness brought you into a world of phantasmagoria, latent images, and Freudian quicksand. Right away, the boundary between *Homo sapiens* and *Canis familiaris* vanished and some different, indefinable unit formed in its place. In the fused world of dog and human, things were sometimes the way they seemed . . . and sometimes they were the opposite. Sometimes a nice person had a nasty, aggressive dog. Since dog club rules were strict about aggression toward humans, such behavior was repressed in the ring and other formal settings. But afterward, the dog would go wild. It'd attack other dogs, eat the picnic ham off the table, and defecate on the living room rug. Look back at the owner, though, and it didn't make sense: You couldn't imagine her running a stop sign. How did she get paired up with such an antisocial animal?

The answer was that she did it on purpose—or, if you like, unconsciously on purpose. Look closely in a situation like that and you'd almost always find a hidden passive-aggressive streak in the owner. The dog picked up the sentiment and, in a very real sense, *obeyed.*

It worked the other way, too. We knew one couple who, for whatever reason, prided themselves on being exceedingly crusty. They cultivated an in-your-face, macho image. Naturally, when they chose a dog they picked a breed with a reputation to match: a rottweiler.

This was an appropriate choice, at least on the conscious level. In the dog world, the rottweiler is the equivalent of a Hell's Angel. It is a tough guy by design, even to the point that in its breeding it has left behind many of the important nerves that transmit pain to the brain. Rottweilers are essentially numb. This is probably an advantage in a dog fight, but it is God's gift to the veterinarian business. A rottweiler will walk for days on a broken leg before it gets infected and the dog becomes aware of the pain and informs its master. The vet bills soon climb higher than the car payments.

But if the macho image that came with owning a rottweiler was worth two thousand bucks to our friends, the reality didn't exactly work out: The dog was as ordered but the people weren't who they thought they were. Beneath their Yosemite Sam exteriors they were among the sweetest people I've ever met.

Now people delude themselves about themselves—we do it every day—but puppies are incapable of such illusions. Perfidy is simply not in their deck of cards. A puppy responds to the reality, not the image, and so the rottweiler puppy figured out our friends in about fifteen seconds. Naturally, she grew up to be a true reflection of the people who called themselves her masters.

The result was an embarrassment. The rottie might look imposing, but she was a happy-go-lucky party girl who trusted everyone, loved to chase balls, wanted to frolic with the coyotes, and would eventually become one of Charlie's best buddies. That's right, the rotty and the poodle. To make it even worse, the poodle was the dominant dog.

The owners were taken aback by this situation. Once, confiding his disappointment, the guy remarked wryly, "At least she *looks* like a rottweiler. I can throw her in the back of my pickup and know nobody will bother it while I'm in the lumber yard."

She did indeed have this psychological effect. Our friend would threaten to sic the dog onto trespassers, tax collectors, and Jehovah's Witnesses, and it always worked. (Fortunately for the illusion, the rottie's tail had been docked, so the offending trespassers couldn't see it wagging.) But her masters would have been a lot happier if she had at least learned to . . . I don't know, snarl? Growl, and sound like she meant it? At least lose the squeak toy?

Another friend, for somewhat similar reasons, had malamutes—huge shaggy animals that they romantically claimed were the closest dog to a wolf. One of their mals was in fact said to be mean, but the other one, Jake, was cut from a different cloth.

Jake didn't look much like a friendly dog. He was huge, and his bulk was emphasized by about six inches of thick hair. Lynn knew I'd love him, but before I met him the first time she thought it prudent to counsel me. People tended to be frightened of his size and looks, she said. But I should hold my ground and not worry. Trust her. He was as friendly as a cocker spaniel.

"Holding ground" talks a lot easier than it lives when a hundred pounds of toothy dog runs at you and leaps at your head. I admit to closing my eyes, which was just as well, since what Jake had in mind was putting his paws on my shoulders and slurping his saddle-blanket-sized tongue over my face. Within the week, he became one of my favorite dogs of all time.

The dogs Lynn and I got to know through Charlie were lovable, or not, and we could love them or not. That part was optional. What it all came back to was not the dogs but the dog people.

It wasn't difficult to pick the committed dog people out of a crowd. Even when they didn't have their dogs with them, they wore dog hair on their lapels and often drove cars with mushy bumper stickers like "I ♥ Dobermans." Coming together, they instinctively formed dog clubs, all kinds of dog clubs. Obedience clubs, hunting clubs, therapy dog clubs, dog-dancing clubs, flyball clubs, Frisbee clubs, agility clubs . . . almost any doggy activity that could be contrived was an ample pretext for forming a club.

Lynn didn't wear dog hair because poodles don't shed, and as a reporter I nixed bumper stickers of any sort. But Lynn was nevertheless in the thick of the dog world, which left me doing what I most enjoy, people-watching. And as I watched the dog people I discovered again and again that if you looked closely enough at the dog, you would find the key to its owner.

◇

The world of purebreds is generally understood only in extreme caricature. This can be laid partly at the feet of my journalistic colleagues: Television crews go to the Westminster Kennel Show each year specifically to record the funny and the absurd, and they always manage to find what they are looking for. The image of a poodle in full lion clip and in the tow of a handler dressed for a state funeral might be sublime to some members of the Poodle Club of America, but to the rest of the world it is pretty ridiculous. Many poodle owners, including Lynn, refuse to put their dogs in such a clip.

So why does the lion clip endure? The answer is in part, economic: Groomers and handlers have a financial interest in maintaining the current standard. It costs a lot to foof up a poodle; the groomers who travel from dog show to dog show know all the right people and generally are able to protect their interests when rules are made.

The other and quite possibly more important force is tradition. Dog owners love to brag on the ancientness of their pet's pedigree. Malamute owners claim their dog is the closest to the wolf; saluki and Afghan owners point to ancient rock drawings to claim their dogs are the oldest. Such claims and counterclaims are the dog world's equivalent of tall stories. Unfortunately for the culture, if not for strict accuracy, geneticists analyzing the various breeds of dogs have concluded that none of them are more than a few hundred years old. If the modern saluki looks a lot like the dog on the walls of European tombs, it is because the canid genome is infinitely plastic and the same shape (and probably temperament) can be produced again and again. All breeds spring eternal from the ur-dog, which of course is the alleyway mutt.

From what we can tell from old texts and our own surmising, the various sizes and shapes of purebred dogs evolved (or *were evolved*, when you consider it was done purposefully by humans) from working dogs. Charlie's ancestors were bred by fishermen for their trainability, on the one hand, and for behavioral flexibility on the other; that, plus their legendary desire to please their human, made it possible to train them for complex tasks. Herding dogs were bred for their ability to herd, guard dogs for their territoriality, and so forth.

Natural "breeds," in other words, usually evolved when their owners simply bred their best performers to one another. Physical adaptation was important, but the quality the owners were after was primarily behavioral. That poodles ended up with water-resistant coats and guard dogs ended up large was a happy side benefit. Charlie might not come off as much of a war dog, but he was very black, his woolly coat made him appear much bigger than he was, and he had a huge mouth full of sharp white teeth. Threaten Lynn, and he could turn into a snarling monster that would seem at least as dangerous as a mastiff. In a nearby town, a poodle nearly killed a thug who attempted to mug its elderly mistress. By the time the police got there, they found the thug on the ground, the poodle sitting on his feet, and the woman sitting on his chest, pounding him with her purse and screaming "Don't . . . you . . . dare . . . hurt . . . my . . . dog!"

In jail the guy became known as the fellow who got beat up by a poodle and an old lady. His life was never the same.

◇

Mostly, the development of breeds was a pretty natural process. Humans, who caught on shortly after the Holocene that like bred like, mated their best dogs to preserve whatever characteristics were most valued at the time. If the fishermen of the Baltic region ended up with poodles, it's pretty sure that other fishermen all over the world came up with their own version of fishing dogs. They might not look anything like poodles, but they did the same job.

This began to change in the seventeenth century, as cities took on modern proportions and more and more country people made the shift to urban life. Many of those people brought their pigs, chickens, and goats with them, or at least tried to. But eventually the price of real estate squeezed out most of the customary rural menagerie.

The city dictated its own lifestyle. City dwellers no longer hunted or fished, at least not for survival, so they didn't need hunting or fishing dogs. They didn't need an animal to guard the chicken coop, because they didn't have chicken coops anymore. Nor did they need a dog to herd the sheep they no longer had, and they certainly didn't need a dog inclined to ferocity toward strangers.

Logically, in fact, they didn't need dogs at all. Psychologically, however, it was another story. The sheep, cows, and goats might go, but the dogs were not negotiable. The defense of the dog's right to be in the city burbled up from some deep chamber in the human psyche.

But humans, being putatively logical creatures, would never settle for an answer like that. They had to have some intellectually acceptable *reason* to stuff into the vacuum. Justification was necessary, else the whole phenomenon wouldn't have fit comfortably in the mind. The average seventeenth-century human just couldn't believe he was feeding an animal that had no use.

This problem was solved in the usual human way. Had dog no use? Then the human would make one up.

A few dogs could be used in sports, as ratters or fighting dogs, to bring glory and winnings to their masters. A few dogs could be used to guard whatever was worth guarding. But as for the rest . . . well, the city was a cultural vortex. Dogs could be whatever people imagined them to be. They could be status symbols, so they were. Certain breeds were even designated for the nobility and commoners were not allowed to own them.

I have to believe that the forces behind these phenomena had much to do with the emergence of a new type (or maybe it was new level) of loneliness—the loneliness of the crowd, city loneliness. In the city, no one counted, no one cared. To paraphrase Harry Truman: If you wanted a friend in the big city, you had to get a dog. Which, of course, is precisely what people did.

A companion dog did not need the specialization that characterized a working dog. *Canis familiaris* was innately a friend to man and woman, so much so that even dogs bred specifically to be fierce (like the aforementioned rottweiler) reverted to type at the first opportunity. It took a lot of training to brainwash a war dog or a police dog to attack a human being; even so, most candidates failed to make the grade. They'd much rather throw their rumps up in the air, wag their tails, lick the human's hand, and be buddies.

Dogs themselves pay no attention to breed, and even size doesn't matter much. The giant malamute, my very furry friend, wouldn't hesitate to pal up with a naked Chihuahua. Nor, in the dog world, does size equal dominance. Put a dachshund together with a mastiff and either one is equally likely to be the dominant partner. It goes without mention that a bitch in heat, whatever her size, will draw every male dog in the neighborhood.

To serve as a human status symbol, however, the dog *did* have to have some visual pizzazz. This, ultimately, would underlie the growth of the breed clubs and their amalgamation into super-clubs, like the Royal Kennel Club and the American Kennel Club.

Another motive grew from humans' sense of history. As the industrial revolution changed the world and citified more and more humans, many canid breeds (like the specialized herding dogs) seemed headed toward mongrelization. This evoked a rising interest among the upper classes to preserve them as they were.

None of this occurred in a vacuum. It was the Victorian era that produced Darwin and, among his social class, an increased interest in animal breeding of all types. But when dog lovers resolved to define and preserve the once-utilitarian gene lines of dogs, the whole story went straight through the looking glass. The breed clubs were engaged in nothing less than an attempt to stop time, and like all such attempts it was doomed from the start. It would prove, once again, that humans have more power than they have common sense.

What happened was not without its humorous side—for example, in the preservation of the classic poodle lion clip. The original German fishing dog had a distinctive clip that streamlined the animal and also kept the major muscles and organs warm. When the French adopted the poodle, the clip was exaggerated into a big mane and foot-and-tail pompoms. So a French fetish dating to the Victorian era came to represent the modern poodle in the American mind. When the doggy clans meet at Westminster, it always comes in for more than its share of television time.

In the case of the poodle it doesn't matter, really—the poodle is an exceptionally tolerant dog with infinite patience toward children, strangers, status-driven owners, and other fools. It is also a ham: After being discovered by the French it was rediscovered by circus trainers, who adopted it for its spectacular trainability. Poodles like attention, and if they have to be clownish to get it, then so be it.

But the machinations of the breed clubs were often less benign. Consider, for example, the English bulldog. The original bulldogs' most distinctive feature was a flattened face, so dog show judges naturally favored dogs with the flattest faces. With fame and even some money at stake, breeders naturally labored to produce dogs with flatter faces yet. The result, over a century and more, was the evolution of a dog that has severe respiratory problems—and not only that but a dog whose head is too large to pass down the birth canal. Today's English bulldogs have to come into the world the way Julius Caesar reputedly did, by means of the surgeon's knife.

The German shepherd is another sad story—especially sad to me, because it's a dog I love. For reasons beyond comprehension, shepherd judges decided that the perfect German shepherd had a profile that sloped in the rear. The eventual result was a dog with a sloping back, all right—and with genetically determined spinal malformations that doomed it from birth to lower back pain. Today's German shepherds are the victims of a deliberately induced genetic disease.

Similar horror stories abound. Cocker spaniels, once delightful and intelligent little dogs, became popular in the 1950s. As the price of cockers soared, unscrupulous breeders set up puppy mills to produce them in large numbers. The most efficient way to do that, and do it quickly, was inbreeding. Within just a few years the cocker had metamorphosed into a stupid, sickly, and often rather nasty dog. A half century later, responsible cocker lovers are still trying to salvage the breed.

The story goes on and on. By the end of the twentieth century breeders had produced a sad veterinary atlas of inherited diseases including kidney failure, deadly "bloat," exotic cancers, eye diseases, epilepsy, heart diseases—and a whole new range of metabolic dysfunctions. In my visits to dog shows, I've seen bug-eyed little dogs, and dogs that couldn't breathe without wheezing. I've seen genetically deaf dogs and hounds that have no sense of smell—roughly equivalent, in the canid world, of being born blind.

I will never forget a cute little teacup poodle that nestled, trembling, in its owner's hands. Was the dog cold, I asked? No, I was reassured, it was just fine. The constant trembling came from the continuous epileptic seizures common to that tiny, bizarre breed.

I always walk away from breed shows depressed. Yes, you can genetically shrink a dog—innards, muscles, skeleton, and all—but you can't shrink brain cells. Make the cranial capacity tiny, and you'll simply have fewer neurons living there. And with the teacup poodle as only one example, you once again have an indictment of human thoughtlessness, bordering on cruelty, in its dealings with nature.

◇

Of all this the breed clubs stood accused, and they were clearly guilty. There were those who would outlaw breeding because of it; I could see their point, at least in theory, but I doubt that any such movement would ever succeed. During the great cultural revolution, Mao Zedong resolved to rid China of dogs. His rationale was that they were eating food that could otherwise have fed people. His fanatic followers went so far as to shoot anyone who was caught with a dog. But people refused to give up their pets. Hundreds of thousands, and perhaps millions, of Chinese put their lives on the line to hide and protect their dogs.

I can't imagine how any other society could succeed where Mao's zealots failed—especially not the American society, which favors squabbling over every picayune detail. In some jurisdictions in the United States it is almost impossible even to pass leash laws, let alone enforce them. No, dogs—and dog breeders—are here to stay.

This is the strength that belies the absurdity of what the cameras seem to show us about Westminster. Despite unscrupulous breeders and health-threatening breed standards, many breeds retain a kernel of their original behaviors. It is still possible, with careful breeding, to restore a semblance of sanity

THE WOLF IN THE PARLOR ◇ 147

to the process. Indeed, among the newer generation of breeders there is a movement to breed for health and personality, instead of just appearance.

Still, there are advantages to having a specific dog breed. If a prospective owner does sufficient research and finds a breeder who is producing good, healthy, friendly dogs, she can select a puppy and have a pretty good idea what she is going to get, in terms of both health and behavior. A mutt from the pound is a lottery. It might be an angel. Or it might be a devil that chews up the couch, empties the trash, and barks every minute you are gone. A dog lives maybe twelve to fifteen years and if you love a dog, that is far too short. But it is a long time to endure a monster.

Of all the things I had learned about dogs, this was one of the ones that struck me most profoundly: Personality and intelligence are genetically determined. A dog can be bent grotesquely by cruel treatment, of course, and the most intelligent dog will lapse into dullness if not allowed to work with its owner. Conversely, the best of training won't make a stupid dog smarter. But it remains possible to open up a dog breed book and pretty much pick out the personality and intelligence level you want. In theory, you have a reasonable prospect of choosing a dog that matches your own personality.

This assumes—a loophole big enough to drive a cement truck through—that you are sufficiently self-aware to know who *you* are.

The subject of distinctive canid personalities always makes my mind leap to the terrier. The basic American terrier was descended from little dogs called feists. I assume that bears some relationship to the word "feisty," and I further assume the personalities, and probably the lineages, trace back (under fences and through various woodlots) to the English ratters.

Rat-hunting dogs were developed in many places, but the prototypical ratter was a low-class sporting dog in late medieval

England. What did an animal have to be to kill a big brown rat in London, circa 1600? It had to be gutsy, for sure, because those were big, mean rats. A ratter had to be quick and stubborn. It had to attack first and think about it later. It had to be nastier than it was smart. Feisty.

Modern terriers are true to their ancestors. With their own familiar humans, they tend to be sweet animals, though practically untrainable. (Think "stubborn"; when the subject is terriers, you've got to always remember *stubborn*.) But let a strange dog, human, or any other animal show up, and a terrier will start yapping, snapping, and growling. A terrier is attitude on legs and, like some diminutive men, is always keen to take on the biggest guy in the bar. A terrier thinks nothing of going head-to-head with a pit bull. I once saw one try to take on Jake, who just stood there in what appeared to be astonishment.

That personality makes the terrier a perfect dog for whom? A basically nice person with a fear of other humans? A cultured person with an underlying frustration? It depends on a lot of factors and the observer, as always, has to be the judge. But spend enough time around a terrier and its owner and you will find the verdict is generally not difficult to reach.

So it goes. Personalities of different breeds are generally obvious (dogs, you remember, don't lie). The collie breeds are friendly enough and very smart, but statistics label them as ankle-nippers. What would you expect with a breed created to move sheep by nipping at their feet? They won't do much damage, but they'll ruin your pants legs. Dalmatians, despite the heartwarming movie, are generally not people friendly—they have jaws approaching those of the pit bull, and without a savvy owner they can quickly turn mean. An amateur with a dalmatian is a danger to himself and those around him.

I think I will leave it there. I will not analyze the owners of standard poodles, except to say that when Charlie was a puppy, Lynn and I always felt underdressed.

◇

After Charlie's training sessions, the dog people would often sit around eating potluck picnic food and talking while the dogs played. I don't know what the dogs talked about, but the human conversations invariably got around to a discussion of breeds. Shelties could be depended on to do so-and-so, briards are good-hearted . . . that kind of thing. One dog story would follow another. It was all quite friendly, but underneath there was a certain edge, a one-upsmanship, with each owner not-so-secretly convinced her breed was best. But "best" depended on what you meant by that.

When it comes to competitions, for instance, the border collies usually come out on top. They are the best working and obedience dog, without a doubt—if you like to hang with compulsives. I don't know how else to describe the border collie, which was bred in Britain as a working dog and which . . . can't . . . stop . . . working. Border collies have to be doing something, all the time, all day long and into the night. They are great flying-disc dogs, except that they put such focus into catching that they will sprain their necks or forget to look where they are going and run into a wall. They take to training, any kind of training, with a vengeance. But once you've trained them, say, to run an agility competition course, then you'd better keep them running that course. Otherwise, they get bored. The bored border collie is sure to find something to do to keep busy. Something, perhaps, in the trash, or in the laundry. A shoe will do, or maybe the arm of the new sofa. We knew a border collie owner who came home one day to find her dog had rearranged the cushions in the living room. He didn't tear them up, you understand, or damage them in any way, he just . . . rearranged them.

That's one of those dog stories you wake up at night thinking about.

Lynn's group also included an Afghan, Prince Frederick.

Frederick was the spitting image of the lion-hunting dogs you see on ancient Egyptian cave walls. In modern times, though, the Afghan is noted more for its elegance and is most often seen in pairs, meticulously coifed and with bejeweled collars, being walked down Madison Avenue by a stylishly dressed woman. In terms of modern reputation, the Afghan is far from a lion chaser. It is an effete sort of dog, born, like the standard poodle, to the silver and the silk. Frederick did have an air of class, I must say. But, as ironies go, of the entire group only he and Charlie were actual farm dogs.

Then there was the rescue greyhound. Greyhound racing trainers usually kill their dogs in late puppyhood, when their running prowess begins to fade. This is the kind of thing that, like dog fighting, is guaranteed to whip dog lovers up into hysteria. When we were in Oregon there was a movement ginning up to rescue these dogs. Greyhounds make excellent pets. You'd think they would be hyper, raised to race as they are, but as a rule they are rug dogs. Maybe they figure they are retired or something; anyway, their preferred position is sprawled in front of a fireplace or, even better, across the couch.

They *will* run, though, if they are in the mood, and a running greyhound is beautiful to behold—what you *can* behold in the few seconds before she disappears over the horizon. Fortunately, greyhounds have a good sense of direction and always find their way back easily enough.

All of that is, of course, generalization, and there are always exceptions. More to the point, dog people all have their own mythology about their favorite breed. If a dog person is talking to you, your job is to nod and not, ever, under any circumstances, inject actual facts into the conversation. This is one of those places angels fear to tread. I have to admit that I am constitutionally argumentative and I learned my lesson the hard way.

Perhaps now, in fact, I should hastily move on.

◇

In the end, dogs are dogs. Breed makes a difference, in that it emphasizes this facet or that and makes the dog more predictable; whether that is critical depends on what you have in mind for them. But they all love their humans, even when the humans clearly don't deserve it. The humans, who as a species are not all that loving or gentle, return the sentiment as best they can. Sometimes we outdo ourselves, mustering up such affection for our canid friends that one has to wish, pensively, that we could show the same emotion toward our fellow humans.

In any event, I certainly liked the dogs, a lot more than I had expected to. Charlie had taught me that he could see and feel things and somehow transmit those sights and feelings to me, and to my delight I now discovered that all dogs had that quality, more or less.

A dog is, ipso facto, an important part of its humans' lives. A horse you can board out; a cat you can more or less ignore; a goldfish you can look at or not look at; a guinea pig or a boa constrictor will stay in its cage until you decide you want to mess with it. Not so a dog. A dog is there, by your side, all the time. If you are in the kitchen, the dog is in the kitchen. If you are sitting around the fireplace, the dog is lying at your feet. When you go to bed, the dog goes to bed with you—often on its own mattress on the floor, though I was surprised to learn how many people sleep with their dog. Or dogs.

I resisted that, with the poodle; Charlie slept with Lynn when I was away, but otherwise he slept on his pad at the foot of the bed. After some pressure I tried letting him sleep in bed, but it didn't work. He was too big. Besides, he pulled covers.

Not all humans love dogs, of course. In that dark part of our minds where phobias live, the wolf in the parlor remains a wolf, and a lot of people are deathly afraid of them. Occasionally a parent would scream at Lynn to get the dog away from her child, though the dog was never very close to start with. In these cases you could see instantly how the parents' fear transferred to the child.

Since the parent usually scooped up the child and rushed away, you never knew exactly what was going on. I asked around, though, when I could, and found that sometimes the parents or the child or both were just plain scared of everything. Equally often, there was some incident with a dog in their background. Perhaps there was a mean dog in the neighborhood (illustrating the powerlessness of animal control agencies), or someone in the family had been the victim of a serious dog bite. On the other hand, Lynn and I had both been bitten as children, and it didn't leave us afraid. But who understands such things, outside a psychiatrist's office?

Sometimes the situation was much simpler. A small child, for example, might see Charlie and spontaneously burst into tears. I thought this was actually fairly reasonable. If I met a dog who towered over me, I might cry too. In these cases the parent, seeing a teaching moment, often inquired whether Charlie was gentle and, finding he was, introduced the child. Lynn always cooperated in this. She'd get down on her haunches and explain the dog to the child.

If the child calmed down, Lynn would show her how to give Charlie commands. Sit. Stand. Back. Bow.

That was effective. The child's discovery that the big black animal with all those teeth would actually *obey* her was guaranteed to change the tears into beaming smiles of discovery and delight. The impromptu sessions always ended with Lynn's caution to the child that all dogs were not so well trained, and could be dangerous. But the child already had the healthy fear; now she also had the knowledge and fascination.

The truth of the matter is that dogs are rarely a problem. They might be perceived as the problem—if you are attacked, how could you think otherwise?—but the issue almost always goes deeper. As any animal control officer will testify, dogs are by their nature gentle and loving creatures; it's human behavior that is dangerous.

Sometimes it is innocence. People just can't admit their own inner hostility, so they transfer it to the animal. Most people with a dog don't really know why they even got the dog in the first place. They just . . . wanted it. Many people are like I was, at first, unwilling to get down on the dog's level and relate to it. Maybe they fear, with good reason, that they might find an important part of themselves down there in the process.

So they have their dogs, but they don't realize that the human side of the bond is responsibility. Their part is to exercise reasonable control—the dogs want it that way, and the neighbors definitely do. But such people, living their unconsidered lives, let their dogs have the run of the neighborhood. When the animal control officer shows up, they maintain vociferously that the dog is harmless—even if it has bitten several people, including the mailman. I'm not saying this happens on some rare occasions. It is common. Ask any animal control officer. For that matter, ask any city or county councilor, because dog issues have a way of getting themselves in the paper and ultimately getting kicked up to the highest political level.

As my understanding of the dog was developing, pit bulls came into style. It was all the rage, then, to have "attitude," and pit bulls were perceived as dangerous. If you had a pit bull with you, no one would dare dis you.

There was something to that, I suppose. Once, walking in Spanish Harlem, I came across a sight I'll never forget. There was a fancy, upholstered black Cadillac parked by the curb of this rather dirty street, and an incredibly beautiful young Hispanic woman in tight jeans, high heels, and a leather jacket was draped across the hood watching the passersby. Beside her on the hood and on the ground next to the fender were two great, sleek brown dogs with black muzzles and dangerous-looking teeth. They were probably mastiffs, but if so they were *big* mastiffs. I had never seen dogs so big. The woman had a spiked leather choker around her neck and matching spiked straps on her wrists and ankles. The dogs, of course, had identical spiked collars. She held them by thin leather straps.

People on the sidewalk glanced at her out of the corners of their eyes, but nobody looked directly at her. Rather, they sped up to get by as fast as they could. The woman watched them with a superior air. There was something very primitive about the scene—sexual, beautiful, and frightening at the same time.

That was what the new pit bull owners were shooting for, usually. But, aside from the moral question of scaring people for the heck of it, the problem was that once such people got the puppies home they didn't know what to do with them. The puppies grew into dogs. The people had gotten them for the wrong reasons, reasons having to do with the emotions of the moment but having no long-term resolution. Usually the new owners were in no position to train their pit bull puppies. They didn't have the time or energy to spare or, if they did, they didn't know how to go about training. And I ask you: Would a person who bought a putatively mean dog go looking for an expert to help him civilize it?

The dog people in Lynn's group muttered darkly about the pit bull situation and shook their heads. Pit bulls were bred for the fighting pit. Their massive jaw muscles, which is what makes their heads so large, are wrapped around some of the most dangerous teeth in the animal world. A pit bull, properly socialized, would probably be a pussycat in the hands of a gentle person. I later saw that happen in several cases. But you had to ask why a gentle person would particularly want a dog like that in the first place, given its potential for problems?

Across the country, state legislators and city councils moved to ban pit bulls, but such efforts were soon submerged in confusion. What was a "pit bull"? Could you prove a specific dog was a pit bull, or half pit bull? And why ban pit bulls if you let people have bull mastiffs?

You can never solve such problems by dealing with the dogs, because dogs are not the issue. People are the issue.

It's an enigma. To carry a handgun, you have to have a permit. Get caught with an unlicensed gun and in most places, you'll do hard time. But to own a mean dog, or even a trained killer dog, all you need is a dog license—and that rule isn't enforced very often. If you shoot someone and wound them, you go to jail. If your dog mauls someone, you get a twenty-five-dollar ticket. The victim might sue you, but then again by that time you might be somewhere else. Your dog, in fact, might be your only possession.

I agreed with the dog people. Something evil was brewing here. Not with the pit bulls, but with many of the pit bull people.

And then there were the animal rights advocates. Many of them were dog lovers, but many also considered keeping dogs a form of slavery. They made their feelings well known and, during one period, they were thought to be poisoning dogs at dog shows. They fed them antifreeze, which tastes sweet and destroys the liver. The logic, to the extent that the story went I could understand it, was to wound the owners. It did, and it struck terror in the hearts of the owners. Lynn and her friends suddenly found it necessary to post a watch over their dogs at shows. Later, these poisonings could not be substantiated, but that the rumor was instantly—and universally—believed was very revealing.

Strange. There were people, like Lynn's friends, who loved dogs. There were people like herders and pimps who found uses for them. There were people who hated them. There were people who hated the people who owned them. People who owned one type of dog sometimes hated people who owned other breeds. But as I first watched and then began to take notes on the world of the dog people, there was one sentiment I never encountered, and that was indifference.

◇

When I added all that stuff up, it simply reinforced my first data point: Dogs aren't about anything reasonable. People might be proud of their expertise with dogs, but expertise is really quite beside the point. Dogs are a vortex of a powerful emotional force that bubbles up out of its ancient wellsprings and engulfs not just the dog but the dog's people. I saw this many times, but what comes to mind is a night in Oregon as I lay on the couch listening to Lynn play the piano.

Henry Mancini, if memory serves. *Romeo and Juliet.*

Charlie, who was just emerging from puppyhood then, was lying at Lynn's feet, half asleep. But as Lynn's fingers flew over the keyboard and the romantic music crashed through the living room, he grew restless. He got up, circled several times, and lay back down. His head went down, then popped back up. He got to his haunches and sat there, trembling with emotion. He started to lie down again and changed his mind. Then he threw his head back, pointed his muzzle at the ceiling, and began to howl.

The howls were punctuated by yips, and the damnedest thing was—the sucker was in tune!

I sat up, awestruck. Lynn, elated, continued to play. Charlie continued to accompany her and then, as suddenly as he'd begun, he stopped. He looked around, seemed to understand what he was doing, and cowered. Tail down, he slunk into a corner. You didn't have to be a dog psychiatrist to understand what was going on; his whole countenance radiated emotion. *The dog was embarrassed!*

Later, I tried to explain it to myself. Charlie certainly had the neuronal apparatus required to reach the state we call "embarrassed." Embarrassment comes from the emotional system, and the dog emotional apparatus is nothing if not well developed. The sweet notes of Henry Mancini had reached down deep into his mammalian brain and touched something, something ancient. Some prehistoric program fired up and started to run, some wolf program, echoing down from the howls of the northland. Charlie had responded. He really hadn't had any choice.

Afterward, having stood revealed, having done something beyond his own control—and having done it here in this household which (for him) was as highly regimented as a submarine, he could only be ashamed of himself. *Embarrassed.*

Lynn, though, was ecstatic. She had discovered a wonderful thing in her animal, and she was instantly determined to pull it out, bring it under control, and make use of it. So it was that, after obedience training, after good citizen training, there would now be voice lessons.

She played, exploring his taste. Not rock and roll, that was soon apparent. When Lynn played "Mack the Knife," the stupid animal didn't even notice—he had the preferences of a pig. Pretty soon we were back to the saccharine Henry Mancini and, oh, yes, "Moon River." "Exodus." "Lara's Theme." Boogie-woogie blues. Rachmaninoff's more sentimental numbers were okay, too. Charlie threw back his head and prepared to howl the night away.

It soon became apparent that Charlie sang much better when I wasn't in the room. When he was singing, he occasionally rolled an eyeball in my direction and once, early on, I couldn't contain myself. I laughed.

He stopped singing, instantly, and went to the floor. Lynn spun around on her piano stool, furious.

I shrunk back. *All right, all right, okay, you win.* I wouldn't laugh at her dog. No ma'am, I would not. After that I didn't laugh. At least not at his singing. Even so, he preferred that I not be in the audience. It took me months to win back my welcome.

As you can see, I was being trained as well.

◇

Among the service activities favored by dog people are therapy dog clubs, which conduct visits to hospitals, nursing homes, and halfway houses. The poodle and his master, both being social creatures, naturally had to join.

For openers, Charlie was thoroughly tested by a supervising expert, to make sure he wouldn't bite if a child or a disoriented old person grabbed him by the ear and pulled. Lynn taught him to keep his paws away from the feet of walkers and the wheels of wheelchairs. A wheelchair can make a mess of a paw. There was a checklist and an exam, after which Charlie became a certified therapy dog.

His singing was an instant hit. Most of the facilities visited by the therapy dog club had pianos, and when Charlie sat up and sang he brought the house down. People who hadn't uttered a coherent word for months suddenly started talking and wanted to pet the dog. Within weeks Charlie became the Frank Sinatra of the dog world, the legendary Singing Dog of the Central Valley.

He was in great demand. I went along sometimes, to gauge his impact on the patients. It was breathtaking. They howled with laughter. For Charlie's part, the attention fed into his circus dog heritage and he sang all the more enthusiastically.

Hey. Waitaminit. They laughed, and he loved it. Why couldn't I laugh?

The answer, Lynn told me later, was obvious. I was laughing at him, whereas his audiences were laughing with him.

In other words, he could tell the difference.

What a remarkable idea. Why would the son of a wolf be able to tell the subtle differences in the quality of laughter of the son of an ape? Where did that sensitivity come from?

Here was another remarkable phenomenon: Charlie could tell my mood before I did, would comfort me before I knew I was depressed. He not only knew what my emotions were, he damped down the hurtful ones, amplified the good ones, and kept them all nicely modulated. Any way you looked at it, his brain was doing something my brain should have been doing but for some reason couldn't.

Around Christmastime, Lynn got an invitation to visit a psychiatric ward in Corvallis, a little town between Portland and Eugene, bringing Charlie and some friends and their dogs with her. Christmas, legendary throughout the Western world for its wretched effects on mental patients, was especially grim in the rainy valley. A nurse let Lynn and her entourage into the locked ward, where they found a dozen patients sitting around the wall, sullen and withdrawn. Outside, rain beat against the windows. At least half the patients had taped wrists.

It took the singing poodle five minutes to warm up the place. The patients wouldn't immediately relate to Lynn or her human friends, but it wasn't long before someone reached out to the dog, and Charlie licked his hand. Across the room another patient came to life, and one of the other dogs covered her face with kisses. Within five minutes, almost everyone in the room was playing with the dogs. In half an hour, several of the patients began to relate tentatively to their human visitors as well.

I'd read about this effect in the literature, but scientific literature didn't hold a candle to the real thing. There was no pain in the literature, and no giggling, either. Literature was emotionless, while the reality was emotion incarnate, perfectly pitched and more powerful than I ever would have imagined.

The withdrawn and depressed patients, absorbed in their own human pain, could not relate to humans. But they could relate to a dog. Dogs know how suffering people feel better than their fellow humans do and, unlike their fellow humans, dogs don't judge them. Dogs just understand the emotional realities and accept them. These mental patients opened themselves up to creatures of another species, and were rewarded by feeling better. When they felt better, it became possible for them to relate to their fellow humans.

This seemed to me to be a wonderful new use for dogs, but of course it wasn't new at all except to me. Freud, I later discovered, commonly used his dogs in his practice. He said they calmed his patients. More important, they seemed to be able to divine the patient's state of mind better than Freud himself. Then, somehow, they passed what they'd learned along to Freud. Freud had taught his students to do the same thing and, to this day, psychiatrists, clinical psychologists, and counselors of all stripes use dogs to lead them into their patients' minds.

Modern science can't tell us exactly why and how it works, but there is no doubt that the doggie effect is both real and powerful. The presence of a dog has been proven to lower blood pressure and reduce blood levels of chemicals like adrenaline, which signifies stress. Elderly people with dogs live longer than those without.

It is phenomenal. In computer terms, it is almost as if the dog is some kind of human peripheral device that plugs directly into the server—the human mind—and adjusts its emotional settings. The evidence is accumulating that somehow, on some level, our dogs know us better than we know ourselves.

CHAPTER EIGHT

All of which leads back to the original enigma. Who are these strange creatures? And what are they doing here, in such numbers?

Dogs? No, not dogs. People. Alexander Pope's favorite creature, self-aware to a grotesque fault, the spirit in the mirror. Pope put his finger right on it: Whatever problem we grapple with, from cosmology to the humble dog, it inevitably comes back to *Homo sapiens.*

In our attempts to study man, we had tried many approaches. We tried art and we tried poetry. We tried literature. We tried philosophy and introspection. Now we were trying science and, with new generations of scanners, were learning to trace the flow of thought through the brain. Many of us had great hopes for such technology.

All the same, it doesn't seem likely that any picture or scan will ever completely capture the human condition. The brain is biology, and biology is evolution—the evolution, in this case, of neural architecture. Who we are today can never be understood without better insight into how we got here and who we once were, because deep traces from our past remain in our behaviors. If our view of ourselves is distorted, if the reach of our knowledge cannot quite grasp our feelings, the reason lies hidden in the past.

I found myself contemplating Hamlet contemplating Yorick's skull. He knew Yorick, he thought. Or did he? Do we, can we, know any of those who have gone before? All they leave are memories shading into legend fading into the darkness of prehistory. All we have left are bones, or the imprints of bones. What can skeletons tell us, aside from the evidence that our remote ancestors, too, suffered from lower back pain? The skulls we examine are hollow vessels, and to figure out what was once in that vessel . . . ah, that was the rub. We don't know poor Yorick so well after all. Yet if we hope to survive for many more generations, we'd better learn about him.

I believed this, anyway; a lot of people did. We believed that our ultimate fate could most readily be divined from our ultimate origins. I'd watched the theories about human evolution fluctuate, decade by decade—watched the scientific controversies. I'd also watched the public's responses.

We might not be willing to put much money into paleoanthropology, but at the same time people were avidly interested in what it produced. Yet the more we studied our ancestors, the more convoluted the problem became. The facts were clear enough, as often as not, but interpretation was treacherous. Even when we had concrete evidence—ruins, written texts, drawings on cavern walls—the meaning of it all was up for grabs.

That left each human generation free to create its own history to justify its immediate agendas. Most people tended to agree, for example, that Columbus first set foot on what Europeans called the New World in 1492. In the United States, most people had long found that cause for celebration. Congress even declared the anniversary a national holiday. But by the end of the twentieth century, Native Americans and their friends were mounting protests against Columbus as the agent of genocide, bearer of measles, smallpox, and syphilis. And who was to say their view was wrong? My mother told me I am one-thirty-second Cherokee, and I had to wonder: Who would I be, were it not for that small scrap of old New World DNA? Was Columbus good or evil? Such questions, being unanswerable, could be paralyzing.

If history is a rewritable pageant, deep prehistory is doubly so. The public attention given to ancestral human fossils creates an impression that scientists have quite a lot to work with but, unfortunately, books and magazine articles far outweigh the fossils themselves. The prehistoric evidence for anything is thin, once you go back further than a few thousand years; beyond twelve thousand, there are only crumbs.

The difficulty is that fossils only form under certain circumstances. First, the critter to be fossilized has to be covered with some kind of sediment; second, it has to be sturdy enough to stand up to the forces of time. Those two facts explain the abundance of fossil shellfish. They lived underwater, where sediment ends up covering everything, and the shells were durable. They could last half a billion years, some of them, even when the rock around them heated up and began to turn plastic under the pressure of continental forces. If they weren't totally melted, or smeared out, they were still there for us to find.

Land animals were sometimes preserved when they happened to inhabit, say, swamps, in parts of the world where the surface was subsiding. That's why we have so many species of animals like *T. rex* and *Brachiosaurus*: They lived in boggy areas that were sinking and filling with sediment. When they died in the mud, their heavy bones could survive almost as long as a clamshell.

Animals that lived on higher ground, such as the plains, are a different matter. Sometimes, by a long-shot chance, they washed into a body of water or were covered, Pompeii-like, with volcanic ash. Otherwise, they lay on the surface and were dismembered by carrion eaters. Their bleached and scattered bones were then pulverized by the elements as the land beneath them eroded away. Sometimes they washed into a stream and hence moved seaward, but by the time they got to the seabed they looked more like pebbles than bones.

The animals least likely to be fossilized lived in the uplands. They were almost never preserved for any significant length of time. Even if their bodies happened to end up in a high swamp, that swamp would eventually erode at the mouth and dump its contents down onto the outwash plains, shuffling the bone fragments and grinding them to powder.

We have more fossils of herbivores than we do of carnivores because they are bigger and there were a lot more of them in the first place. Bird and proto-bird fossils, being fragile, are exceedingly rare. Upland primates, being both upland and relatively rare, usually vanished without a trace. Human ancestors, perhaps the rarest of all upland primates in the ancient past, were almost never preserved.

I happened to know this because once, at a physical anthropology meeting, I blithely mentioned the "fossil record." Afterward, a scientist pulled me aside and scolded me for having more words than good sense. Fossil record, indeed! If I took all the existing bones of humans and pre-humans older than twelve thousand years, he told me, I could put them in a single steamer trunk and have room to spare. And there, he said, was my "fossil record." The rest was supposition.

I was stunned. The knowledge certainly cast the matter in a different and far dimmer light.

◇

Sometimes I remembered the laughable innocence with which I had set out to "look up the dog." Hell, I couldn't even look up the human with any confidence, and if the origins of my own kind were but shadows around the glow of a long-cold campfire, *Canis familiaris* was but a pair of red eyes in the dark. I no longer had any illusions about being able to answer my question about the dog with any scientific certainty. I'd be lucky to answer it to my own satisfaction. Yet I couldn't stop.

So there I was, once again, back around to basics, human basics.

What *do* we know about ourselves? What do we *really* know?

For openers, we are primates, and primates are inherently tropical animals. That means we came from Africa or, to avoid a technical argument, either from Africa or from the southern part of the Indian-Asian supercontinent. The African arguments are persuasive, at least in my opinion, but new evidence might turn the whole thing on its head next week. However, it is certain that we began somewhere warm, and that there were lots of trees—big ones, because that's where our ancestors were adapted to live.

So, originally, we were arboreal animals, eaters of fruit and (when we could get them) insects and other small creatures. It follows that, like other arboreal animals, we were prey to big cats. We were afraid of falling, as arboreal animals had darned well better be. Most people don't know that monkeys fall out of trees all the time, dying of their injuries on the ground. The other monkeys, rubberneckers, gather around to watch the death throes and to learn the lesson: Don't fall.

We also shared an environment with some very venomous spiders and some very deadly snakes; some of those snakes killed with poisons, others by squeezing us to death. If there were fossil programs in our skulls, which most experts believe there must have been, then we can see them today in our common phobias.

Geology tells us that, at some point around three million years ago, there was a drastic change in the east African habitat, brought about when the African continent drifted north into the underbelly of Europe. That cut off the ocean currents that had once flowed across the top of Africa, and that in turn changed the climate. The jungles of eastern Africa, where the Old World primates lived, dried up. The trees died and the primates—what few survived—found themselves on the ground.

Turned out of their jungle homes, our ancestors were ill equipped for their new life. They were especially vulnerable to predators. They couldn't run very fast, had no real weapons, and were probably quite tasty. Leopards, in particular, loved them. Proto-humans were such a frequent item on the leopard menu that we even knew how a mama leopard carried them home to the family. The leopard straddled the dead primate and picked it up by its head. One set of fangs pushed into the eye sockets and the other set pierced the top of the skull. The body was dragged between the leopard's legs. We know this because we have the fang-pierced skulls to prove it. Today's leopards and tigers still have a hankering for primate, and on the Indian subcontinent man-eating tigers continue to exist into the twenty-first century.

The lone human ancestor, in this scenario, was not likely to survive. Individuals had a prayer only if they teamed up with others like themselves. The argument was, in fact, that the dangers of the veldt might well have prompted the formation of the first tightly bound pre-human social bands. The same precarious circumstances may have been the impetus behind the development of the first stone weapons, in which case the human love of killing machines may have begun as a defensive reaction.

By a million and a half years ago—long before the first true humans appeared—our ancestors had discovered fire. Tools and weapons became more sophisticated and the primates slowly came to more resemble today's humans. Then, skipping way ahead and playing rather loosely with the millennia, we got to those wolf skulls in Lazaret Cave in southern France. Arranging those skulls was a pre-human act, since it happened about 150,000 years ago, probably tens of thousands of years before the first recognizable humans appeared in Europe. It might be said, then, that our species grew up with the wolves.

The first more or less modern humans, it is currently thought, came out of Africa about 100,000 years ago. A rump group of anthropologists still think we developed in the northern world, but for the moment the out-of-Africa explanation seems to best fit the facts. At that point, the more modern versions of humans took over. I felt safe in assuming that the primate-wolf relationship, whatever it was, simply continued under the new management.

◇

By the time the first true humans worked themselves north and began following the great hoofed herds, they had developed a sophisticated hunting and gathering culture. They lacked inherited instincts for their new niche, and they had to make up for that lack with culture. They not only had to know how to kill large animals and tan and sew together their pelts, they also had to be able to pass that knowledge along to their children.

Humans began as omnivores whose diet emphasized plant matter, but their metabolism evolved to allow them to digest high quantities of protein and to do a passable job of processing fats. They still ate plants, of course: They almost surely ate whatever they could get their hands on. They hunted and foraged, following the migrating animals from low ground in the winter to high ground in the summer. Over lifetimes, they probably established traditional camping sites in these locations and left implements, and perhaps shelters, at those sites for use on their return. If those strategies were used, they constituted the first tenuous step toward settled life.

We don't know how plentiful these early humans were. There may not have been many of them but there had to be enough to survive local disasters that would wipe out the occasional band. We know that they were smart—smarter than we are, if that extra 5 to 10 percent of brain mass meant anything. Any way you figure it, they were a successful new animal.

But they had a lot of design flaws. They had been cobbled together in a hurry, both physically and behaviorally. Nothing of their life was "natural" to them, in the sense that a wolf's life was natural to the wolf. The wolf had had fifteen million years to perfect its act, but humans were forced to make things up as they went along. The humans must have looked at wolves with no small amount of envy.

The early relationship between humans and wolves must have been complex. They were competitors, in that they occupied the same territory and hunted the same game, but from what we know of their ecology there was plenty of meat to go around. In that great protein factory of the north, there was no cause for either species to go hungry, or for their competition to grow into rivalry.

Despite the great differences between the *Homo sapiens* and *Canis lupus*, there were also some remarkable similarities . . . and humans, being a noticing kind of animal, must surely have noticed. Both formed bands, both nurtured their fellow band members as well as their offspring, and both hunted cohesively in groups. Humans, by this time, surely had symbolic language: Their brains and probably their larynxes were built for it. This set them apart, sort of. Yet it couldn't really be said that the wolves were inarticulate.

The cubs barked and the adults howled, and after watching Charlie sing I do not think their noise lacked meaning. Wolves also had an intricate body language that included syntax. For example, there is a body posture (rump up and front feet extended) that specifically means, "All that follows is play." That body sign, called a "play bow," allows them to roughhouse knowing that the other guy would pull his punches.

There was another thing, too: Wolf cubs are cute.

This is more than just a human judgment. Psychological studies show, throughout the animal world, a certain inborn tenderness for the individual with relatively big eyes and a foreshortened muzzle. These features trigger a nurturing response in the wolf, as they do in the human, and might explain why an adult of one species would adopt an infant of another—dogs have been known to adopt kittens, for example. Babies are cute, across the spectrum of mammalian life. That's just the way the world is built.

We know another thing about these early people: They lived like pigs. They were messy. In their heart of hearts they were trailer trash long before the first trailer. It was in their nature to live in trees, where the whole concept of housekeeping was irrelevant. Eat a fruit? Drop the pit wherever and it'd disappear down through the foliage. Defecate wherever you liked, it didn't matter; the waste would drop down to that great garbage pit called the earth. When you died, you'd . . . you'd fall to earth as well. To this day, the idea of "the Fall" figures prominently in our mythology.

We did not lose our careless mind-set when the jungles died and we became a terrestrial animal. Then as now, wherever humans went they left a trail of garbage, and when they finally settled down they lived in their own trash. Over time their trash and garbage built up so high that they had to jack their houses higher. The remains of those garbage piles were their gift to archaeologists, who have since come up with a nicer word for them: "middens," or, if the piles are city-sized, "tells." But, if a rose is a rose is a rose, then a garbage pile must have stunk whatever it was called.

Wolves, however noble in mythology, will happily eat carrion if it isn't too ripe. They don't have the innards of buzzards, but they'll gnaw bones and eat human leftovers. Today, where wolves are still extant, as in Alaska, a good place to look for them is around the town garbage dump.

From these facts comes the supposition that, as early humans moved across the landscape, some wolves learned to scavenge from their leavings. At first the wolves might have eaten what the people pitched out and then gone on their way, but an injured, old, or orphaned young wolf might stay and follow the source of the garbage at a safe distance. Add a few millennia and the result would be a class of "camp-follower" wolves.

All of the likelier scenarios of dog origins begin with the appearance of such follower wolves. Those would have been the wolves humans were most likely to see and interact with, and they were the wolves most likely to be drawn closer and closer into the human orbit.

The follower wolves would change over time. Some would die, others would leave the group and be replaced by newcomers. There would be cubs, some as a result of breedings between follower wolves and others because of outbreeding with independent wolf groups. Many follower groups would have disbanded and been replaced. The population would have been very fluid, particularly at first.

Over time, however, the environment would have placed different demands on follower wolves than on the truly wild ones. The follower wolves would probably have to be more metabolically flexible, for example, so that they could both eat human leavings and forage when necessary. Follower wolves would also benefit, tangentially, from the humans' use of fire. Cooked meat was more easily digested (and therefore more nutritious) than raw food. Wolves could not digest raw grain at all, but once grain had been milled, cooked, and presented to them as scraps of bread, they could eat it and readily extract nutrients from it.

Follower wolves would also grow to be comfortable with a hu-man presence nearby, while other, wilder wolves might shy away.

These were small things, perhaps, but given the extreme flexibility of the wolf's genetic code the changes would accumu-late. The follower wolves could still breed with other wolves, for example, but they might not do so as frequently as before.

This would have been critical to the ultimate separation of wolf and dog. The idea that the ability to produce fertile off-spring defines species is a gross oversimplification. Species often split apart not because the various subgroups can't interbreed but because they choose not to. Mating behaviors might evolve in different directions for otherwise identical animals until, fi-nally, you have two animals that look and act quite different though they occupy the same territory.

That would have been true, surely, of the follower wolves. If wolf groups had cultures, as experts claim, the culture of the fol-lower wolf would be different from that of the truly wild wolf. The groups would each go their own way and, while they *could* breed, the act would become quite rare. That isolated them ge-netically despite the surrounding ocean of true wolf genes.

Behaviorally, the niche occupied by the follower wolves would have put a premium on generalization. The animals would need to be able to follow their human bands, eating what-ever came their way, being friendly or flighty depending on the necessities of the moment. These pressures favor childlike be-havior: Across the board, immature animals are typically more curious, friendly, and adaptable than adults. The best-adapted follower wolf was probably one who never quite became an adult, psychologically. Thus, by a process known as neoteny, follower wolves slowly became more cublike . . . which is to say, puppylike.

This brings several likely scenarios to mind, none of them exclusive of the others. Modern humans love to coax wild animals into eating out of their hands, and follower wolves might have been thus enticed. And, much as the wolves used the humans, the humans would have used the wolves. Fully developed wolves would probably be pretty strong, tough, and stringy in the pot, but cubs are said to be tender and delicious. As the human scraps sustained the follower wolves, those wolves donated some portion of their offspring to the human pot.

The implications cascade. I could close my eyes and imagine a prehistoric woman planning supper, perhaps in a lean time, and deciding that puppy would be good. She takes a cudgel and wades into a pack of follower wolves, looking for a young one. She finds several. Some lick her hand. Others snarl and try to bite her.

Now, I ask you: Which one is she going to bash? The friendly cub, under these circumstances, was much likelier to live long enough to breed and thus pass its behavioral traits to the next generation. This vision also fed into my growing suspicion that women had a critical role in the creation of the dog.

Over the millennia, as the follower wolves became increasingly puppylike, other critical changes would have taken place in addition to their growing friendliness. Adult wolves are notorious singers, but they rarely bark. Cubs, on the other hand, do sometimes bark. As the follower wolves grew to their increasingly puppyish adulthoods, their tendency to bark would be critically important to the human band.

◇

Humans were predators by this time, but when caught off guard they were still relatively defenseless and thus not very fearsome. The other animals who shared the landscape were probably commensurately less shy. A lion or tiger, coming upon a group of sleeping humans, would probably think in terms not of terror but of supper. So might wild wolves.

The most feared of all animals would have been other humans. Humans, in addition to being messy, were also inveterate thieves. We know from studies of aboriginal peoples that they commonly raided neighboring human bands not only for goods but for wives. This may have been a good thing genetically, especially from the point of view of the marauding band, but for the victims it was all downside. So humans had many reasons to fear the night. The only way for the band to sleep soundly was for one of their number to stay awake and stand watch.

Having once been a sailor, I can testify personally to the energy cost of standing watch. Evening watches aren't so bad, but when you spend four hours standing a mid-watch, from midnight to four A.M., you end up seriously sleep deprived. You stumble through the next day on grit, and grit alone, and you aren't worth much to those around you.

When the follower wolves developed the ability to bark, the terms of human existence would have changed dramatically. The puppy-wolves, with their superior ears and noses, would have been much better at detecting intruders than the best human sentry. With such animals to start a ruckus if a stranger approached, there was no need for human sentinels.

This was no minor contribution; given a full night's rest for everyone, the band would become significantly more efficient and energetic the following day. They would hunt and forage better and, as a result, they would throw away more leftovers.

In the course of my research I had a long conversation with Forrest Smith, a biologist at the University of Akron. He recalled how once, while he was doing research in eastern Africa, his group camped half a mile from a Masai village. After their tents were pitched, a local fellow dropped by to warn the researchers that there was a rogue lion in the area. The scientists and their entourage were understandably apprehensive, especially when, a few mornings later, they found the lion's pug marks near their tents. After that, rest was difficult to come by. Smith remembered lying on his cot at night, listening for strange noises, sleep eluding him.

Every now and then, as he stared into the darkness, he could hear the Masai dogs going berserk. Through those long, fitful nights, he grew to envy the Masai. They, unlike the scientists, could sleep soundly. Few lions would come near dogs, and if one did, its approach would be loudly noted.

Smith wished—oh, how he wished—he had one of those dogs.

CHAPTER NINE

U p and around Spinoza's spiral I went, my naïve questions
that led to no answers replaced by more sophisticated
questions that likewise led to no answers. And always,
with every loop around the spiral, I again faced the fundamental
strangeness of my situation.

*There was a wolf in my parlor. What on earth was it doing
there?*

Charlie was of a species that could date its existence to before the beginning of the ice ages. I was so new that by any reasonable standard you'd have to call me a prototype. Aside from
the fact that Charlie and I were both social animals, we were
about as different as two mammals could get. We were different
in biology and we were different in psychology and we were different in pretty much everything in between.

Every time I came back to this juxtaposition of species, it
seemed stranger than before. But I found myself homing in on
the two key differences between us: eyes and noses.

My world, the human world, is a world of images. The sine qua non of *Homo sap* is its eyes—its eyes and, of even greater importance, the huge optical processing center that occupies the back third of our brains. Not only can we acquire and develop superb visual images, we can also extract an amazing amount of information from them.

Charlie had eyes too, of course, but they were different from ours in several critical ways. They weren't as keen, generally, although they were much better at detecting movement. On a scale of 1 to 10, Charlie's eyes were about a 5. That was no insult; wolves don't live by their eyes, nor do their doggy heirs. Charlie's forte was the realm of the nose.

I had a nose too, of course, but it wasn't one of those attributes I thought much about. I'd look funny without it—I'll give you that—but as long as it was there we primates didn't tend to brag about it. Quite the opposite: We tended to look down on big noses. People go to surgeons and endure great pain and expense to have their noses made smaller. Perhaps there are also people who go to the surgeon to make their noses larger, but I have never met one.

But compared with Charlie's, my nose was scarcely a nose at all; it was a travesty of a nose. It was too short, by his standards, with room for too few odor receptors. I was so smell-blind that . . . well, shucks, if Charlie's kind ran the world I'd probably qualify for disability.

Worse, even those things I *could* smell weren't all that useful because the information was poorly processed. The primate brain just doesn't have the neural circuitry to do justice to the olfactory world. An odor, to a human being, usually means a stink. We spend billions on soap and perfume to rid ourselves of it. We also get odor fatigue: If we smell a particular odor for very long, we cease to perceive it.

Our eyes were another matter. Human eyes are the best in the known universe. Granted that the eagle has telescopic vision and the owl can see in almost total darkness, neither of those fine creatures has much in the way of visual processing equipment.

In humans, though, the whole back end of the skull is stuffed with what amounts to a neuroanatomical movie screen, all wadded up so it will fit. I'm not making a metaphor here—the anatomy is that straightforward. Each of us has our own digital cinema, designed to play whatever scene is unfolding in front of our retina. We live most of our lives through this medium, dwelling in a world replete with visual cues and visual instincts. "Eye candy" is a phrase that would make little sense to most other animals, but the first time I saw it I knew instantly what it meant.

The power of the human eye goes back to our earlier existence in the treetops. An animal that jumped from branch to branch, high over the ground, had to know *exactly* where that next branch was. It'd also better be able to compute, on the fly, how much weight that branch would hold. As our ancestors evolved, their eyes moved around to the front of their heads, so that overlapping visual fields enabled the occipital cortex to show its mind-movies in three dimensions. In the treetop world, those with poor depth perception didn't survive.

Something startling emerges when you put the triune brain under a microscope. The ancient mammalian and reptilian brains appear to have developed on a rather ad hoc basis. The various nodes of intersecting neurons are scattered in a way that looks at first glance to be haphazard. This is an illusion, of course: Nothing in the brain is truly haphazard. But you can't put a slice of the mammalian brain under a microscope and readily deduce nature's design. The whole thing seems like a tangle, with the neurons and their wiring running off in every direction. Generations of neuroanatomists and physiologists have earned their dissertations by trying to tease those various centers apart and figure out what each one connects to and what on earth that might imply.

The primate brain tissue, on the other hand, looks positively . . . well, rational. Given the right magnification and stains, one can see that the gray cells are arranged logically and hierarchically, each group organized inside a honeycomb-like unit. The units are neatly placed, side by side, to make up the working surface of the primate brain. Even the casual amateur, seeing a picture of this tissue or perhaps peering through a microscope, is struck by the obvious orderliness of it all.

My immediate thought, when I first saw photographs of those honeycombed layers of cells, was that they looked exactly like what they were: computer processing units. I suppose I'm dating myself, but they were strongly reminiscent of the tubes that used to form the basis of all things electronic, from radios to early televisions and computers.

Today, the word that leaps to mind is "digital"—and, indeed, the human visual process seems to follow digital strategies, making clear distinctions and pursuing reductionist solutions. This is in sharp contrast to the mammalian brain, which deals in murkier stuff, like emotions, hunches, and psychic comfort zones. In the deep brain, it is difficult to find conceptual edges. You just can't put numbers to emotions.

The digital nature of the primate brain makes sense, since our primate ancestors evolved to live in a visual world and visual worlds are basically digital. The visual spectrum, for example, might be a continuum, but the human mind can parse and split it into distinct wavelengths—colors—with breathtaking precision. If you have any doubt, you only have to look at the work of Monet or Van Gogh.

This being the case with the visual cortex, it isn't surprising that the frontal lobes evolved in the same direction. Indeed, under the microscope the "logical" part of the human brain, the prefrontal cortex, looks pretty much like the visual cortex. There's the same orderly march of honeycombed tissue, row after row after row. Not only do we see the world digitally; we think about it that way, too.

If the back of the brain can reduce the spectrum to colors, the front of the brain can go it one better: It can define the colors and even learn to mix and filter them. Our logic circuits can pursue reductionism into the far abstract reaches of our imaginations, parsing the magnetosphere into the points of the compass, parsing the animal world by species and subspecies, parsing our own language into parts of speech.

We are, come to think of it, the parsing animal. Give us a problem, and the first thing we do is parse it, divide it up into its component problems. That is our operational faith. Our primate brain assumes that big problems, if divided into smaller ones, will be more solvable.

John Locke, the first great democratic theoretician of the Enlightenment, posited that at birth the human brain was a tabula rasa, a blank slate, to be written upon by experience. We know now, more's the pity, that we're not all born so equal. Some of us have perfect pitch and others, like me, have no musical sense at all—and I'm color-blind, to boot. No amount of learning will allow me to see certain shades of red.

But when it comes to the part of the brain we think with, we do in fact find a certain rough equality among humans. The forebrain is like an empty computer memory, waiting to be programmed by . . . well, by anything. Most of all, by experience.

All that, just because our remote ancestors were tree dwellers.

◇

Once I let my mind wander down this bio-philosophical path, I gained altitude (or was it depth?) very rapidly. There is a rule in biology, for instance, that form follows function—that things are built the way they are because that is the form that best serves the purpose. A wing is shaped like it is because it has to be shaped that way, if the bird is going to fly, and at the same time a creature with such an appendage is bound to take to the air. In the same way, the architecture of the brain defines the architecture of the mind and determines not only how and what we think, but what we think about.

Being visual thinkers, for instance, we are born with an appreciation for geometry. Being visual thinkers, we are born to paint on rocks and dye our clothing. Being visual thinkers, we are inevitably fated to be visually greedy, to build microscopes and telescopes to collect light and give us ever better pictures of our universe. We use those images, sure. But the first thing we do, when sighting a new object, is take immense pleasure in it—and in ourselves, for having sighted it.

So we are indeed a creature of light. "Light" is a magic word to us, godly even. Another word, "vision," also takes on a multitude of meanings. We live in a world of shape and color, and our visions, whether they come in through our eyes or are manifest only in our dreams, have sharp, clear lines and textures. We see similarities among shapes, no matter how subtle. We incorporate visual patterns into our thinking, dividing the *things* in our lives by visual class. No two leaves look exactly alike, even when they are on the same tree, but we know what a prototypical oak leaf looks like—the theoretical ideal oak leaf—so, with a little training, we can always tell the oak from the maple and the beech. No two human beings have identical faces, but upon sighting one of the variations we automatically understand that here, before us, is a fellow human. These abilities are not confined to humans, of course. But it is in the human mind that they have their clearest expressions.

The spiral takes us around and around and around, up and up and up. Our ways of seeing and modes of thinking slide back and forth between the mundane and the abstract. It is perfectly reasonable to say I can see a can of cola, but I can also "see" a solution to a problem. Our best thinking is "visionary." We have "insights." Even in our religions we are defined by our visions—or are those hallucinations? We are so good at both that we are often unable to tell the difference.

To live in the world of eyes is to think optically, and to think optically is ultimately to think digitally, which metamorphoses into logic. To think logically is, finally, to think in abstractions. This was the happenstance by which the human animal made the unlikely transition from a tree-leaping knuckle-dragger to the creature we see today, drawing abstractions like $E=mc^2$ on blackboards and painting images like the *Mona Lisa* on canvas.

Abstract intelligence, when it evolved, was a new force in the world. Nature, in her incessant gene-shuffling experiments, had stumbled on something big (and, we hope, enduring). She has kept the human prototype, at least for the time being, and improved on it. Our ancestors prospered wildly while getting smarter and smarter with every change.

At first glance, this seems wholly in our favor. We not only had experiences, we considered them deeply, thought them over, digested them mentally. All animals had experience, but we had *considered* experience. With considered experience we filled our brains with knowledge and know-how, which generated theories and even dreams—dreams, perhaps, of longer spears, sharper stones, lighter and stronger baskets.

All this, and moment-to-moment experience as well, filled the mind with activity. Put a functioning human head into an fMRI scanner and the monitor screen will show us for exactly what we are, a creature metabolically burning with intelligence.

We are the pondering animal, uniquely well equipped to do mental work. Every thought we have goes through a multiplicity of higher-level processing steps, being examined this way and that and compared to other thoughts and observations. We build our model worlds and try out living in them, to see how they might be. Thus dreams become plans, and our plans become our realities.

But our ability to ponder has a strange side effect. The languages of the intellect and the languages of the heart are different, and we don't seem to be able to handle them at the same time. When one comes to the fore, the other seems to fade. Clearly a buffer has evolved between our mammalian brain and our primate brain.

Such a barrier may have been necessary, but it was not our friend. If you were going to admire us for our smarts, you eventually had to ask yourself, Okay, but what other animal would end up going to a shrink because it wasn't sure what it was feeling, or didn't know whether what it was feeling was what it was *supposed* to be feeling?

So it went. As we became masters of our universe, or at least aspired to that status, we learned to see things as they were. This included things we did not want to see; worse, once having seen them we found it impossible to unsee them. Burdened by our own past, wizened by experiences we could not forget, we reduced them to symbolic stories to memorize and hand down for our children, our grandchildren, and their grandchildren to ponder even after we were ourselves gone.

And that idea . . . of being "gone" . . .

Now, *there* was a sobering idea.

Gone.

The issue of personal mortality popped unbidden into the human mind and rattled around without any place to attach. We didn't evolve to understand *gone;* there would have been no purpose. So every hypersmart human being was doomed to struggle with it, to deny it, to find the denial unacceptably weak, and to struggle some more. To other animals, death was an event that happened once. The animal with the big brain, though—with the visual, logical, foreseeing, imagining brain—that animal died again and again every day.

I watched Charlie carefully, and was pretty convinced he didn't have much sense of his own mortality. True, when he met that cougar he certainly got out of the way fast enough, but that's a different matter. I don't believe he thought about death, and I'm positive he didn't obsess on it. The idea that out there somewhere there inevitably lay another cougar, or maybe a Mack truck, or some other emphatic end was simply beyond his ken.

Charlie didn't *have* to think of it for the simple reason that he *couldn't*. Lacking the neural equipment to project out into the abstract future, he didn't do it—and he didn't have the equipment to worry that he didn't. For all practical purposes, in the minute-to-minute scale upon which life is lived, this rendered him immortal.

Humans, on the other hand, are smart enough to see that we are all going to die sooner or later. We see others die, and it shakes us to the core. It makes us wonder what death is like. We've seen it, of course—but . . . from the inside, how might it feel? What happens to the "us" inside . . . well, our hearts? Suddenly, we have crossed the threshold into religion.

Scientists, of course, look to the material universe even when contemplating the spiritual one. Psychology is one result, though there is precious little comfort there. But as a new generation of biologists thought it through again, they have gotten a somewhat different handle on it. Religion, since it exists, must have evolved. To believe, you need the neural circuitry with which to believe. So . . . what was that circuitry and how did it evolve?

Hobnobbing with neuroscientists, I heard a lot of theories—or, to be precise, a lot of informed speculation. If I had to lay down a bet, though, I'd put my money on the idea that God was a workaround.

A "workaround" is a small computer program that comes into play when two incompatible programs collide. The workaround makes them disengage, or it translates between them. Workarounds are commonly used by big computer programming teams who design parts of a mega-program and then attempt to put them together. Life being what it is, all the pieces don't necessarily play nicely in the same cybernetic sandbox. Some tend to pull the program in unpredictable directions, or to overdo or underdo the design specs. When that happens, a workaround is written to make allowances, cancel out unacceptable answers, bridge between incompatible programs. Without workarounds, no program would function unless it was perfect, and perfection is an elusive state.

The workaround theory of religion goes something like this: The brain got bigger and bigger and we got smarter and smarter until finally we began to realize that we were going to die. All of us. No exceptions. Eeech. *Shouldn't have thought that thought!*

But by that time, you'd thought it, and you couldn't unthink it. So there it was, the big hairy Socratic reality that all men were mortal. It couldn't be unseen. It stuck there in the mind like a cocklebur.

Hey! We didn't want to die, the same way Charlie didn't want to meet the big yellow pussycat. This was a visceral fact, not an intellectual one. One simply did not make peace with death, not really. Besides, if we were just going to die anyway, why do all this other stuff, this difficult stuff? Why mate with someone else who was also going to die, and produce children who, no matter how much we loved them, were going to up and die too?

Look straight into the maw of the obvious. The knowledge of death was depressing. Depression made us less able to cope. With the realization of death, the intellect ran full tilt into the emotions of paralysis. Paralysis was another form of death. We were trapped.

This was not merely another pothole on the way to human evolution. It was a four-hundred-pound gorilla. We couldn't afford to be smart, much less to get any smarter, if getting smarter made us morose.

How did we escape this psychological dilemma? We didn't,

not totally. But nature, who is at least as smart as the average programmer, took the edge off it by evolving a workaround. Whenever we started dwelling too much on our own deaths, well . . . *voilà*! Suddenly we were thinking about God. God would make sense of it all. With apologies to Margaret Mitchell, we'd think about it tomorrow. Meanwhile, back to feeding our hungry children.

The God workaround was akin to a short in a computer system: Think about death, and your brain changed the subject to God. It didn't need a reason and it didn't need your permission. This made it possible for us to continue getting smarter without the system freezing up.

Whether you buy into the details of that explanation or not, it illustrates how our evolving intelligence complicated our lives. Being smart was an advantage, sometimes, but it could also be a disadvantage. With our propensity for abstraction, we could find ourselves making war over a flag or a banner—and especially (savor the irony) over a god. We became so involved in our intellectual activities, whether doing math or selling insurance, that we forgot to laugh or cry. Even with our puny human noses we could smell the fragrance of the flowers, but mostly we didn't bother. We rushed right by them, hell-bent on the obsession of the moment.

We so lost touch with ourselves that we forgot who we were. We even found ourselves arguing with each other over the meaning of "self," and whether it was socially constructed or not, and even whether there *was* any such thing as self. If I turned out to have a triune brain, then there was no *me* at all, but rather a committee. And if each of the three turned out itself to be a committee of many sub-brains, each with its own prejudices, interests and wants . . . where did that leave me? Dare I even continue to use the word "I"? Or was the royal "we" more accurate.

Which brought us to a very odd moment, a sort of soft spot in the biology. Or was it in the philosophy? Either way, knowledge was not an unmitigated good. There was a serpent in the garden; worse, the serpent was inseparable from the garden. We couldn't get rid of it and still have the garden that fed us.

If you think about these things, you end up investing a lot of mental energy in the workaround. The workaround keeps us from understanding ourselves too well, which makes you wonder how much we could know if there were no workaround. Might there be some way, maybe philosophically, to work around the workaround and see what is there?

Or maybe the brain tissue that would have let us work around the workaround isn't there anymore. Maybe, with disuse, it just disappeared—like, for instance, our ancestors' tails.

That was an odd thought. We'd spent millions of years building our big human brain, proceeding all the time as if one couldn't have too many neurons. Then, suddenly, around twelve thousand years ago, we lost a big chunk of what we'd so laboriously built. At the same time, we seemed to suddenly get smarter. Had some part of the brain started getting in the way? Did 90 percent of the brain rise up in rebellion and kill off the other 10 percent?

Was *that* the workaround?

I hit that thought and left it there. I didn't know where to take it.

Chapter Ten

Charlie was dogged by none of these issues. He had a forebrain, but it wasn't weighty enough to get itself mired in some philosophical tar pit. He had eyes, too, and an occipital region to go with them, but not so much that he could afford to waste any of the circuitry on illusions, optical or otherwise. He saw what he saw, and what he saw he took pretty much at face value.

This was immediately apparent on those rare occasions when Lynn and I watched television or a video. Charlie promptly sighed and went to sleep or, if sleep didn't come, he concentrated on working a bone. Even a dog appearing on the screen, or barking out of a speaker, failed to impress. His two humans might be dumb enough to project their imaginations into the big square eye-thing, but the dog innately understood that it was pure poppycock. The television emitted no odor: Ipso facto, it was not real.

Reality, canid reality, begins with the nose, and the nose knows things of which you and I can only speculate.

Oh, we can study the subject of odor, and do a bang-up job of it. We can intellectualize odor practically to death, laying factual brick on brick. With the tools of analytical chemistry, we can name the molecules and chart their reactions both inside and outside the nose. We can determine molecular weights and describe cascade reactions; we can model the shapes of the compounds in question and suss out the valences of the atoms that make up the receptor molecules. We can even count the numbers of receptors, more or less, and we can figure out what they connect with in the brain.

Or we could, if we ever got around to it—which, mostly, we hadn't. True, we had done a modicum of research for medical purposes. For reasons that are mostly mysterious, for example, the human nose sometimes goes completely blind. Don't laugh; it's a serious matter. We might not have much of a nose, but we use what we do have to determine whether there is a gas leak and whether our food is spoiled. Smell-blind people can't open the refrigerator without running a small but real risk of poisoning themselves.

There is also some commercial interest in odor research. The people who make perfumes care about smell, as do vintners and, perhaps to a lesser degree, tobacconists. Such people are curiosities on their own merit, demonstrating that the human nose, while inferior, can nevertheless learn. Experienced perfumers and wine tasters are proof that the odor-sensing part of the human brain has retained at least some of its intelligence—minimal intelligence, but intelligence nevertheless. That is to say, the nose can be trained. Anyone with a normal nose can learn to differentiate between major groups of wines and perfumes. The world's greatest noses, though (and that's what they are called, noses, as in "Sally is a nose") are probably born as much as made.

As for the perfume industry, most of its research is wrapped in trade secrecy and impossible to penetrate. It is easy to figure out, however, that a lot of this work involves pheromones, volatile molecules that the animal world uses as, among other things, sexual signals.

When the nose is genetically attuned to them, these signals can be extremely powerful. Many male moths, for example, have complex antennae studded with receptors so sensitive that a single pheromone molecule can set the moth on a path toward a female as far as a mile away. More practically, commercial breeders of animals, including swine, use pheromones to get their animals, uh . . . in the mood.

Pheromones fascinated perfumers in part because they work below the level of consciousness. The olfactory circuitry is so closely attached to the emotional circuitry that you can't tell them apart. From all we can tell, the animal itself thinks it is acting of its own volition, although in actuality it is behaving like a biological robot. The boar probably thinks (if pigs bother to think under such circumstances) that the female turns him on because she is beautiful, in her piggy way.

In this context, one can easily understand why finding a human pheromone has long been the holy grail of the perfume industry. It would be a perfect love potion. It should work as well with man as with pig, and, *oh, oh, OH* think of what the consumer would pay for such a product.

Despite reports to the contrary, however, no human pheromone has ever been found. Given the almost vestigial state of the human nose, that is hardly a surprise. Our primate ancestors responded to pheromones, but most of the scientists I have talked to think humans had long since lost their receptors. The sex-pheromone ads that adorn the pages of men's magazines have one, and only one basis in fact: There is a sucker born every minute.

Since the dog's world is olfactory and ours is visual, any attempt to gain a deep understanding of the dog's world eventually runs up against the unyielding wall of biology. The primate nose is simply not a very sharp tool. You can train it, sure; but then again, if you really wanted to you could probably train a pigeon or a cockroach to do ballet. But the result would never be pretty.

It all comes around, ultimately, to yet another manifestation of Pope's commandment. The proper study of man is man, and smell, being not terribly relevant to humans, is the least respected of the human senses. As a result, it has never evoked much curiosity on the part of those who train and fund scientists.

But even if we did our scientific thing and produced a blizzard of journal papers on smell, the result would still be mere information, and therefore ultimately unsatisfactory. We can study the nose, we can parse it, we can run slices of tissue through the electron microscope, but we can never do the one thing that really counts. We can never, ever, smell the smells and feel the feelings they trigger.

We're hopeless. We human beings have maybe ten million odor-sensing receptors in our noses, which sounds like a lot until you consider that Charlie has more than 200 million. What's more, his smell receptors are simply better than ours. Not only can a dog smell more acutely than we can, he can keep it up longer and more reliably.

I once lived close to the Blue Plains sewage plant in the District of Columbia (I was in the Navy, and the military always get the finest housing locations). Even as sewage treatment plants went, Blue Plains had an odoriferous reputation. When people visited us they screwed up their faces and made disgusted sounds. How, they wondered out loud, could anybody stand to live there?

Truthfully, we didn't really mind. Within two days of moving in, our receptors were jaded and we could no longer smell the sewage. "Odor fatigue" might be one of nature's small mercies. Or perhaps she didn't want us to be distracted by smells.

Or, more likely, it was just that an animal that lived in treetops didn't have much use for odors, which, being mostly heavier than air, tended to hang close to the ground.

The dog, though . . . I didn't have a dog when I lived next to the Blue Plains plant, but I should've. My dog would have been in doggie heaven. It would have arisen each morning to some new and slightly different eau de Nation's Capital, depending on the particular combination and yields of yesterday's laundries, showers, garbage disposals, and toilet bowls. And the dog, unlike the human, would never become even slightly resistant.

So the dog is fundamentally different. What's more, we will never understand exactly how different it is, because we can never peek even for an instant into the dog's world. Even top-tier biologists talk about having "a feeling for the organism." True understanding, in science as in the rest of life, is rarely achieved on the basis of abstraction alone.

This, I understood by now, was at the root of the enigma of the dog. We wanted to understand the thing, but, jeez, we couldn't even actually *see* it, because it was something that couldn't be seen.

We looked at the dog, of course, and thought we saw it—assumed that we saw it, that the image reflected on the movie screen in our heads was the real thing, the actual *dog*, the creature that *was*. But all we saw of the dog was the part that reflected and absorbed light. We didn't see the creature that emitted and absorbed odoriferous chemical compounds and vibrated to them like an emotional tuning fork. We didn't even know that we ourselves radiated chemical information the same way we radiated infrared light. The whole universe of smells was utterly alien.

We lived in our world, accompanied by an animal that lived in an utterly different world, and the part of it we saw—the visual image—was so superficial it might as well have been an illusion. So we ultimately had only a trivial comprehension of the dog (which was probably why we tried to breed it into different shapes and colors) while the dog, by virtue of our chemo-emotional emanations, knew a great deal about us. Stuff we didn't even know ourselves.

Though the limitations of the intellect were clear, it was nonetheless the only tool I had. So I shifted my focus a bit and, for a few months, read everything I could find on the subject of the dog's nose. It was fascinating stuff, as far as it went. I learned, for example, that the nerve cell that carries the olfactory receptors on its surface extends all the way through the tissue of the nose and into the brain. The nose, in other words, is the only sense that is a direct extension of the brain.

That makes the nose the only sense organ that directly connects the brain with the outside world. All the others pass through intermediary cells. Images from the eye, for example, have to travel several inches along the optic nerve. In the process, the cells in the optic nerve rework those images—sharpen them up and give them emphasis. Some bits of information are sent along with high-priority tags and other bits are pretty much ignored. That helps make our vision sharp, on the one hand, but on the other hand, it means that what we see is prejudged before we ever "see" it. What the eye sees is not what the mind gets, in other words, which is the root of optical illusions.

What Charlie smelled, though, was exactly what he got. In a real, physical sense he was in closer touch with the world of biology than I was.

◇

The directness of the link between the nose and the olfactory/emotional brain also speaks to the ancient nature of this sense. Chemical sensation, as the experts call smell, was probably the first sense to evolve. Even bacteria can perceive the chemicals around them and can move up, down, or sideways in relation to gradients—can navigate, as it were, by the chemical wind. A lot of scientists think this ability was probably present in some early bacteria.

Everything I read regarding the nose seemed to carry deep philosophical implications. Was the nose, of all the other sensory organs, the one least likely to lie to us? Did its primacy give odor some mysterious power? Was the poor performance of the human nose a testimony to our species' estrangement from the earth that gave it birth?

On the other hand, we were still able to appreciate at least some of the olfactory beauty on nature's smorgasbord. Take the classic example: the rose. Why did it smell so lovely, and how did it capture a place in our hearts?

I found a book in the library.

The smell of the rose comes from a specific mix of chemicals released by the flower in bloom. Long ago, humans discovered that some roses smelled sweeter than others—the same way they discovered that the pollen of certain poppies could improve one's mood. The early rose-lovers (like the early opium-eaters) learned to breed for the plants whose flowers accentuated the desired effect. Eventually, over many generations of humans and roses, botanical geneticists created the fragrant roses we smell today. In the process the rose became one of *Homo sapiens'* rare windows onto the world of pleasant smells, as opposed to the world of stink. But it was man-made and, being man-made, bore little relationship to the actual world of smell.

Humans could tell, just by watching how smell affects animals, that the olfactory world is intense. The direct link between the olfactory nerves in the nose and the emotional circuitry on the underside of the brain confirmed that perception. It was so difficult to tell where smell left off and feelings began that the first generations of neuroscientists decided that the whole underside of the brain was the "smell brain." The region was called that well into the twentieth century, when it was finally understood that most of that tissue didn't process odor, it generated emotions.

The region where smell meets primary emotion is not a place that the average human encounters very often. Thanks to the complexity of our upper-brain filters, the emotions evoked by smell come to us (if at all) as distant echoes. They are subconscious and so, by definition, can never be fully conscious. Even so, we file certain smells away and keep them, along with the emotional sensations they trigger, in a filing cabinet in the brain.

We know they are there, though—at least we know it intellectually, because every once in a while they erupt with amazing emotional power. Given a combination of stress and circumstance, a wafting odor can trigger a circuit that floods our minds with powerful emotional memory.

The trigger can be almost anything; often it's a childhood experience. Perhaps we are walking through a busy city when we smell something that instantly takes us back to our childhoods. The smell of baking turkey, for example, might haul up memories of long-ago Thanksgivings. Baby powder can evoke memories of our own childhoods, or of our once-young children.

Sometimes, though rarely, this moment is amplified by the setting and our mental condition. When that happens, the lid is ripped off our inner world and we feel emotion at such a pitch and of such purity that we are temporarily overwhelmed.

That only happened to me once, but it's not an experience one ever forgets. In my case it had to do with apocalypse . . . that, and doughnuts.

The doughnuts were a fragment of my childhood and a summer my family spent in a tenant shack near Anadarko, Oklahoma. My mother, in her boredom, learned to cook doughnuts in oil heated on a kerosene camp stove. So the doughnuts were real, or had once been, although by the time of which I speak they were long since eaten.

In 1960, I was a grown man on an aircraft carrier in the northern Pacific and my mother's doughnuts were all but forgotten. It was night, and I was standing a midwatch on the flight deck. We were somewhere in the neighborhood of the Aleutians, and the sea was so rough that the carrier deck pitched and rolled. A high wind laced with salt spray howled out of the north and found its way under my foul weather gear.

We were on one of those interminable cold war alerts when the world seemed about to obliterate itself in one orgasmic burst of nuclear fire. This alert had gone on for days. We were flanked, a sonar-shack buddy told me, by two Soviet killer subs. Two FJ-4B Furies sat on the catapults, each with a nuclear weapon hung below its starboard wing, destined for targets in Mongolia and northern China. Far away, in what we then called Formosa and we now call Taiwan, a confrontation was brewing. Chinese artillery shells were streaking across the Formosa Strait to land on the Taiwanese garrison island of Quemoy. From both Washington and Beijing came threats and counterthreats. The Strategic Air Command was on full alert and the Chinese were bellicose. John Foster Dulles, the father of brinksmanship, played Strangelovian chess in Washington, provocatively ordering us here and there.

I had a new daughter at home, according to the telegram in my pocket. I wondered if I would live to hold her.

The midwatch was the loneliest and coldest watch of all, stretching from midnight until four o'clock in the morning. These were the ghost hours, and they passed slowly. I paced the flight deck, growing colder and colder, checking tie-downs on the aircraft, doing my meaningless little part to bring the world closer to its end. Once the aircraft on the bow were launched, we knew they would not return. There would be no ship to return to. One of the Russian subs we knew were out there would put a quick end to us with a nuclear-tipped torpedo. It would probably be for the better. Who would care to live in a world reshaped by nuclear war?

But that was just philosophy, and what was philosophy when you were cold, scared, and homesick?

And then, in the wee morning hours, as the watch was drawing to a close and my metabolic cycle and psychological state had reached its nadir, I happened to pass the exhaust pipe that vented the bakery shop, six decks below. Without warning, I was hit in the face with a warm blast of air laden with the smell of frying doughnuts.

It wasn't a smell so much as it was a perception—as I suspect a pheromone might be—and it traveled through my limbic system like a burst of electricity from a neuroanatomist's probe. The emotional explosion knocked me to my knees. For an interminable instant I was home again, in that little shack in the blackjack forest of southern Oklahoma, seeing my mother's familiar back to me, my long-dead sister sitting in her high chair, as the aroma of doughnuts sent an expanding shock wave through my mind.

It only lasted a moment, but when the watch was relieved half an hour later I was still shaking uncontrollably. The watch officer, fearing I had hypothermia, sent me to sick bay.

Such is the raw power of the nose, even the deeply flawed human nose. Our species defends against such experiences with elaborate cortical filtering systems made up of layers of intellect and training. Only under a lot of stress does the direct connection between nose and emotions erupt into the oh-so-carefully-arranged conscious mind. When it happens, it is an event of a lifetime. My experience was so acute and unusual that I can remember it in detail going on half a century later.

But for wolves and their dog descendants, pure unadulterated emotion is the basis of experience. We can be pretty sure of this because we've made the observations and traced the circuits. Emotional circuitry dominates the dog's brain and, unlike the human, the canid has relatively few prefrontal buffers to modulate or muffle its feelings.

The high science of modern neuroanatomy, in other words, has confirmed what anyone who's ever watched a dog can tell you instantly: Dogs think with their emotions. They live the life poets struggle for, the *felt* life. Charlie was feeling incarnate.

As for me, my studies were changing me. Sometimes, now, as I sat there watching Charlie, I realized that he was studying me back. If he was dumb where I was smart, might not the opposite be true as well?

◇

I had to keep reminding myself that the dog is a fundamentally alien animal. The world we humans see is the world we live in, the only world we can conceive of. But that is wrong, all wrong. Even the phrase "the world we see" is chauvinistic, because the word "see" is used to signify not visual sight but understanding. Charlie *sees* his world as sharply and crisply as I see my own, and never mind eyes. Eyes are great instruments, and quite useful for an animal that is compelled to parse everything, but when it comes to the knowledge of the gut, the nose is a far, far more acute organ.

As I accepted Charlie's otherworldliness, I could watch him living and reacting in the world of chemical information. In Charlie's world, facts floated on the wind. Each breeze carried a wealth of intelligence that was beyond my ability to imagine. Some of the chemicals were specific, like moth pheromones, and so he didn't have receptors for them. The moth's world had nothing to do with him. Many of the other molecules, though, were invested with meaning.

I could only see in straight lines, but Charlie's world was nonlinear. I could see faraway stars, which was a cool trick, but it wasn't nearly as practical as Charlie's ability to see over hills and around corners. Charlie, sitting on the deck, could "see" a deer herd on the other side of the hill. He not only knew that they were deer but he knew how many there were, because each individual had a slightly different scent. He could tell how many were bucks, how many were does, and how many were fawns.

He could even tell if they were healthy, because an unhealthy animal has an unhealthy scent. After all, what is the body but a chemical system? And all chemical systems emit specific effluents which, if analyzed, reveal exactly what is going on in the factory.

There is a lot of lore about these "chemical fingerprints." At least as long as a hundred years ago, some medical scientists had observed that sick people smelled different from healthy ones. Some psychiatrists even thought that schizophrenics might have a distinctive smell but . . . well, it was hard to tell. Put three scientists together around a patient's bed and maybe one thought he smelled something strange. The second one might not have enough of a sense of smell to tell, and the third one— well, he relit his pipe and thought the whole idea was silly.

In hindsight, the perception of a distinct schizophrenic smell was probably the first tip-off that mental illness is a metabolic malfunction. In recent medical history, the idea that odor might be used in diagnosis recurs over and over, in one form or another. After all, a person is a biochemical creature and as such *has* to produce a distinctive odor. Otherwise, how could a dog differentiate between two people just by smelling their dirty socks (apparently an enjoyable and fascinating experience, if you're a dog). There must be some way to put that odor specificity to work, aside from tracking. Periodically someone would try.

I did a story once about Army scientists at Aberdeen, Maryland, who were trying to build a "smell chamber" for the purpose of sniffing human beings in great molecular detail. They figured that a smell profile would be an amazingly accurate identity stamp, which was what justified the Army doing the research. But the scientists confided in me that they were really more interested in the therapeutic possibilities. A working smell chamber, if it was sensitive enough, could conduct a thorough physical examination in a couple of minutes. A couple of sniffs and you'd know whether the patient had a cancer, and if so where. Likewise, the chamber might diagnose kidney disease, say, or incipient gall stones.

The fellow I interviewed could hardly contain his excitement. He was visualizing himself as being a leader in a medical revolution. But his dream never amounted to much. The theory was fine, but the science of smell wasn't very advanced.

The Aberdeen scientists ran into the same brick wall as everyone else who has tried to study smell: priorities. The proper study of man is man, and man isn't a nose animal. Light . . . now, *there* is something that matters to humans, and in the age of discovery the investigation of light was first priority. Hundreds of years ago, the human species had learned to make and use magnifying lenses. They brought the stars closer and revealed the lives of cells. We even learned to use light from the edges of the universe to see backward into the past. Electron microscopes gave us photographs from deep in the cellular machinery. If it could be seen, we wanted to see it and would somehow find a way. We even figured out that there were light frequencies below and above the range of our visual perception, and we learned to use them to see through the otherwise opaque human body.

Smells, though . . . smells didn't excite the same interest. If you were a primate, why would it occur to you to magnify smells, especially when so many of them were negative sensations? All you had to know about body odor came in a cake of soap. The skunk was pungent enough as it was, thank you, and the same was true of skunk cabbage. Smells were signals of the bestial world—dogs and horses and rabbits and all that—and thus beneath our notice. Sheesh, if you wanted to know what animals smelled like you could go to a state fair and tromp around in the manure. You could pet the pony and admire the prize bull. It was all very interesting, once a year. Then you went home and took a bath; afterward, likely as not, you'd smear deodorant under your arms to keep you from smelling like some kind of big stinky primate.

So the technology to make a smell chamber work just wasn't there. The scientists working on the project simply couldn't identify such a large array of molecules quickly enough, and even if they could have identified them, they wouldn't know what they meant. Arizona had been mapped. Patagonia had been mapped. The world had been mapped—hell, *Mars* had been mapped. But it had never occurred to anyone to map the spectrum of smells.

By the beginning of the twenty-first century, scientists were still trying to construct the simplest of artificial noses—noses that could, say, sniff out bombs. In an age of terrorism we had cause now to build a "nose telescope," but we'd never done the basic work that would allow us to get very far. In fact, our olfactory knowledge was several hundred years behind our knowledge of light and vision. That whole branch of chemistry had been not just ignored but *studiously* ignored, and now that we needed it we had to start from scratch. In the meantime, people charged with our security did it the old-fashioned way, which is to say they used dogs. The handler supplied the brain and the dog supplied the nose.

And what a nose it was!

I read somewhere that if you put a dog on the ground floor of a ten-story building, then release a single drop of butyl ether (the volatile fraction of sweat) on the upper story, the dog will detect it within seconds. Volatile molecules disperse *that* fast, and a dog's nose is *that* sensitive. A single molecule is all it takes to bring a dog to full alert.

The more I learned about such stuff, the more attention I paid to how Charlie used his snout. He didn't just breathe through it, the way I breathed through my nostrils. Charlie was a connoisseur. Sitting on the deck beside me, he seemed to focus his mind as he sampled every zephyr.

I had meanwhile bought a book on dog anatomy and, once, I brought it out onto the deck and sat, watching Charlie, with the book open to a cutaway of the canid nose. Inside, the organ was a maze of surfaces and baffles designed not only to provide surfaces for receptor cells but also to catch samples of scented air and hold them for more leisurely study. When Charlie caught a whiff of something interesting, he paused to concentrate, the way a wine-taster might. From the book, I learned he was trapping the chosen molecule in the baffles that lined his nose—trapping it, savoring it, matching it to smells he had smelled before and experiences of his past life. Turning it into *knowledge.*

Charlie was not at all relaxed about the process. It wasn't roses he was smelling, but something far more basic to his being. When an interesting odor wafted his way, his whole body tensed. His back legs cocked as if to spring into action; at moments, he'd lift his rear off the deck as if prepared to leap. He pointed his nose this way, and then that. Sometimes he picked up a stray molecule of something remarkable and he went on red alert, snapping his head around, nostrils flaring to better smell the world.

When he was occupied with smells, the flaps of his nostrils moved like vanes. According to the literature, he could use those vanes in tandem to triangulate distance and direction, the same way humans use their own binocular visual system to create a three-dimensional world. But there was argument about this and, in the end, there was the sense that if there is such a thing as the "wisdom of the nose," it (like so much else about the dog) might well be beyond a primate's ken.

Still, you couldn't help but ask the question. At least I couldn't. Not when I hung around with Charlie, because every now and then something would happen to make me wonder . . . and maybe even sense the vacuum in understanding created by my own olfactory blindness.

I remember one bright spring day when for some reason we

were all—Lynn, Charlie, and I—stopping by the campus. We were in the parking lot with the windows rolled down when one of my students came hurrying around the corner.

As it happened, he wasn't just any student. He was a young man with a very serious mental illness that might well make it impossible for him to live anything approaching a normal life. He'd told me about his struggles, and I was trying to help.

When he came around the corner, he saw me and we both raised our hands in friendly greeting. But Charlie, in the backseat—Charlie, gentle Charlie, who I had at the time never seen even bare his teeth in anger—Charlie went nuts! Barking, snarling, snapping, paws clawing at the half-open window as he tried to get out of the car and attack my student. It took both Lynn and me to hold him down, and he didn't really settle until the student was on the other side of the mall.

Later, we puzzled over it. There was no denying that Charlie had picked something up, almost certainly a scent that he identified as sinister. I told Lynn about the Army smell chamber, and the old theories about mentally ill people smelling different from the rest of us. Whatever the case, Charlie smelled something powerful enough to change his personality, at least for a few moments.

Take it as a baseline that, under normal circumstances, Charlie was your average friendly pooch. When someone knocked on the door he barked his alarm, but when Lynn or I showed up and let the visitor in, Charlie went all suck-up friendly. He wagged not just his tail but his whole body. He jumped around, trying to get petted and, not so incidentally, get a sniff of the visitor's underarms and private parts. He'd jump up and lick your glasses if we let him, which we didn't.

But once more, some years after the incident with the mentally ill student, he had another strange reaction to a human being. The university at which I was teaching had hired a new administrator, to whom I had taken an instant liking. So I was surprised and dismayed when Charlie met him and, after beginning to greet him, seemed to have a sudden change of mind. He backed away with his tail between his legs, went to the far corner of the living-dining room and stayed there for the rest of the evening, keeping his distance while keeping a careful eye on the new guy.

Charlie's obvious suspicion embarrassed me, though I don't think the administrator noticed what was going on. Later events proved me hopelessly naïve; the smiling man was no sooner established in office than he went after me and everything I stood for, and we ended up locked in the kind of quiet, almost polite psychological battle to the death one sometimes sees in academic settings. That taught me a lot about academia but, more important, it taught me to *always listen to the dog.*

That experience set me thinking about what I guess I'd have to call "emotional judgment." Up until then, I generally thought of emotions as forces to be resisted in favor of logic. One has to learn to control one's limbic system with one's forebrain, starting with potty training and ending who knew where. The neocortex literally sits on the limbic system, and it sits hard. I want to do a lot of things I'd damned well better not do. I am also afraid of a lot of things that pose no threat to me—spiders, heights, and, on another level, people who look and act different from me.

I have learned to ignore those desires and fears, mostly. For this, I am rewarded. People who are different from me—Africans, Asians, Latin Americans—turn out to have a great deal to offer. Because they have had different experiences, they expand my world.

On the other hand, letting one's emotions go can be quite pleasurable. It feels good to yell "Kill the umpire!" or to sing the national anthem. But if you don't keep a tight rein on such emotions you can get into serious trouble. It isn't wise to slug someone you don't like, or to steal that computer you can't afford.

Your forebrain tells you that to do such things are, in the long run, counterproductive. So emotions are like the crazy aunt down in the basement. You have to manage her, and you seldom take her out in public.

But now the dog had me thinking about emotions in a way I never had before. If emotions were so misleading, then how come most mammals seemed to do just fine with them? Left to their own devices, they simply seemed to do what they want, assuming, of course, that their desire wasn't overwhelmed by fear. Obviously, they were living as their emotions evolved for them to live. Their brains had adapted over millions of years, settling into the subtleties and exigencies of their environments, whereas my brain had come into existence in an evolutionary flash, with no time for my emotions to catch up with my new reality. If I let my emotions do my thinking for me, I'd make a monkey of myself.

This conclusion seemed to me inarguable. However, it ran directly counter to another human assumption about the relationship between heart and mind. We thought of scientists and other thinkers as being cold and somewhat inhuman; the rest of us, the theory went, were in much better touch with our hearts or, more accurately, our limbic systems. We see this theme throughout literature and in popular culture. Moviemakers love to paint scientists as unfeeling, and by implication less than human. Think of Dr. Frankenstein. Think of the scientist who brought the dinosaurs back to life in *Jurassic Park*. Think even of Dr. Strangelove. People loved those stories.

Yet the limbic systems of animals aren't dissimilar from ours. Ethnologists have demonstrated time and time again that our feelings aren't much different (if at all) from those of a chimp or bonobo, and a primate's emotional circuitry isn't much different from that of a mouse, rat, ferret, or most other kinds of mammals.

Feelings, in other words, don't make us human. What makes us human is our abstractions, our cold calculations, our fine eye for reality, and damn the emotions. This makes the scientists and philosophers the most human of us all.

A dog occupies a different niche. More than almost any other animal, a dog can be trained to hold its appetites in abeyance. Charlie's desire was to eat whatever smelled good but, thanks to Lynn's reprogramming, he could suppress that desire. Put a sandwich on the floor, and he'd nose around it, point at it, indicate he wanted it—but he wouldn't touch it until Lynn said, "Okay." For the son of a wolf, that represented an incredible exercise of mind over desire.

Unlike other animals, he seemed to desire to please humans. He heeled beside us when he would rather have been running. He went into a down-stay when he'd rather have played.

But then again, the control he exercised was tenuous. Sometimes his desire welled up and overwhelmed reason; a rabbit jumped up in front of him and he forgot himself and broke after the bunny.

Lynn could always call him back, of course, and he'd come. It was hard on him, though; you could see it in his body language. He'd rather have kept chasing the rabbit, and as he came toward Lynn's commanding voice he'd chance a yearning look backward, at the way the rabbit had gone. You could almost hear him lament, Damn! *I coulda had that sucker!* But his mistress called, and he came; inexorably, he obeyed. Lynn had spent an enormous amount of time and effort training him so that her voice could cut through his desire.

No, that wasn't quite right. Her voice, her companionship, her approval *was* his greatest desire. When he had to choose, he chose her.

But, oh, the rabbit, the rabbit!

Such thoughts floated around in my head for a while before they began to congeal and I realized the psychodynamics of what I was seeing. Lynn was using her forebrain to sit on, and control, Charlie's limbic system. It was she who taught him to refuse food offered by strangers and to stay out of the street. It was she who fed him and took him to the vet. It was she who filled the minutes of his life with love. His entire psychological existence depended on the companionship of a human being—which left him the freedom, when it was safe, to be the thing we called a "dog."

That was the canid condition, and such it had been for ten thousand generations or more. It had taken me years to recognize it, but the exchange was embarrassingly obvious.

Charlie in fact *did* have a big neocortex. It was just that it wasn't in his skull.

It was in Lynn's.

CHAPTER ELEVEN

So there was a psychological leash between Lynn and Charlie. That meant he got to have it both ways. When he was
under her control, he was not only a pretty smart guy (he
liked that!) but he had Lynn's undivided attention. When she
dropped the psychic leash, he had boundless emotional freedom,
untouched by anything approaching common sense. Life was
wonderful, the air was full of delicious smells, the sun was shining, and existence offered nothing but opportunity.

There was one morning, for instance, when we were still in
bed but Charlie sensed something outside. Lynn let him out and
came back to bed. But she wasn't there for long.

Charlie flew around the corner of the house and, beneath
him, where the garden stretched down toward the valley, were
three huge black creatures. They were just standing there, like
they were stupid or something. Maybe they'd like to play. He
gave an inquiring bark.

One of the steers moved nervously away. Instantly, the dog

brain processed that fact and its implications. These big things, despite their size, were afraid of him.

What we heard was Charlie's joyous yip-yip-yipping as he dashed down the hill. That, and the thunder of hooves. We got to the deck in time to see three full-grown steers thundering at full speed off into the forest—in three different directions.

The farmer, our neighbor to the west, stood with shoulders slumped, near the back door, watching his cattle disappear. Charlie stood at the edge of the yard, barking the doggie equivalent of ". . . And don't come back."

"I almost had them cornered," the farmer said, his voice laced with frustration and resentment, "when that big black bear came charging down the hill. Now I've got to round them up all over again."

The same thought went through Lynn's head and mine: "What you really need, Harry, is a border collie." But for a change we both had the sense to keep our mouths shut.

As for Charlie, he never detected a hint that everyone on earth didn't love him. Around people or dogs he was full of himself; when he learned to perform, he quickly bypassed the dog-trick stage to settle into his life as a star. Give him a command, and he did tricks—and then took his bows. The curtain calls frequently lasted longer than the tricks.

He understood the concept of fans, and he accepted his responsibility to meet and greet, whatever the circumstance. In a nursing home, no senior would be ignored and few, even those deepest into the nighttime of Alzheimer's, failed to respond.

As a star, Charlie also quickly figured out paparazzi. People took a lot of pictures of him, and with the passage of time he figured out that whenever someone pointed a camera, he was expected to pose. He'd freeze in place (don't want any blurred pictures of Sir Charlie!) and show his best side.

This was humorous when you were, in fact, trying to get a Charlie picture. But at other times it could be downright embarrassing. If someone tried to snap a family photo, Charlie would dash to center stage and strike his pose. Lynn would have to grab him and lead him away from the camera, him protesting soulfully with every step, *But my fans! What about my fans!*

Shame? What was shame?

It was difficult not to envy him and his ability to immerse himself in the world, to be a dog in full. I was Charlie's pal, because to hang with Charlie was to share at least to some degree in the joy he could find in the most mundane of events. Sometimes he even taught me lessons that applied to my own, ultra-abstract professional life.

These were the 1990s, the years when the once-grand newspaper business was beginning to crumble around the edges. Some of us, me included, saw catastrophe ahead. I was visiting papers and newspaper organizations to argue that journalism needed to be more reflective of the everyday world, which was emotional. In other words, one could report emotion as accurately as one could report fact.

The counterargument, embraced by practically every editor I knew, was, "Sheesh, who needs that stuff?" As readership fell, they fired their best (and most expensive) writers first. This made papers all the more dull, and readership slid further and further. Somehow I could not get through to the editors that emotional satisfaction would bring readers back.

Part of my problem was that I didn't know quite how to articulate my point. To editors, emotion seemed like fluff; that was their peculiar blindness and I didn't have a metaphor that spoke to them. Then, one bright Oregon summer day, Charlie gave me a lesson in psychology that perfectly fit the bill.

It was our practice in those days to take an afternoon walk through the forest. Homeward bound, we approached the house from the valley. From this aspect, the high deck jutted out over the walk-in ground floor. I'd strung bird netting from the ground up to the deck, hoping to train a clematis to climb the post.

Clematis grows wonderfully in Oregon, and I had visions of blossoms draping the high deck.

So far, though, only one clematis tendril had begun to make its way upward. Otherwise the netting was bare.

On the day in question we were returning from the forest when, about a hundred yards out, Charlie emitted a yip and took off toward the house. I charged after him, pumping and panting. By the time I reached him he was in a full point, his nose aimed at a spot about four feet up the bird netting. There, trapped in the netting, was a full-sized gopher snake.

Once I saw the snake Charlie broke his point and started jumping around, woofing and whining and yipping ecstatically. The snake, on the other hand, was not pleased at all.

It was not a good day for the snake. He'd tried to climb the netting, weaving through the perforations, until he somehow got caught. The more he thrashed, the more tangled he got. Finally, to top it all off here were a human and a big black dog sticking their noses into what was none of their business. The snake struggled mightily, trapping yet another coil in the net.

Gopher snakes are not venomous and are generally laid back. This one, though, was in a foul mood. I had a sharp pocket knife to cut the netting, but no gloves to protect my hands. I went to get them, leaving Charlie to guard the snake, practicing his whole range of barks and growls. When I got back, some time later, his excitement was undiminished. The snake, for its part, had given up and sagged against the netting. When I started work, of course, he revived with a vengeance, trying to get an angle where he could bite me. I started, prudently, at the tail, cutting away one plastic thread after another. I mean, this guy was *really* tangled. Charlie was neither still nor quiet for a single moment during this process. It was quite a scene, barking dog and writhing snake and highly focused human trying to dodge the fangs as more and more of the four-foot creature was freed. Finally I got my glove tightly around the snake's neck, snipped the last piece of plastic, and let the snake drop to the ground.

For an instant I feared Charlie would be on it and would get himself bitten. But I'd underestimated him. He stepped back a respectful distance while the snake got itself together. It didn't coil to strike, either because that is not in the nature of a gopher snake or because it was just sick and tired of the whole thing, but instead slithered away downhill in search of a friendly gopher hole or something. Charlie followed, not barking now but intensely curious. He came when I called him back, but reluctantly.

That was life in Oregon with the poodle. After a while he settled down and, utterly exhausted, curled up in the sun and went to sleep.

But if the snake was gone, it was not forgotten. The following day, as we returned from our walk, Charlie again broke for the house a hundred yards out. He ran directly to where the snake had been the day before, and scoured the vicinity with his nose. He waited, in tail-wagging excitement, until I got there and did an inspection. Nope. No snake.

No snake, but Charlie had had great fun anyway, just in the anticipation of snake, in the memory of snake past and the possibility of snake future.

So it went the next day and the next, until it became obvious that while the snake itself may have been exciting, the memory of snake also made the canid blood run hot. And memory of snake, unlike snake, was lasting. All summer and into the winter, Charlie continued his daily investigation of the snake scene; well into the following year, that corner of the house held a disproportionate interest to him.

After a while I realized what I was seeing. There were two things: snake, and memory of snake. Snake is exciting. Everybody is excited by a snake, which is why young boys carry them into classrooms and wave them around. But we overlook, or at least I had overlooked, the power of the other thing, *memory of snake*. To Charlie, memory of snake could be more powerful in the long run than snake itself. Finally, all this was going on in the mammalian brain, which humans and dogs share. So the dog story could apply to people, could be used as a metaphor.

When I next found myself trying to convince editors that an occasional zowie-knock-'em-dead feature story was worth it no matter how much it cost, I invoked the snake. Give the readers a story with emotional impact, and they'll find themselves looking at the paper the next day as well, and the day after that, and the day after that.

An occasional editor got it; most didn't. What, was I saying people were like dogs? *Yuk, yuk, yuk.*

Which I suppose, looking back, is in itself a sad metaphor for what befell a once grand industry. Maybe an epitaph. Editors are apparently not as perceptive as Charlie but, unfortunately for them, their readers are.

◇

Meanwhile, as Charlie wallowed in the joys of life, I slogged through the deep mud of time long past. The more I studied the dog, the slipperier the ground seemed to get.

Dr. Olsen had insisted the dog couldn't be traced back more than eight thousand years, and at the time that was a pretty well accepted number. Within a couple of years, though, the evidence had shifted in favor of twelve thousand years, making the first dogs contemporary with the old man in the grave. Then, with the passage of a few more years, it was becoming clear that follower wolves dated back fifty thousand years and more. That surprising news was based on evidence from studies of mitochondrial DNA, the same kind of work that established the existence of the famous "mitochondrial Eve" in Africa some 140,000 years ago.

This complicated the enigma even further. If wolf and proto-dog branched off so early, then there had been follower wolves at least five times as long as there had been dogs, indicating that a lot of wolfish evolution took place before the first dogs appeared. And the follower wolves didn't look a bit different from their truly wild cousins. Not according to their fossils, at least.

So what was going on, evolution-wise, in the intervening millennia?

The most likely answer was that the follower wolf *was* evolving, but not in ways that would leave fossil evidence. The wolves' bones weren't changing, nor were their teeth or the length of their snouts. What was changing was the organ of personality, the brain.

We know that the most plastic part of the canid genome is the DNA that specifies the behavioral code, and we also know that behavioral changes would have separated the line of wolves from the line of proto-dogs every bit as effectively as physical changes. Wolves, after all, are very finicky breeders. In each pack only one pair breeds, and the selection of that pair seems to be an intricate social affair. Proto-dogs might have looked like wolves but they didn't act like them, and that would have made them losers in the breeding caucus. So while wolf and proto-dog might have been biologically able to interbreed, in practice they would rarely have done so and the gene pool would have divided.

Once behavioral differences began to develop, *Canis lupus* must have been exquisitely susceptible to the widening genetic split. In addition to being finicky breeders, wolves are extremely territorial; a pack will usually kill an outsider wolf that wanders into its area. The follower wolves would not have been allowed free travel in and out of the local wolf pack domain. Yet as they followed the human pack, they would naturally have to cross wolf pack boundaries, making them vulnerable to attack. This would make follower wolves stick together at least as tightly as ordinary wolves. It might also have been one of the factors that drove them into closer physical proximity to humans. Their wild counterparts, though not yet acutely people-shy, must by this time have recognized *Homo sapiens* as a formidable opponent. The closer the follower wolves could get to the humans, the safer they would be.

Shift the subject to human gender. Granted, in an enlightened age and a Western culture we have strong feelings about how men and women should treat one another. But in earlier societies? Men and women specialized in different jobs. Almost universally, men hunted and fought and women gathered, cooked food, and made clothing. It appears that women would have also been the driving force in the transformation of wolf into dog.

Imagine a Paleolithic camp, consisting of four or five shelters. Assume that the hunters have had bad luck lately, or perhaps just been lazy. Or maybe it was just that everyone was sick and tired of moose.

Dogs, or more specifically puppies, are said to be delicious. Even today certain ethnic groups eat dog, mostly in the part of the world—northern Asia—where the dog is thought to have made its first appearance.

Juggle these suppositions in your head. Consider the menu options. Consider who generally makes up the menus. Consider who decided which dog to club to death. Consider who skinned it and cooked it. Who kills chickens, on the farm? Who plucks them and fries them?

So we come once again to mama among the pack of follower wolves, her appraising eye sweeping over the puppies and her club coming down on the one that snarls. That's dinner. And perhaps, if the mood struck her or there was a child or a sick person in the camp, she might tuck the friendliest cub under her arm. In the Australian outback this happens even in modern times. A dingo puppy is wonderful for distracting children or comforting the ill—tasks also deemed generally to be women's work.

As the wolf cub grew older, of course, it would become more wolflike, and eventually it would abandon its human family.

The same thing happens in modern times, with captive dingo puppies. As puppies, they behave pretty much like dog puppies, but when they approach adulthood they hear what Jack London termed "the call of the wild" and disappear into the outback.

But thirty or forty thousand years ago, in the case of the wolf, even a brief stay with humans was a step toward domestication, and a big one. It also fits my growing suspicion that women, not men, were the primary force in the appearance of the dog.

I can't prove a word of that, of course, at least not in scientific specificity. Most of the really interesting questions in archaeology are impossible to answer definitively. Instead, our picture of what happened—of where we came from and why—is a fragile, loosely woven fabric of facts knit together with reasonable supposition. In this regard, my scenario is as good as the next guy's. It also has the gestalt of the evolutionary process.

By now I was pretty certain about one thing, though: Humans did not domesticate the wolf. Being short-lived and having no written language, prehumans were in a poor position to observe evolution at work, let alone figure out how to turn it to their own advantage. Conscious human motive, in the Paleolithic, was a weak force that did not much endure. It was difficult to imagine that Paleolithic humans could think ahead in centuries, let alone millennia. To domesticate a wolf would have simply taken too many generations to be maintained as a conscious process. Even to produce the follower wolf may have taken between 50,000 and 100,000 years.

Besides, these wandering people had never seen a "dog." There were no other domesticated animals, either. Even if they could have conjured up a dog by magic, where would they have gotten the idea?

No, the dog had to be a product not of human design but of some environmental necessity. Nature did it, not man; that much was clear. *How* was a different issue.

Part of my answer was in place, anyway. First, and for a very long time, there were follower wolves. The follower wolves separated themselves from other wolves by the nature of their movements and behavior. As time went on, they bred less frequently with the totally wild stock. As mama brought down her club on the most aggressive pups, her selection became natural selection. As she brought a cute puppy back to camp and fed it directly out of the humans' pot, she performed another act of natural selection. When mama's great-great-great-great-granddaughter waded into the pack looking for a puppy for dinner, she might not even have seen any aggressive ones.

Then time passed, great gobs of time, and those Paleolithic women metamorphosed into blue-jean-clad women leading their dogs into a nursing home as earlier women might have taken a puppy-wolf to a sick child.

Women, always women. Just recently I was explaining my thesis to a friend and his wife. My friend was a retired virologist of more than a little note—a trained observer, an expert in natural history and the evolutionary process, and a lifelong dog owner.

I told him about the dog's language, about the play bow and the lip curl, and about how this body language even had a syntax. I told him about the mysterious behavior in which the dog dropped onto one shoulder to wipe its body against something rotten. That was about when he interrupted me.

"My dog," the scientist said with a snort, "doesn't do those things."

I looked over to his wife, whose face had cracked into a wide grin.

"*His dog*," she said, with measured ironic emphasis, "*does all those things all the time.*"

She didn't say anything about the many inadequacies of the Y chromosome. But she was thinking about them. I could tell.

CHAPTER TWELVE

That incident left me thoughtful. Not that long ago, I'd been as oblivious to dog behavior as my friend was; suddenly I realized how much I had changed. It was as if I had hiked up a conceptual mountain, a mountain so high that the trek itself had come to occupy my full attention. Then, when I suddenly found myself at a viewpoint, I was shocked by the height. It's a feeling familiar to most hikers: You look down and, gee, you had been way down *there*. Now you were *here*, with the whole beautiful world laid out at your feet.

It wasn't long ago that I hadn't paid attention to dogs, either— well, not quality attention. I didn't take dogs seriously. Why should I have? They were peripheral. Nice to have around, perhaps, sort of the way it was nice to have a tree in the yard or a rug that matched the walls. Then Charlie had appeared in my parlor, eliciting a mild curiosity. I had pursued it, as I was trained to do. I'd thought learning about dogs would be straightforward, like looking up some word I didn't know, but the answer hadn't been in the library. This in turn had piqued my curiosity further, and led me to wonder why so little of substance had been written about the origins of our most common household animal.

I had, after all, been trained to wonder about things that weren't there but should have been, as in the Sherlock Holmes story of the dog that didn't bark in the night. So the dog became . . . well, an intellectual spiral of the most Spinozan sort. The more I studied, the more complex the question became.

I was reminded of Nietzsche's maxim, that you should be careful when looking into the abyss, because the abyss will also be looking into you. There are truths that, once seen, can never be unseen. But it took something like my encounter with my friend the virologist and his wife to make me realize how profoundly the enigma of the dog had changed me.

I, however, had not much changed the enigma: I still didn't understand what the dog was all about. I *did* understand, now, that the dog mattered, that it was worth paying attention to, and that its existence made my world a different place. The human condition was still my primary interest, but now it seemed as if every time I put my mind on the strange case of *Homo sapiens* the dog intruded, tongue out and tail wagging . . . and every time I tried to focus on the dog, a human edged into the picture.

It was as if the dog, like Nietzsche's abyss, had the power to change you—if you looked at it long enough, you found yourself looking at yourself. It appeared that dogs and humans were utterly inseparable, all the way back to that mysterious old man who'd shared his grave with a puppy. So I had to take the next step, ask the obvious question: If the human was integral to the evolution of the dog, might the reverse be true as well?

When I looked back on my long journey to the dogs, my earlier blindness made me squirm. It wasn't that I'd become an animal rights activist; I was still a speciesist, especially where me and mine were concerned. Pope's imperative lived on in my psyche, uncomfortably sharing mind space with Charlie. But all the same I had learned that dogs matter and that my earlier refusal to acknowledge them had made me a much shallower human. More and more I found myself searching more widely for scientific papers about human evolution that, even if they didn't mention the dog might, on close reading, imply something about it.

Since I had begun my quest in Oregon there had been a definite increase in publications about domestication of all sorts. The whole vague question seemed to be floating to the top of a lot of good minds. We seemed to be realizing, as a culture, that we were not alone, and that the fact was strange and unexpected. We were growing more interested in domesticated animals. All of them, that is to say, but the dog.

The ethnologist Juliet Clutton-Brock coined a phrase that captured the thinking of the 1980s and 1990s: "walking larder." In the days before refrigeration, it was easier to keep live animals than dead ones—plus, the live ones carried themselves.

A pregnant goat, captured and tethered, would eventually drop its kid; then there would be two goats and, as a boon, goat's milk. The same, with the obvious exception of the milk, applied to pigs. All kinds of animals from sheep to the forerunners of modern chickens and cattle folded nicely into the pattern. Given a few thousand years, domestication would follow.

Clutton-Brock's domesticates were all herbivores, or omnivores capable of thriving on plant products alone, often plants that humans could not digest. They did not compete with humans. Wolves, and the dogs that were their changeling progeny, ate pretty much the same stuff as humans.

The fact that we eat the meat of herbivores, such as cows and chickens, instead of the meat of carnivores, isn't random or a result of preference. Scientists say it's a dictate of the metabolic world order.

All energy, including the energy required to drive life, comes from the sun, and it comes first through plants, which use it to make sugars. Herbivores eat the plants and extract the sugars—or, that is, some of the sugars—to make their flesh.

Biology, like physics, follows Newton's dictate: With every transition of energy, there is considerable waste. If the herbivore is eaten by a carnivore—say a wolf—to produce wolf flesh, there is another dramatic drop in efficiency. This is why the land can support many more herbivores than it can carnivores, and why you won't see tiger in your local supermarket. Tiger meat, per pound, would be hideously expensive to produce. So we cut out the middleman and, instead of feeding our chickens to tigers, we just eat the chickens.

True, people did eat follower wolves. They ate what they could get, and in pre-Holocene times, the puppy was the only animal they could reliably get their hands on without expending much effort to chase, trap, or otherwise catch it. But once sheep, pigs, and chickens came along, producing great quantities of protein while eating things people couldn't eat anyway, the consumption of dog tended to fall.

Unfortunately for my obsession, the Clutton-Brock scenario didn't fit what we knew about the dog. For one thing, the other domesticated animals appeared several thousand years *after* the dog, and they appeared in a burst. It seemed as if human beings, after working with the dog for several thousand years, suddenly had a eureka moment in which it occurred to them that other animals might also be enlisted into the human cause. Once they made this leap of imagination, a burst of domestication followed. Sheep, pigs, goats—almost the entire menagerie appeared in what must have been a creative frenzy, and the human animal established itself as a master species.

It was clear, then, that humans created those domestic animals, but did not consciously "create" the dog in any similar way. The dog was unprecedented. The dog just happened. Nature did it, and she probably did it by slamming the wolf and the human together with such force that they were fused for all time.

So the dog wasn't a "domesticated animal" in the traditional sense. It was never exactly a walking larder, though it functioned that way in part. Mostly the follower wolves were just out there, on the periphery of the camp, and had been as long as the mind of man remembered.

But I could not put my finger on what the force that joined these two creatures—man and wolf—might have been. After all this time, I had to wonder if I wasn't spending far too much energy on the quest. Yet it wouldn't leave me. Awake and asleep, somewhere, somehow, a dog trotted blithely through my mind.

◇

In the absence of much hard fact, scientists sparred over such things as where and when the main domestic animals had been pulled into the human orbit. By the 1990s, archaeologists were beginning to pay attention to (and sometimes preserve) the animal assemblages associated with human habitation. There still wasn't all that much being published in the journals, but every now and then I'd find something truly stunning.

One of my scientific contacts was James Serpell at the University of Pennsylvania. He was kind enough to send me the manuscript of a book he was editing, *The Domestic Dog: Its Evolution, Behaviour and Interactions with People.* The book was a compendium of current knowledge about dog evolution, with chapters by most of the main players. It was full of good stuff, but one idea in particular utterly stunned me. According to Raymond Coppinger and Richard Schneider, the wolf, like the cougar, had an inborn program that governed its behavior during a stalk and kill.

To be sure, the wolf was more genetically flexible than the

cougar, but the patterns were definitely there. One tactic included the wolf pack running circles around the selected victim, then the lunge, bite, and tear. Subprograms apparently kicked in prompting individual wolves to play a particular part, some harassing the animal from the front—grabbing the moose's nose, for example—while others slashed at the flanks in hopes of severing a major artery. Still others concentrated on ripping open the belly and dumping the entrails.

The follower wolves, subject to the same harsh ecological pressures that governed their truly wild brethren, might have lived even if mutations disrupted those behavioral programs. After all, they had humans to feed them. In fifty thousand years and more, the follower wolf's skull must have positively rattled with loose genetic behavioral springs and gears.

Coppinger's theory was that a follower wolf that chanced to lose certain parts of its kill program chain might be less of a wolf but would be of enhanced value to the human band. Say, for instance, one line of follower wolves lost the genetic program that governed the kill phase of the hunting routine but retained the earlier segments. Such wolves would select, isolate, and harass the prey but not kill it. Then, when the animal was totally exhausted, human spear bearers could step in to execute the kill at almost no risk to themselves or their wolfish partners. In time, the follower wolves might even be trained to help the humans drive herds of mammoths and buffalo over cliffs.

Other scientists criticized Coppinger's idea for various technical reasons, but I thought it was brilliant. It drew a lot of possibilities together, made them make sense. Injuries sustained while closing in on a wild, frightened prey were a chief cause of death among both wolves and humans. The Coppinger scenario would make the process much safer, thus allowing both creatures to survive longer and produce more young. Over time, the changeling follower wolves and the humans who learned to cooperate with them would come to predominate. Humans, no fools they, would probably have understood that like produced like, and would have favored not only the most valuable follower wolves but also their pups. How long would it be before the most useful follower wolves bestowed bragging rights on their humans?

This all seemed pretty convincing to me, but it could have happened at any time. Why did it happen at the end of the Pleistocene, at the precise moment when humans themselves underwent some dramatic change? Why not ten thousand years earlier, or twenty?

What was missing from the picture was a precipitating force—an ecological force, since the puzzle was evolutionary in nature.

When the question was thus stated, there was an obvious answer: The great change occurring at the twelve-thousand-year horizon was the end of the ice age and the dramatic climate change that occurred as the last ice sheets retreated toward the poles.

As the ice retreated, the fertile, earth-girdling grassland that nourished the endless herds of herbivores and the carnivores who fed on them began to change. Due to the drying effect and the loss of moisture from retreating glaciers, coupled with changing ocean currents and weather patterns, the grasslands and forests gave way, slowly at first and later with much greater speed, to tundra. The winters became harsher. Life, never easy, became more dangerous and difficult.

Hunger had always driven the actions of creatures large and small, and now that hunger increased. The great herds diminished, putting pressure on the predators who followed them. Where there had once been enough protein for all, now competition became intense. It was a dying world, and the losers would be legend: the saber-toothed tiger, the dire wolf, the mammoth, the giant elk . . . all soon gone—they, their lines, and the ways of life they supported.

When the world changes, the only way to survive is to change with it. We had always assumed that humans survived for precisely that reason: their ability to change. But now, as I reviewed my notes yet again, another possibility presented itself.

Was it the humans who changed? Or was it the dogs?

To a reporter, the audacious and unexpected question is golden. With it comes the possibility of altered paradigms and, perhaps, a revised understanding of the world. I responded like a dog who'd caught the scent of a rabbit.

Competition. Wolves. Conflict.

As the herds shrank, the two main predators, humans and wolves, would have come head to head. Wolves were even more territorial than humans. In fact, the only time one wolf was likely to attack another was when a territorial boundary was crossed. The follower wolves, who moved with the human band, would have retained that instinct but without a stable sense of territory. The range of the follower wolf wouldn't be marked by this ridge or that creek—it would have to be marked by the proximity of the human band. In this, human and follower wolf would be of the same mind.

Knowing what we know now about the profound genetic plasticity of the canid, it's obvious why the genomes that governed their complicated hunting sequences would start to break apart. Some of the follower wolves would lose their kill programs, as cougars sometimes do. Others would lose programs that led up to the kills. The program that told the wolf to cut out and harass the chosen prey animal could also be deleted or truncated. Some wolves would be prone to circle not just the victim, but the entire herd, and that herd would become, in effect, part of its territory. It would naturally challenge an encroaching wolf from another group. In a time of scarcity, then, the herds would by default become the property of the owners of the follower wolves, which was to say humans.

By now, the follower wolves would also be capable barkers,

and they would bark at intruders. Those barks would bring humans. A wolf seeking to encroach on the humans' herd might engage a follower wolf easily enough. But the added presence of humans would cause it to back off so that it could live to try again another day, with a different prey. The follower wolves would have become herders, and that would have tipped the balance decisively in favor of the humans.

By the time the follower wolves were guarding the humans' herds from their brethren, the wild wolves, the follower wolves probably weren't really wolves any more. Now they would be of recognized value to the human band, an integral part of the human survival strategy. In their new role as guardians of the herd, they would be cared for and their offspring would be well fed. They would lose those wolfish characteristics they no longer needed, such as wile. Humans were better at strategy, anyway. This was when the follower wolf would have lost a fifth of its brain mass and become unable to prosper without human companions to take care of it and tell it what to do. It would, in other words, have become a dog.

Dogs have even shorter lives than humans, so the humans would naturally have sought to continue the lines of the best herders. They would have bred favorites to favorites, not with the idea of creating a new animal but simply to ensure that they and their sons and daughters would have canid help in keeping the herds together and the real wolves at bay. But as always, human intent would have been mixed with human desire, which was so often defined visually.

One human aesthetic is known for sure: We humans, being flat-faced ourselves, prefer foreshortened faces. This is a scientific fact. Among the studies that back it up, my favorite involves that much-loved imaginary critter Mickey Mouse. Walt Disney originally created him with a long nose. In the early comics, he looked definitely ratlike. Not exactly the lovable face he has today. But over a few decades, as popularity dictated form, Mickey's nose grew progressively shorter until today he looks more like a stuffed toy than an actual mouse. And, of course, he is greatly loved by both adults and children.

Something similar must have happened to the dog. Wolf puppies naturally have short noses but with maturity they lengthen. Normal genetic variation, though, dictates that some will end up with shorter noses than others. If human psychology favors shorter noses, and if humans were the key force of nature for the dog, then by all means the dog nose would shrink. The descendants of wolves could afford to lose an inch or two of nose—their sense of smell would still put their humans to shame.

So Olsen was right: Foreshortened snouts were the sure mark of the dog. But while he drew the line at eight thousand years ago, other experts began to push the origin of the short-faced wolf back another few thousand years. Their evidence was sketchy, probably too sketchy for Olsen, but the timing fit the emerging picture of the climate change that followed the recession of the ice. Also, the definition of the dog finally rests with its behavior, and the first follower wolves to become herders probably didn't look much different from wild wolves. The difference was in their brains, which of course left no fossils. The nose wouldn't begin to shorten until breeding was controlled by people, and, considering this was the first time humans had done such a thing and they were working without a plan, it may have taken a while: three, four, or five thousand years.

Strikingly, the most recent research indicates that the dog showed up almost instantaneously all over the northern hemisphere. At first blush, the safe guess seemed to be that many different dog breeds appeared simultaneously all over the world. I sort of liked that idea, because it emphasized how intense the selection pressure must have been. Things were so bad that humans and follower wolves either teamed up or neither would survive.

The first DNA studies, however, pointed to a different scenario. All dogs seem to be descended from dogs that first appeared in northern China. It might be that those dogs instantly became so critical to our ancestors' existence that they spread by trade all over the human world. Another explanation would be that the people who had dogs survived, prospered, and spread across the world, while those who didn't have dogs, or couldn't get them, perished along with the other doomed fauna of the Pleistocene.

Another question hung there by a thread, largely unanswerable. There was no evidence that our closest late-Pleistocene cousins, the Neanderthals, had ever had dogs. Might they, in the crisis that marked the Holocene, have died off as a result?

We do know that humans changed almost as dramatically as dogs did. Set aside for a moment the shrinking human brain; by all functional evidence, humans got smarter. Suddenly they were master of the animal—the wolf—that was king of the other animals. Human numbers exploded. There was more time, while tending the dogs that tended the herd, to develop their own skills. Human flintwork became finer and more intricate. Humans carved things. They pondered their world and increasingly tried to represent it in rock art and cave paintings.

I thought the enigma was beginning to yield a little. Most of the pieces were in place and I could see the picture quite clearly. There was a certain gloating satisfaction in that, but also chagrin because there was yet one piece missing—the most important piece. The Popean piece. I wrote, "Set aside the shrinking human brain," but that was simply not possible.

Why the dog lost 20 percent of its brain was obvious: It had humans to think for it. But why did the human lose 10 percent? Here they were, these bipedal animals, poised on the brink of the most remarkable invention of all time, the invention of culture; why, at this moment, when we seemed to become smarter, did we lose a significant portion of our brain?

I was stumped. How did a smaller brain make us smarter? The universe was a strange place, but was it really *that* strange? "Less is more" was a nonstarter, when it came to neurons.

I didn't have a clue. I didn't even have a sense of where to look for one.

CHAPTER THIRTEEN

The next chapter of the ecological saga is much better understood. As the ice retreated and the northern forests and grasslands vanished, leaving tundra, the caribou herds were gradually reduced. As the centuries passed, the carnivores who depended on the herds found ever thinner pickings—except, of course, for the humans, who with their wolfish companions hoarded more than their share of the protein.

The herd animals protected by the follower wolves provided humans with a ready supply of protein for the taking. The hunt, with its dangers, was minimized. This was important enough, in the ecological dynamic, that it helped humans survive and prosper while other species died out.

Over the next few thousand years, the human hunters and their follower wolves evolved into herders and their dogs. By eight thousand years before the present, the dogs were definitely dogs, even by Olsen's stiff standards.

There were pressures on the human population, of course.

The ecology of the north did not return to its former productive self, but there was opportunity to the south. In the once parched lower latitudes, where there had been globe-circling desert, the end of the ice age had brought rain. Trees grew and veldts appeared Human dog communities found abundance in these emerging ecologies. There were wild goats, sheep, and pigs to hunt, as well as a rich variety of edible plants.

All this happened too slowly to be seen in a lifetime; the stories of the changes, if they entered the verbal tradition at all, did not endure. At first, what happened was not deliberate, but as time passed it took on a much more thought-through quality. People came to pay serious attention to the breeding of both their herds and their dogs.

Meanwhile the people, their dogs, and their herds, if they had them, were nomads. Nomads, but not wanderers. They tended to come back to the same places seasonally, in search of what they had found there in years before. It was a matter of desire and, of course, hunger.

But mostly, it was all about people being people. As our western ancestors migrated from the Caucasian forests, where apples grew wild, they naturally took all the fruit they could carry. Because they could carry only so much, the apples they took were the best of the lot. As they traveled they ate the apples and, being litterbugs by nature, they threw the cores by the trail. As a result, apple groves grew along the migration paths, where earlier there had been none. In the process, because the seed they scattered had come from the apples they considered the best, the fruit in the new groves was not typical of that in the original groves. Voilà, and by the grace of the gods, the new groves produced exactly the kinds of apples that people liked most.

This totally unplanned process was repeated with grains, wild vegetables, and herbs; whatever the humans liked best tended to become more abundant and also to become more finely tuned to human taste. But the changes happened slowly, over many generations, and it was not likely that any individual man or woman had much understanding of what was going on.

At some point, almost certainly by the time the old man was interred with the puppy, another force had blossomed in the human brain: religion. Religion may or may not have been a new thing, but most of the archaeologists I talked to believed that these wandering humans tended to sacrifice their best finds to the gods. They ate what grain they could, but they saved the very best as an offering to the earth that had provided them. In burying these sacrifices, they took the randomness out of the cycle of growth and inserted human value into the evolutionary forces at work on those grasses and weeds. Human desire, but not yet human design, would ultimately change those plants into barley, oats, and wheat, the manna of life, what we needed forever tangled up not in what we knew but what we *wanted*.

These nomads did understand, though, that they had somehow come to occupy a special place in the world. As later scripture would describe it, the gods had given man and woman dominion over the earth, and at the same time charged them with the responsibility for husbanding it.

Dogs and humans, meanwhile, had become as inseparable as sharks and pilot fish. You rarely if ever saw one without the other. Equally important, the dog was not just used; it was loved. The dog was loyal, obedient, and nonjudgmental. Far more than other animals, it was part of the family. When it whelped, its puppies were admired, played with, fed. When it died, it was buried, often with great reverence. Later, artists would draw their dogs heroically and bards would write poems about their sterling qualities.

Or look at it the other way: Who would ever write that you could trust a cow, or that a goat would lay down its life for you, or that a pig would be your friend for life?

Not until the late twentieth century did scientists come to truly appreciate (and admire) the way our ancestors had pulled other living things into their vortex. Until then, our big egos had blinded us. Whenever we credited early humans with deliberately domesticating the dog, we had not only been wrong, we had been wrongheaded.

It was a natural enough mistake, given that we ourselves lived in an invented world. Everything around us was invented by humans, so it was only natural to assume that had always been the case. From that myopic point of view it had seemed obvious that early humans had "domesticated" plants and animals as part of a plan, or as a series of "Eureka!" insights. But the mistake, however natural, had effectively blinded us to the wondrous nature of what had actually happened.

In fact, none of the underpinnings of modern civilization— not the dog, not domestic animals, not even agriculture—was "invented" in any way that involved conscious purpose and forethought. It all just . . . well, *happened.* If humans won the genetic lottery and emerged the world's masters, that might have been of their desire but it was hardly of their planning.

We had not understood that invention itself had to be invented. People had to look around, see what was there, and draw logical conclusions. This implied time, energy, and inclination to ponder, as well as to act deliberately on the fruits of that pondering. We apparently did not do this, at least not with respect to animal domestication, until the rise of the first Egyptian kingdom.

Unlike their forebears, the Egyptians put it all together, consciously and purposefully. If like begat like, then a person of foresight could choose particular characteristics of an animal and exaggerate those characteristics by careful breeding. One could capture wild animals, tame them, and by breeding for behavior eventually produce domestic animals that would not return to the wild.

So it was in Egypt, at precisely the moment that history changed from the oral tradition to the written one, at the time when pictograms emerged to foreshadow writing, humans tumbled to the idea—call it "inventive intervention"—of actually creating new animals. With all due respect to the folks in white coats, the Egyptians were the true developers of genetic engineering.

While we remember them most for their pyramids of stone, the far more important legacy of the Egyptian kingdoms was the development of the first sophisticated, thought-through animal husbandry. It was not biological science, but it was close, and it set history onto a path that would inevitably lead it to science. By the time the pyramids began to crumble, their builders had established a knowledge base upon which would rise the greater and more enduring pyramid we call civilization—a civilization that, as its various forms rose and fell, would eventually make *Homo sapiens* what it is today.

This mastery would allow many things, among them the luxury of forgetting that it had all begun with the dog.

How far we had come—and how mindlessly. How much we had forgotten in the long millennia since the old man and his puppy went to their grave at Ein Mallaha. Pope's favorite animal, for all its sterling qualities, was not a grateful one.

◇

The people of the Nile, having perceived as much about breeding as they could without actually knowing molecular genetics, put an unprecedented number of heretofore wild species to work. Ancient paintings show, for example, trained lions, leopards, and ocelots. Perhaps most famously, the Egyptians apparently harbored the first ancestors of the modern cat, which derived from the North African wild cat, a creature not noticeably different from the average cat of the modern world. The theory goes that they welcomed cats into their midst because the cats killed the rodents that, in ancient times as in today's third world, were the chief threat to stored grain and other food.

The small cats, unlike the larger ones, were pack animals, genetically destined to bond with others. This key similarity to wolves ultimately destined them to make common cause with humans. The Egyptians' more ambitious experiments in the domestication of the big cats, though, were pretty much failures. The big cats were not, strictly speaking, pack animals—a "pride" of lions was a harem, not a pack. This meant the animals could not adopt humans as part of their social unit: Lions might be gentled but never quite tamed and the human attempt at close association with them was ultimately, and prudently, abandoned.

It was with the dog, though, that the Egyptians best showed their masterful talent for breeding. Catching on quickly to the plasticity of *Canis familiaris*, they produced a broad range of breeds, large and small and of various behavioral predispositions. In other words, they not only bred, they invented: war dogs, guard dogs, herding dogs, greyhound-shaped dogs (used to chase animals such as lions), and a plethora of small canines used for purposes we don't know. Some, to judge by their size, were pets, and many were important enough for their names to appear on stelae and in murals: They had names like Brave One, Reliable, Good Herdsman, North Wind, Antelope, Blackie, and even (my favorite) Useless.

Though the dogs of Egypt made for fascinating reading and study, the humans were as always the more interesting animal. Egyptians respected the dog enough to mix it thoroughly into their pantheon. Osiris was a dog, as was Anubis, the god of death. To this day Sirius is known as the dog star and its highest rise marks the "dog days" at the end of summer. It was as if something in the human psyche remembered the central role of the dog in human evolution and wanted to pay it homage.

Yet at the same time the Egyptians also tended to belittle the actual, living, defecating, tail-wagging, hand-licking household dog.

The language, as usual, told all. While creative pejoratives like "running dog capitalist" and "yellow dog Democrat" would not come along for a few more millennia, the Egyptians had the idea. "Dog" and "slave" were the same. Despised humans were referred to as dogs, and prisoners were known as the king's dogs.

If the Egyptians took priority in the invention of new dog breeds, Asians would soon challenge them for creativeness. Starting with different stock, they developed the same sort of specialized war and hunting dogs that the Egyptians did, but to my mind their greatest success was in extreme physical configurations. It was the Chinese who first developed animals like the noseless Pekingese, along with tiny dogs that the women of the court kept in their sleeves for comfort and companionship—called "sleeve dogs" for obvious reasons. I am especially fascinated by these "sleeve dogs." They remind me of the old man in the grave, and the puppy he took with him. Sleeve dogs also foreshadow our more recent discovery that dogs are pretty good psychotherapists—and that brings me back to Freud and his dogs.

I could only wonder what the good doctor would have said about our ambivalence toward dogs, and our tendency to see them at one and the same time as both loving companion and filthy cur. It was almost as though, in despising the animal that most loved us, we were despising ourselves.

◇

For all of that, our love was real and it was enduring. Though scientists and historians had only recently begun to take the dog seriously, dog lovers had been tireless in piecing together what happened between ancient Egypt and modern Westminster. There wasn't much truth to the resulting accounts, but they preserved the principle of what the Egyptians learned, and the technology of dog breeding was never in danger of being lost. Wherever man and woman wandered, they took the dog with them, and in the process made it into helpmate, status symbol, and genetic Play-Doh.

In Europe, by the high Middle Ages, one could find the full range of dogs, from sighthounds to war dogs to herding dogs. Gutsy little dogs with short legs and shorter tempers were created and trained to "go to ground," meaning to follow foxes, badgers, and the like right into their dens.

In Germany, fishermen were using dogs to swim out and set their nets. They favored dogs with heavy wool instead of fur, because wool kept the swimming muscles warmer. By trial and error they learned to take the woolliest dogs and shave their sides to increase swim speed: To protect their swimming muscles they left the wool thick in the area of the chest and upper back, and over the muscles of the back legs. They also left a lot of wool on the tops of their heads, to tie colored rags around. When there were multiple dogs in the water, the rags helped the fishermen to identify their dogs and shout or whistle their commands accordingly. This valuable if unusual dog would eventually become a "poodle," after the root of the German word meaning "to splash."

Good dogs were highly prized for their usefulness, if not necessarily their beauty, and they were an important item of trade. By the medieval era in Europe, dog breeding had been firmly established as a cottage industry. Every noble of any importance had a breeder, often doubling as gamekeeper. The dogs he raised shared the castle with servant and lord, traditionally dining with them and grabbing bones, bits of gristle, and other tidbits thrown from the table. Dogs may have changed dramatically from their follower-wolf ancestors, but they still functioned as walking garbage disposals.

As the medieval population grew, more and more people began gathering around the castles, both for protection and also to practice their trades. They were blacksmiths, weavers, merchants—specialists, in effect. The world was still primarily rural, but the process of agglomeration into proto-cities had begun.

These people, having come in from the farms, naturally brought as many of their animals as they could. In the great castle environs of the Middle Ages, one could also find pigs and cattle. Even today, in rapidly urbanizing areas like Mexico City you can still awaken to the sound of roosters crowing and goats bleating from the rooftops. But rural menageries didn't really fit in to the urban setting. Ground was too valuable, for one thing. For another, prosperous tradesmen were too busy to raise what they could buy from local farmers. Garden plots shrunk and pigpens largely disappeared. Horses were rare except among the aristocracy; if a peasant owned a horse, it was too valuable as a draft animal to keep for pleasure. Goats, like chickens, hung on for a while in the cities but slowly diminished in number.

The big exception was dogs. Country people who moved to the city were ultimately willing to rid themselves of their other domesticates, albeit with some reluctance. They could live without their own pigs and chickens. They could buy their goat or cow's milk from a farmer. But in almost all the cultures I've read about, people absolutely refused to give up their dogs.

As these new city dogs made their slow transformation from utilitarian companion to personal friend and status symbol, kings led the way—or perhaps their dog-loving nature was just more apt to be recorded. One tale, based on a twelfth-century manuscript, relates a bidding war followed by bloodshed over an Irish wolfhound named Ailbe. Ailbe was owned by King Mesrodia of Keinsternien, and two other kings wanted him. The king of Connacht offered six thousand cows for him; another king, the king of Ulster, offered the same sum. As bidding turned to squabbling, the high bidders drew their swords and fell on one another. The manuscript doesn't say how many were killed or who won the dog.

As the aristocracy of Europe became increasingly centralized, dogs lost their traditional utility, at least for the ruling class—which doesn't mean the dogs vanished. Instead, following in the footsteps of the Irish kings, the royalty turned their dogs into status symbols. If you were a person of worth, you employed a master of hounds who tended kennels full of dogs specially bred and trained to hunt everything from rabbits to foxes. When the long gun was developed, other specialized dogs were bred to point and retrieve.

What applied to the king was no less true for the common man; commoner and king, after all, derived not all that many generations ago from Holocene hunters and farmers. Every class had its canine status symbols, from the dalmatians trained to run beside coaches to the ratters down by the wharves.

The ratters make a particularly good example of the illusions that surrounded the city dog. Ratters were owned by people far too poor to justify the care and feeding of a dog, and the argument that they helped rid the city of rats was a transparent rationalization. In modern times, with rat populations having dwindled in most places, ratting societies are alive and well. People catch their own rats, or breed them, and then put them in a pen with the dogs. Stopwatches are set, and the ratter who kills the most rats wins.

Similarly, the coon dogs of the American South are useful in treeing raccoons, and when prepared properly the raccoon does indeed make a toothsome meal. But by no metabolic calculation can the protein in a raccoon possibly balance the calories expended in the chase, not to mention the effort spent in breeding the coon dogs and the amount of time the owner spends bragging about them.

Sometimes, of course, dog owners just cut to the chase. Dogfighting is entertainment and sport, insofar as gambling is a sport—and so addictive that dogfighting has proven to be impossible to wipe out even in the twenty-first century.

◇

This was the context from which the so-called "purebred dog" would ultimately emerge. A specially bred dog, it could be argued, was more valuable than a mongrel on the face of it, and in any event breeding could bring out certain valued behaviors, which could be guaranteed to the customer. By the 1800s scientists like Charles Darwin were drawn to the kennels, where they studied breeding under the master of hounds. Darwin, polishing his theory of evolution, was fascinated by how these dog experts could predictably breed not only for physical characteristics but also for temperament and personality. It was these dog breeders who ultimately convinced him and his cousin the scientist Sir Francis Galton that individual behaviors were in large measure a function of parentage—a theory that was famously misused to reinforce the class system.

One thing built on another, and in every case the human relationship with the dog was justified and justified again, but the reality was always at least two notches more romantic than could be supported by logic. Dogs remained dogs, but the culture of dogs grew increasingly bizarre. As a case in point, English royalty (for some obscure reason) chose for its dog a short, fat, quarrelsome, nippy, and difficult-to-train dog called the Welsh corgi. Kings and queens were often seen with as many as a dozen of the creatures fanned out before them on leashes. The saluki became another royal dog of choice. French aristocracy took the high-stepping, tangle-woolled poodle, foofed it up, trimmed its wool to resemble a lion's mane, and put a ribbon in its hair where once it had worn rags. And so on, and so forth, until the western world had hundreds, if not thousands, of distinctive breeds.

Pedigree counted, if only because . . . well, pedigree counted. That was what made kings and queens, wasn't it? Pedigree? So it seemed reasonable that high status might rub off on the commoner who, while not pedigreed himself, owned an animal that was.

If pedigree conferred bragging rights, primacy of pedigree was frosting on the cake. The poodle went only back a few hundred years—yesterday, to saluki or Afghan owners who claimed that their dogs' lines were traceable back to the pharaohs. Husky owners claimed their dogs went all the way back to the wolf. Pug owners claimed their dogs went back to Asia and 400 B.C. As far as I can tell, their convictions have not been affected one whit by recent genetic studies showing that few (if any) breeds are more than a couple of hundred years old. If the modern Afghan looks like a dog on an ancient tomb wall, that is because the genetic package that makes up what we call "Afghan" has been teased out by breeders again in the modern era, and quite possibly many times in between.

But, of course, pedigree doesn't really matter. It always comes back to the same thing: The critter that matters in the dog-human relationship is the two-legged one.

The great twelve-thousand-year drama of human and dog boils down to nothing more than what I'd discovered when Charlie came into my life. Walk the dog, in ancient Egypt or Napoleon's Paris or modern Washington, D.C., and your dog will encounter other dogs, attached by leashes to dog owners. The dogs sniff and the owners talk. They fuss over one another's dogs. They compare notes. This leads to gossip. Gossip is a binding force. Thus all the dog owners in a given neighborhood know one another and, if their dogs are threatened, will stand together.

Human beings, even more than their canid friends, are social animals, and purebred owners love nothing more than to give their packs a name. Then, of course, they make rules, elect presidents and secretaries, and presto, kennel clubs, which band together to become royal kennel clubs or national kennel clubs.

So pervasive is this drive to conglomerate that by the late 1800s even a country as relatively backward as America had its own kennel club. Eventually dog owners who chafed at the AKC's rules and exclusivity would break away and form alternative kennel clubs, like the United Kennel Club and the World Kennel Club.

Clubs, of course, aren't clubs unless they have meetings—or, for the doggy set, dog shows. In the United States, the Westminster Kennel Show gets once-a-year headlines, of course, and the reporters usually zero in on some fluffy on a silk pillow. That is always good for a laugh. But for dog lovers, shows are no laughing matter. Shows are how one gets titles and ribbons. Shows are . . . well, dog shows are critical to life as they know it.

Every weekend, save none except maybe at Christmas, dog shows erupt in cities and towns across the United States. Anyone who wants to see a dog show need only watch the coming events page in the local newspaper or Web site. No town, however small, is immune. There will be obedience matches, herding trials, conformation competitions. This Saturday, somewhere near you, there will be competitions in everything from Frisbee chasing and dumbbell retrieving to scent tracking and, probably, silly dog tricks.

Are such things really needed in a modern society? Obviously not, at least nationally. Yet there are few civilized societies without them. Dogs, and dog lovers, are an inseparable component of human existence.

Chapter Fourteen

In many ways, *Canis familiaris* is a perfect psychological match for *Homo sapiens*. Faced with an egocentric human, dogs are almost endless fonts of submissive awe, sympathy, and loyalty, aspects of character that seem to have been largely deleted from the human genome. They like to play and so do we, but we are guilty and self-conscious about it; when we have a dog we can always say, "Heck, the dog needs to play." We don't get nearly enough exercise, most of us, but the dog is a perfect excuse to walk. While the dog reads the pheromonic newspaper around the edges of the lawns, mailboxes, and fire hydrants, we listen to the bird calls and sniff our neighbor's roses. The dog pulls us to meet people we have no logical reason to want to know, but we are surprised at the joy there is in the most casual acquaintance. The dog is an emotional amplifier tuned exactly to each owner's individual psychology.

But one conspicuous and terrible incongruity remains. The

human lives what, to the dog, is practically forever—and if our own lives are unsatisfactorily short, the dog's life is ever so much shorter. A wild wolf lives, on average, two years. Given the far less dangerous life of a well-cared-for dog, that lifespan can be dramatically extended, much in the way that a human's is extended. Dogs of full-sized breeds generally live for twelve or fourteen years; small dogs can live longer. Sixteen years is not unheard of, but the last few of those years are usually racked by the same physical agonies and frustrations that afflict very elderly humans. That's just the way it is.

We who love dogs ignore this reality, the same way we skitter around the irrefutable knowledge that our days, too, are numbered. But reality always intrudes.

Just before Charlie's twelfth birthday, Lynn came home from the vet's office crying hysterically. *"Charlie has cancer!"* she screamed in agony, and threw herself into my arms.

I was surprised and shocked, which served the moment: I was able to direct my energy to support Lynn. But the day passed, and the grief didn't. It spread.

The cancer was a lymphoma, common enough among old dogs. It could be treated, and we tried that, but an old dog has few physical resources to fight the effects of the chemical sledgehammers we use to kill malignant cells. The end, when it finally came, was the result of an agonizing decision based on our love for our old friend and the considerations of what we so euphemistically refer to as "quality of life issues."

It didn't hurt. I was told this. And then, Charlie was dead. *Charlie was dead.*

I was shocked by my own reaction. After all, he hadn't been *my* dog, at least not exactly, and as the attachment between us had grown so slowly I was unprepared to suddenly find him gone. I heard howls of pain, and thought they were coming from Lynn, but they weren't. When I could scream no more, I sobbed myself into exhaustion. So much for the Popean man; the heart knows things far below the mind's shallow ken. I had been prepared to comfort Lynn, but it was she who comforted me.

After that, the hours passed and then the days. Life went on, but it was a significantly different life. I was acutely aware of a blankness around the edges. I did my work. I wrote well. I ate, I drank, I slept. But the work did not hold my interest to quite the same degree, the food was not so savory, and the dreams of the night were dreadful enough for me to resort to the artificial slumber of the sleeping pill.

As the days turned into weeks, the acute pain receded. The blankness did not. Lynn wanted to get another puppy immediately, but I was against it. It seemed disloyal. It was too much like buying, say, a new computer because the old one had gone bad. It was too utilitarian and mechanistic. I felt as if a puppy would somehow detract from Charlie's memory. It just didn't seem right. We should wait a decent interval.

But Lynn was the one with dog wisdom, not I, and when she insisted on at least investigating the possibilities, and vetting the breeders, how could I object? Among other things, it seemed like therapy for her. It was something to do and it made her happy. Her happiness was paramount.

My doctor noticed my funk, consulted Lynn, and suggested Zoloft. I did as I was told, and Lynn said I began acting more like myself. That was good because, again, it made her feel better. But in truth? The blankness remained. I tried to remember: Had it been there all along, until Charlie came? Hard as I tried, I couldn't recall.

Lynn, meanwhile, mounted a determined and energetic charge into what we quickly began to call "the puppy project." She reviewed the recent scientific work on dog genetics and the health consequences of inbreeding. All purebred dogs are inbred to some degree, of course, since the breeders are going for specific qualities. A careful and knowledgeable breeder can produce a healthy dog, a poodle in this case, that is unlikely to have the genetic problems common in its type: hip dysplasia, sebaceous adenitis, progressive retinal atrophy, Von Willebrand disease, to list a few. Poodle owners, unlike those of many breeds, have invested serious money and effort to define these diseases and to create breeding databases that include not just appearance but also temperament and disease resistance. In her studies, Lynn made friends with a geneticist in Canada.

The thing that struck me, as a bystander, was that some breeders pay attention to this stuff and some don't; Lynn's first chore was to compile a list of thoughtful breeders. Once she knew which of these were best known for healthy dogs, she called them up and spent hours on the phone "talking dog" with them. By now she was also chatting with her scientist friend in Canada on a daily basis.

When all the facts were sifted, all the pros dissected and the cons weighed, when all the considerations had been considered until I could no longer stand to talk about it, Lynn zeroed in on a short list. One breeder was in Texas, one was in Canada, and another (to my quiet delight) was only an hour or so down the road from where we lived.

Nancy McGee was a retired financial expert, a widow who had fled California in favor of a nice house in the woods and the company of . . . what, a dozen poodles? Two dozen? Suffice it to say she didn't live in a home, she lived in a poodle kennel.

Her charges had everything a poodle could possibly desire: companionship, the run of the house, the best veterinary care imaginable, and a set of large fenced runs in the backyard. More important, and the fact of which she was most proud, all of her poodles were healthy and had friendly dispositions.

As Lynn investigated Nancy's poodles, Nancy investigated Lynn. The process reminded me of my Navy days, when I had to get a top secret clearance and the investigators questioned people I had, personally, forgotten I'd ever known. Lynn called everyone, including not just owners of Nancy's poodles but their friends and even sometimes *their* friends. She rooted around for the enemies that everyone had, and she found those too. As a reporter, I thought she did a good job of rifling through Nancy's closet and, at the same time, I'm pretty sure Nancy was doing the same thing to Lynn. It was like an old-time courtship.

On Lynn's third visit to Nancy, I was instructed to come along. Clearly, Mr. Lynn was expected to make an appearance so that Nancy could look him over.

At about this time, Nancy had decided we were qualified to own (is that the right word?) one of her poodles, so she allowed us to visit more often. I'm sure she and Lynn discussed my gloom, and Nancy declared we were badly in need of a weekly "poodle fix." This coincided with the birth of a litter of puppies to a bitch named Jade and a stud—well, gentleman poodle—named Galt. The two parents sniffed me over, apparently approved, and we were introduced to the puppies through a sliding glass door.

Lynn and the breeder were so caught up in estrogen-driven excitement that they were almost jumping up and down. Babies of any species will do that to women. My own experience, though, is that neonates in general are overrated in the beauty department. My own newborn children had been no exception and neither, as it turned out, were standard poodles. They were squirming black blobs the size (but not the heft) of a pear— sightless as yet, though a puppy's mouth and nose are neuronally connected and working at birth, so that the pup can find the mother's teat. They did seem to be good at that. It was difficult to imagine them ever being good at much else.

The two women stood there, peering through the glass and talking poodle genetics. Lynn could throw around the names of champion sires with the best of them. Charlie, she explained, had borne the seed of a poodle named Dapper Dan. Yes, the breeder knew the line well. Dapper Dan was . . . Yadda, yadda, yadda and the this and the that and the royal family of dogs. I quickly grew bored. Royal or not, I figured Dapper Dan, like any other dog, would happily eat coyote shit if he'd ever got the chance. I moved across the deck to sit on the top step and look out over the yard beyond.

Serious breeders rarely work in cities, where the law books bristle with antidog ordinances, and Nancy was no exception. Beyond the fenced runs there was a cornfield and then, in the far distance, a tree line. Above that the sky was the light powder color they call Carolina blue.

I sat there, essentially unengaged, my mind wandering, idly fixing on the remarkable way the newborn nervous system is wired. The puppies beyond the window, like human babies, had been born with almost a full complement of neurons. But most of the connections weren't insulated yet, and too much electricity leaked out for them to fire coherently. This is one of nature's classier tricks, wiring up the brain before birth but not adding the bulkier insulation until afterward.

The two-step development of the nervous system is a key to mammalian evolution. Newly hatched reptiles emerge from their eggs pretty much ready to go, but mammals have to pass through a birth canal. So we are all, man and dog, born twice—first physically, then mentally. The latter is a more leisurely matter, dependent on specialized cells called (who thinks up these names?) oligodendrites.

These servant cells are sort of like slugs, laying down slime trails wherever they go, only the oligodendrites' trails aren't slime. They are the cell's own specialized skin, or membrane, which is made almost entirely of fat. Myelin, it is called. Soon after birth, these servant cells get busy, hundreds of thousands of them crawling around the axis of each nerve cell, laying down insulating layers of myelin. As the layers of insulation reach a critical thickness, various parts of the infant's body switch on. First, the nerves to the eyes start firing, and then the eyes open. Then comes the face. The priorities of the dog brain are such that the pup gets wired from the head back. When the tail starts wagging, you know the whole puppy is now under at least the nominal control of its central nervous system.

The skull grows rapidly during this initial period, to make room for the myelin. Then the myelination process continues more slowly. In the dog, most of it is finished in eighteen to twenty-four months. In people, it continues in spurts through adolescence, accounting for the bizarre behavior of many teenagers.

A female acquaintance once accused me of hiding behind my intellect. I was surprised at how angry she was, and I still don't quite understand why. But that day at Nancy's it was engaging to sit in the warm sun, tuning out the women's chatter and thinking of the evolutionary mechanics of the brain. It gave me something to think about other than missing Charlie.

At some point I heard the patio door open and looked up to see the puppy's mother, Jade, walk out: break time for mama. She stepped into the sun and stretched, clearly pleased to be away from the puppies for a moment; she paused to greet me as she went down the steps, then trotted into the backyard to sniff out the right place to empty her bladder. I wondered, idly, what her criteria were.

The sky had been perfectly clear when I sat down but now, above the distant horizon, a line of puffy clouds had appeared. I knew exactly what they were. Convection cells, carrying hot, humid surface air into the higher, colder strata. As the air cooled, the water sweated out into fog. As I watched, the line of puffs merged and built, changing shape, becoming ever larger as they moved across the landscape. They billowed up white against the blue until their bottoms began to turn dark.

The plasticity of clouds has always mesmerized me. One moment there is a clear blue sky beneath a hot white sun and the next moment . . . It is a kind of Genesis: Lo, let there be clouds. Then the clouds come, springing from nothing, billowing up white against the blue, moving, building, differentiating into this form and that, merging, sending out new lobes, mushrooming. If you didn't know better, you'd think they were alive. Somewhere back along the genetic chain of existence I'd bet that my own ancestors once thought precisely that.

Clouds were *like* life, in the way that they interlaced and confused cause with effect. We call them clouds because we can see them, whereas we can't see the rest of the atmosphere around them, of which they are a part. So that part of the sky, the noncloud, doesn't really have a name. All the same, it's there.

Clouds seem to have lives of their own, but they are really just effect. They are produced by certain conditions of the atmosphere, which contain them by strict, if unseen, forces. They are water vapor in an invisible mold, responding to the gas laws, pushed about by the winds, condensing according to the dictates of temperature differentials and humidity. What can be seen is not what matters, and what matters cannot be seen. All you see is what was wrought, the secondary effects.

But it is so easy to imagine that clouds are not produced by a force, that they are forces in themselves, independent entities. And maybe, as you watch and woolgather, your mind sees in the clouds shapes of horses and pigs and dinosaurs and all the other images the human mind imposes on clouds. Maybe it doesn't matter much to you how much you know or don't know about clouds, they are hypnotic and beautiful.

Suddenly I was jerked back to reality by realizing I was not alone. Jade had paused halfway up the steps and was looking at me, her head cocked inquisitively. She was enough like Charlie to make my heart jump, but she was not Charlie. I couldn't tell you exactly how she was different. She had the same nose, the same body, the same coal-black wooly hair—but she was different.

There was no Charlie, not anymore, and there never would be again. Inside, something was hollow, and it ached like the socket of a newly pulled molar.

Jade took a step toward me and nuzzled me with her nose. She sensed the pain and was trying to help. I'd seen Charlie act that way when he was working at being a therapy dog.

I petted Jade, ran my fingers through her wool, and after a few moments she moved up and sat down beside me at the top of my steps, leaning into my body. There was a time, long ago, before Charlie, I would have assumed that she wanted my attention. But no, that wasn't it at all. She wanted to *change* my attention, manipulate it away from the pain. Without thinking, I threw my arm around her. She licked my hand.

I sat there, idly stroking the dog, increasingly aware of springtime bursting around me and thunderclouds building. The day was suddenly vivid, the earth dynamic.

I didn't connect this change of mood with Jade's presence, at least not instantly. The past several weeks had been long, miserable, and morbid, and it was enough to feel good once more about being alive, being a human being on a beautiful day, wondering and thinking, thinking about the brain, watching the clouds, breathing the fresh air.

Two snowbirds landed in the short grass right in front of us. Jade pointed her nose at them and the quiver in her body passed through my arm and into my mind. I couldn't help but follow her eyes. Together we watched the birds, all dressed up in their pleated Confederate gray with white tails, on their way to the Arctic. They danced across the lawn in an elaborate waltz, up and across and over, chirping and flitting. Their behavior, I reflected briefly, was probably a mating ritual—like the clouds, produced by invisible forces. That the forces were psychological in the birds' case and physical in the clouds, made no difference.

I sat with my arm around Jade, the air charged with energy, life, and awareness, intellect and emotion in a temporary truce, just me, enveloped in the present, joyous in my own momentary sense of completeness.

I don't know how long this went on, thinking in such human abstractions, but it must have been a long time. The big poodle beside me was infinitely patient, infinitely there, leaning delicately against me, allowing herself to be used while watching nature unfold around both of us, her eyes following the birds and the activities of the other poodles in the runs, ears alert, nose pointing this way and that, the delicate black vanes of her nostrils flaring and closing.

She didn't watch the clouds, though, of that I'm pretty sure. I've seen no evidence that dogs care much about the sky. The sky is for the imagining animal, the dreamer, the abstractor.

In this instance, Jade was missing a good show. In the time that Lynn and the breeder had consumed talking dog, the harmless-looking poofs of clouds I first saw had puffed themselves up, climbing now until their bases turned dark and merging until they stretched across the far horizon. Then the first stroke of lightning flashed somewhere inside them.

The lightning itself was invisible, but it illuminated a dark sulcus between two cloud convolutions. The clouds seemed to pulse with the stab of illuminating energy, as if something were coming alive and, I realized with a shock, something was. The little clouds that before had been the products of the immediate environment had now become the determinant of that environment—a force that perpetuated itself, sucked up more air to create more cloud to suck up more air. Nature, in her endless motility, could do anything, anything. In this case she had turned herself inside out, converted effect to cause, created the clouds, and then set them loose, more or less, on the bright spring day.

A visible hair of light crawled along the bottom of the clouds. It reminded me of the primordial warm pool where, it was thought, life was long ago created when lightning fused two inert molecules into a single one—a magic molecule capable of becoming its own cause and reproducing itself.

The squall line was moving now, toward us and slightly to

the east. I could as yet hear no thunder but Jade suddenly turned that way, tilting her head and perking her ears. She heard, even if I didn't. She heard *for* me. I heard *through* her, felt at one with her, my cares anesthetized for the moment by Jade's aura. It was a moment of Zen surrender, when the intellect relaxes, yielding control to deeper and older forces, when the human ego surrenders to the law of the scaled lizard and the furry mammal, when intelligence is freed from logic and transmogrifies into knowledge.

I saw clearly, then, the metaphors in the sky. Clouds too insubstantial to be touched, mere fog banks, produced bolts of lightning and blasts of tornado-spawning winds no different in nature from the motion of the continents or the dynamics of evolution. The forces of the environment built single cells just the way they had built the original little pooflets of cloud, and eventually from those they built fish, and then fish with legs, and then all the rest from thunder lizard to butterfly. We humans have come to understand this, very slowly and only with the intellect. It seems beyond our emotional understanding, which is why, even now, some see evolution as repugnant and atheistic. It runs counter to our ego and, anyway, it's something we can't see happen around us. Species develop, split, come together again over such long periods of time. Our individual lives allow us but a glimpse of the process.

Yet if we could speed up time, we could see the continents slide across the surface of the planet just as dynamically as clouds move across the sky. The stone under our feet boils with convection currents, heating and cooling itself with its own processes of friction and compression. Hot rock rises, cold rock sinks. Along the leading edges of continents plumes of magma billow up and break the surface as volcanoes.

The timetable of evolution is somewhere in between the timetable of tectonics and the timetable of clouds. On this time scale, teeth and bones grew from nothing, the product of forces unseen. Organs formed like clouds, beginning as smears of protoplasm, gathering strength with each generation of cells. Brains. Brains, the organs that excreted thought—they were products, too, of outside forces. They built like clouds, larger and higher in order. Fish, lizard, bird, dinosaur, mammal.

It took a long time to build the brains of higher mammals, but they could be altered in a geological heartbeat. We see that with dogs. In the same way that we can breed a big dog or a small dog, we can breed one that is friendly or mean, smart or dumb—a dog that doesn't care about people or a dog that wants nothing so much as to please. In a few generations, anything can happen. In geological terms, brains are as plastic as the clouds— clouds which, by now, had built into spectacular white columns with undersides almost as black as Jade's fur. Continual strokes of lightning illuminated them from inside. They glowed with the spirit of electrical charge.

I could hear the thunder myself, now, rumbling like a distant cannon. A fork of lightning shot between cloud and ground, and then another. One of the cloud tops, penetrating the strato- sphere, was being sheared off by stratospheric winds, blowing flat to form a classic anvil. I had to crane my neck now to see it. I felt an anticipatory puff of chilled air. A warm June day had be- come something quite different. Nothing stayed the same for long. Not the day, the cloud, the poodle, or the man. Everything was plastic, even boundaries.

But clouds are not a metaphor for nature. Metaphor is a hu- man medium, not nature's. Nature doesn't do metaphor. Nature works in brutal forces, carving her desires in flesh and blood.

My mind flipped from clouds and drifting continents to memories of the old man in the grave. There was such yearning in the way he reached for the puppy, it was almost a tangible force. Twelve thousand years later, we still reached for that in- estimable, harmonic *something* that the puppy had, and that we so desperately needed. We had no older bond than that between us and the dog. It was as if we overlapped at some level, as if something had happened at some time in the past that was irrevocable for both dog and man.

Finally, after all these years of searching, of wondering, of blind alleys and dead ends, scientific papers and dog shows, books and interviews, confusion and angst, ego and despair . . . a key turned in a lock, the enigma rotated, and human ego factored out. The ego had been the obscuring force. Ego aside, it was almost mathematically logical.

When the wolf became the dog, it lost 20 percent of its brain mass. This we attributed, reasonably enough, to human influence. So why hadn't we immediately attributed the human's loss of brain mass to the propinquity of the dog? Why was it so hard to see nature's impartiality? How could the forces at work on the dog *not* be working, simultaneously, on the human?

More realistically, each animal changed the other.

The dog had shed 20 percent of its brain mass because the human had agreed, biologically, to do its thinking and scheming for it. In return, the dog had agreed to carry 10 percent of the human's burden, so that the human brain could shed 10 percent of its brain mass. Considering the comparative sizes of the two brains to start with, it had been a more or less equal trade.

That explained how we lost brain mass and at the same time got paradoxically smarter. We hadn't actually lost that brain matter; we had just handed it to the dog to carry. The dog was more than guard and hunting companion: It was our beast of emotional burden.

We knew what the dog had given us to carry: intelligence and shrewdness. But what had we given the dog?

That was not so hard to answer, at least in a general way. The dog was keeper of the deep emotional past. It was our emotional guide dog.

Emotion was as clearly the dog specialty, as thought was ours. We went to the dog when we needed to be more animal-like, when we needed to feel. At the same time, the emotional engines the dog carried for us could be quickly turned off. With just a little effort, the dog could be trained to settle quietly at our feet, put the emotion to rest. With our minds freed of emotional static, we could then do our thinking. Our key adaptive strength was thereby strengthened.

Think of it in computer terms. Our wetware contained a complex of emotional programs that we sometimes needed desperately, but that dramatically slowed down our operating system. The dog had the same program, so we threw ours away and instead used the dog's. Our program was now a peripheral (aka "the dog"), running on a detachable drive. When we undertook to do serious thinking, we unplugged the peripheral drive. That dramatically streamlined our mental capacity. With the overlapping psyches of the dog and human, we could have it both ways.

Obviously, there were no wires to connect us. But baby and puppy both came with a complex and subtle language that could easily be developed into a rich, multimodal, emotional communication system, consisting of everything from human words to body language to (at least in the dog's case) chemical messengers.

If we're depressed, the dog knows it and comes to do emotional repair. If we want to explore, we hardly have to call the dog; he's there. Conversely, we are constitutionally unable to avoid certain dog signals of alarm. A barking dog will keep us awake as surely as a crying baby. This wireless connection is much more effective than anything the hardware guys have yet devised.

That, or something very like it, was what must have happened twelve thousand years ago. The deal was struck in nature's court of law, and it allowed both animals to survive and prosper through the great, heaving ecological changes that accompanied the end of the ice age.

But there was a Faustian clause in the contract: Once signed, the deal was forever. Once one animal started turning vital functions over to the other, once symbiosis was begun, it was irreversible. We could not quickly re-evolve the brain tissue we lost. That was the price of symbiosis: To become one with another animal, to lose one's discrete identity.

If *Canis familiaris* now needed the human, the human was equally dependent on the dog. Humans don't just like dogs, we cannot do without them. They are our only touchstone to an emotional past we have forever lost, and yet desperately need.

And that explained why there are so many dogs in the world. It also established that it would always be so. Finally, it explained why the old man shared his grave with the puppy, and why he was reaching for it. He wasn't complete without it.

I remembered once again that day, long ago now, when the wolf had first entered my parlor. Charlie was a puppy, newly arrived. Lynn had gone into the kitchen and was moving around in there, making kitchen noises, staying out of the way while Charlie and I bonded.

I'd sat there on the couch, not quite knowing what to make of the situation. Charlie had positioned himself in the middle of the oriental carpet and stared back at me, clearly unimpressed by my magnificent forebrain.

I am here to stay, he said, *and the sooner you get used to that, the better it will be for everyone.*

How much intellectual agony had I invested to discover that Charlie was right?

Chapter Fifteen

So there we sat, Jade and I, on Nancy's back steps—quite a pair, when you think of it, a rare highland ape and a prodigal wolf. Different animals, yet neurologically attached by a bond that might as well have been made of steel. Psychological symbiotes, each toting a piece of the other's brain.

How do you parse the taxonomy, once you recognize psychological symbiosis between human and dog? What? *Homo canis sapiens?* Or *Homo hog,* for "human-dog?" No, "hog" is a nonstarter, only in part because the name has already been taken.

Let the taxonomists worry about it.

Mostly it doesn't much matter what you call us. Give me another name, and I would still be me; if I am one animal in two brains, I'm still who I am, no more and no less. This changes my understanding of the human condition, but fails to alter the condition in any way.

Nature didn't care about any of that, of course. All nature

cared about was what worked. Humans and dogs bonded out of desperation. We paid a price, but it turned out to be worth it. As the ice retreated and the global climate changed, there was a great era of dying. Other fiercer and mightier creatures than us disappeared: the mammoth, the giant elk, the saber-toothed tiger, the dire wolf, the giant sloth . . . hundreds of species, thousands.

So that was what happened twelve thousand years ago: the dog. The old man and his puppy, still alive, walked the earth together. They survived but, very specifically, they survived because they had each other. So, it was in the confused splendor of the birth of a new environment, as the ice melted and the giant beasts disappeared, men, women, and dogs walked out of the mists of time. Together.

When you solve a problem, as when a reporter discovers the real significance of a story he's working, everything re-sorts itself. All the facts remain, but are now rearranged. We see them in a different way, as part of the new matrix of understanding. As my odyssey ended and I rearranged the pieces, I was amazed by how much had been hidden in plain sight.

The truth was already embedded in our language and culture. We argue, for example, about whether we own our dogs or our dogs own us—but we argue sniffishly, the subtext being that Shucks, we know we're the top dog. Or animal. We never for an instant *really* thought otherwise.

The dog is man's best friend, we say. Yeah. Okay, almost. But substitute "shrink" for "friend" and the mind rebels. We are an animal with a phobia about having a need for emotional assistance. So we step lightly around it. We say things like "My puppy stole my heart," which is the almost-right idea and the almost-right set of facts. But the anatomy is all wrong, totally and completely wrong. The theft isn't of the heart, it is of the brain's limbic system. What the puppy had stolen was a piece of our mind.

◇

I felt a cold nose in my ear, accompanied by a soft woof. It brought me back to Nancy's steps and the building storm.

Jade's large brown eyes were deep as the universe and seemed to hold some humorous accusation. I looked away, and then back. She was still staring at me. In adoration, if I wanted to interpret it that way. Or perhaps it was amusement at the depth of human illusion, stubbornly resistant to a truth the lowly dog knew all along.

Jade continued to stare at me. Dogs blink, but not as often as humans, and she didn't blink at all. She just kept watching me think, the mysterious human who had to laboriously process the emotional knowledge she, Jade, had been born with.

Then Jade looked up, and I followed her gaze. Lynn was standing above me, purse in hand. She was ready to go, hoping to beat the rain.

She drove. I sat, mind lurching out of control, as the pieces continued to fall into place, rearranging my perception not so much of the dog as of myself.

In the weeks that followed, we made the drive to and from Nancy's many times. Lynn wormed herself into Nancy's heart and, more important, into the nursery pen. There she would sit, cross-legged, half-covered with puppies that were larger and more alert with each visit. Watching from beyond the barrier, I couldn't tell one from another, but Lynn was soon able to identify each one from a distance and to discuss (at what seemed to me tedious length) their distinctive personalities.

Which personality would be best for Lynn? They narrowed the candidates to three, then two, and finally one. Lynn named him Sam, after Samuel Clemens. And so, in the fullness of time, we headed home once again with a black puppy sitting up in a box, looking around at the world and—I could tell—incorporating it all into his dominion.

The transition was much easier this time. For one thing, I knew where I stood, and I'm sure Sam sensed that; there was no need for him to repeat Charlie's admonition that he was here to stay, and that it would be easier all around if I just got used to it. I was already used to it. I slipped imperceptibly into my accustomed role as butler and omega wolf.

◇

So Alexander Pope had been right all along: It *was* all about the human. Work your way around to the other side of the dog enigma and what you get is . . . a mirror. The dog is us. The enigma exists only because recognizing the fact threatens our view of ourselves as self-contained and supreme.

At about the time we brought the new puppy home, I realized I now had the answer to a question that had been simmering in my mind for such a long time.

I admitted many chapters ago that I'd once spent a day with a dogcatcher. I admitted that, but I didn't admit what happened that day, an occurrence that I couldn't explain and couldn't forget. But it haunted me, appearing sometimes in my dreams and sometimes in broad-daylight flashbacks.

One of the dogcatcher's calls that morning was to a suburban house north of Baltimore. The dispatcher said there was a dog to be picked up.

The door was opened by a man dressed in slacks, starched white shirt, shiny shoes, and a power tie. There were two children, a boy and a girl, who crowded into the doorway with him, eyes wide. The man said something about getting this over with quickly so he could go to work.

He and his wife had given the puppy to the children as a present, he explained as he led us through the house and out the back door. But as it happened, the puppy just didn't fit their lifestyle. Maybe later, but not now.

The puppy was about twelve inches tall, still in that generic puppy stage with big feet and foreshortened nose, aquiver with life and energy. It was attached to a steel stake by a chain about six feet long; within that radius, the lawn had been reduced to fine dust, and in that dust you could see the concentric circles of the chain links, a testimony to the thousands of trips the bored puppy had made around the edge of its small world. As soon as the puppy saw the children, it started lunging against its collar, tongue lolling and tail wagging furiously.

"Go ahead," the father said to the children, "take a minute to say good-bye."

The children ran to the dog and hugged it. The joy of the dog was incandescent. It licked their faces, wiggled against their torsos, and slathered their faces with doggy kisses.

The man stood back about ten feet, waiting impatiently. After about a minute he ordered the children to step back. They obeyed. Sensing his cue, the dogcatcher moved up, kneeled beside the puppy, and fumbled with its collar snap.

"This nice man," the father told his children, "is going to find the puppy a nice farm where he will have plenty of space and be very happy."

"Isn't that so?" he said to the dogcatcher. "A nice farm!"

The dogcatcher froze in his half-kneeling position, puppy in his arms. He was still as a statue, his eyes fastened on the ground.

"You're going to find a nice farm, isn't that right?" the man said again, more insistently, in the commanding voice one uses on recalcitrant employees. But the dogcatcher didn't move a muscle, make a sound, or meet the man's eyes. The man glared at him and the moment stretched on for several eternal seconds, until finally it was broken by the father's voice.

"That's right," he said to the children. "There's a wonderful farm out there waiting for him."

The dogcatcher stood, puppy in his arms, and without a

word exited through the gate. The children stood there and waved, tears in their eyes, and then they all went back into the house. The father adjusted his tie and closed the door.

Back in the truck, the dogcatcher continued his stony silence. He pulled the truck out into the street, drove a block, and turned off on another street. He pulled over as soon as he was out of sight of the house, and his frustration and rage exploded. His fists beat on the steering wheel hard enough to make it bend and vibrate. "I hate that," he screamed. "I hate that, I hate that, I hate that. There ain't no damned farm. Don't they know that? Don't they care? *There ain't no fucking farm.*"

The pound was already full of puppies, so that evening I watched while the dogcatcher handed the puppy to a technician, who set it on a wooden table. The puppy sat there, perky and inquisitive, looking around. The technician expertly ran the long needle between the puppy's ribs and injected the chemical that instantly stopped its heart. He caught the floppy form before it hit the table and tossed it on a pile of other dead animals next to the incinerator door.

I couldn't forget that scene, and I didn't know why. As a child on a farm, I had seen animals slaughtered, had even done it myself. I didn't like it but, as my mother explained to me, it was the order of things. Later, as a science reporter, I had seen many people die in places like the Baltimore trauma unit. I didn't like that, either, but, again, it was the order of things. Those scenes did not appear in my nightmares, or erupt without warning as flashbacks. But I could never get that puppy out of my mind.

Now I knew why. What I saw was *not* the order of things. It was not based in reality, in evolutionary biology, in logic—except the logic, of course, that we had to do something with the excess dogs we bred and bought and decided we didn't want. The dog had been a fantasy in the minds of that human family. When their fantasy didn't match the reality, the reality had to be done away with, quickly and out of sight. And so it was.

◇

Killing puppies is an ugly business, but sometimes it may be necessary. What so disturbed me about the day with the dog-catcher was the pattern of events that led to the killing. It felt . . . perverted. Dishonest.

If humans and dogs are neurological symbiotes, *Canis familiaris* is in a different category than goats, pigs, horses, cattle, and the rest. Those are clearly separate species; clearly we created them and now possess them, almost in the way we can possess a lawnmower or a Mercedes.

In the case of the dog, though, a biological deal had been struck in the court of natural law, under which the dog would carry part of our psychological burden—would become a peripheral animal, our emotional caddy—and we in turn would do the thinking for it. The dog, in other words, was us. Now that the situation has changed, and the natural world has been conquered, we want to renege on the deal and turn our back on our partner. That is why we need to hire someone to go out and pick up loads of dogs to kill.

The issue is not the dog, has never been the dog. The dog is not confused about what it is. The issue is our own comfortable lies to ourselves, and the blindness those lies impose. And of all the things man is, he is certainly the fantasizing animal. If an obligation is inconvenient, we look the other way.

For us to see the dog as part of ourselves would be to admit to our own emotional frailty. We would have to concede that we don't control as much as we think we do—that we are as much a product of nature as is the dog. We would have to accept that we did not conquer the world without help. Even more contrary to our self-image, we would have to admit that our brains, which is to say our selves, are incomplete. To admit we need the dog, *we really need it,* simply requires more courage than most people can muster. As a result, every word written about the dog, every thought, every observation recorded, is poisoned by hypocrisy.

At some moment, long ago, the symbiosis was out on the table, acknowledged by both sides. That's why the old man was buried with the dog; otherwise, he would have gone to the after-life incomplete and he knew it. But by historical times that clar-ity of shared existence was gone and the dog was seen, as the wolf had once been seen, as a separate creature. There was no symbiosis. Today dogs may not be buried in human cemeteries.

The thing about fantasies, though, is that they are, in the end . . . fantasies. The reality, our special relationship to the dog, simply continues beneath our notice. People will have, keep, and love dogs, and never mind the reasons they make up. It is our lack of candor that makes things go badly, and why nothing we try to do about dogs will ever quite work out.

The result is visible all around us.

Take the confused case of city dogs. It is easy to argue that dogs shouldn't be in cities, that they have no place there, that their presence is illogical—but that is a waste of emotion and po-litical energy. It's not an issue of logic, it's an issue of psychology. If Mao couldn't successfully ban dogs in Beijing, what are the chances of the city council succeeding in New York, where it's politically difficult to maintain leash laws and impossible to en-force them?

One thing follows another. Once we accept that there are go-ing to be city dogs, no matter what, we face the corollary: There is also going to be dog poop. Yet why should New Yorkers, when walking around their great city, have to keep their eyes on the sidewalk directly in front of them? Why is this most powerful of all empires defeated by the movement of a dog's bowels?

As a reporter, mine is not to specify a solution. Mine is, first of all, to express my fascination for the power the denial of the dog has over us.

Not that there aren't ideas flitting around. There are. Dog

parks, for example, where dogs can run off leash provided they are still under their human's control. My guess is that there are many ways to mitigate, if not solve, the city dog problem. If we put human ingenuity to work—if we called in the sanitary engineers and the city planners and the architects—some elegant solution would surely be found. After all, we solved the much larger problem of people poop, an advance which, not so incidentally, allowed Western civilization to grow and flower.

◇

On the other hand, the world is becoming smaller and more crowded. Increasingly, we are dealing with a society so complex that none of us can understand much outside our own field of expertise. We are increasingly isolated and alienated, adrift in a world we did not evolve to tolerate.

At the same time, scientists with their scanners and genetic manipulations are learning more and more about what and who we are, and we are discovering that such self-knowledge is to the good. Legions of otherwise normal people have discovered that they are better, more successful and happier, and more themselves if they start their day with Zoloft.

The point is that many of us need a shrink, but there aren't enough shrinks to go around and besides, they're expensive. If you acknowledge our increasing alienation, and if what the evidence suggests about our psychological symbiosis is true, one predicts that over time there will be an exponential increase in the number of dogs. We may not realize that we are getting, in addition to other things, a live-in shrink—but at some point we will simply *have* to look the dog straight in the eye.

Humans, being what they are, cherish their illusions above all else and wrestle painfully to keep them. But the illusions are part of our cultural childhood and no longer serve us well. The mythology of heroic violence, for example, runs afoul of the difficulty of changing the world with military force. The mythology of true love collides dramatically with the difficulty of maintaining a marriage and rearing children. The mythology of freedom and choice denies the evidence that we are increasingly a nation of proles led this way and that by politicians and a media that feed us what we want to hear. The world is desperate for cultural and social improvement, and that requires not just knowledge but wisdom. In each case, our illusions are the chief barriers to wisdom.

Against this background, the issue of the dog-human animal looms large. Aside from the unhappiness that mismanagement causes, the fantasy that we can do it all ourselves cuts off any hope of using the dog as it evolved to be used. It destines us to be forever alone and, in the process, converts what could be a human asset into a stubborn social problem.

It didn't matter so much in the days when our ancestors were learning to plant seeds along the rivers of the Middle East. But as human societies grew and became more complicated, the dog was increasingly sand in the gears of civilization. With every generation, the status quo Canis became more expensive and disruptive. The relationship cried out to be made transparent—our inadequacies admitted, our secret tail-wagging psychiatrist acknowledged, the door opened, and the dog allowed to enter our lives as he was, instead of as we fantasized him to be.

◇

If a solution is to be found, it will have to be based on the original compact between man and dog. The dog agreed to carry an emotional weight for both of us. Our ancestors agreed, in return, to do the thinking for the dog. As long as we insist on ignoring our part of the bargain, our best efforts will always fall to pieces, because rather than acknowledge the human's responsibility, we blame the dog. Thoughtless acts committed by dogs can only be dealt with by homing in on the animal who's supposed to be doing the thinking.

Lay out the equation in its harshest form: When a dog bites someone, what we decide to do with the dog is irrelevant. But its owner should be charged with the appropriate level of assault.

The human's responsibility is not a simple one, but the cardinal rule is quite straightforward. Pay attention to the dog. Pay attention even before the dog is acquired.

The prospective dog owner should question his knowledge of what, exactly, *is* a dog. How will it fit into his life? What inconveniences will it cause? Who will feed the dog? Who will take it to the vet?

Beyond that, what kind of dog do I want? This is a deep question, full of tiger traps and punji stakes. For example, there is a macho and very American prejudice against pedigreed dogs, probably because in the land of the common man we are all created equal. That's an interesting belief, given that some of us are born rich and some of us are born smart, but never mind. With dogs, the myth simply doesn't apply and can cause heartache.

All dogs, mutts or not, have personalities—often quite strong personalities. To choose a mutt is to guarantee the amount of time and energy required to train a possibly recalcitrant animal. With rare exceptions, a purebred dog purchased from a responsible breeder will have a predictable set of known personality tendencies. You can look them up in a book. This makes it possible to predict a little better how the dog will fit into the family as well as the level of commitment it involves.

Even then, forget any fantasy that the dog will slide smoothly into its place in the household. Puppies are like babies. They have no idea what's expected of them. Like babies, they have to be shown—often again and again—and then allowed to grow into their knowledge.

What is "knowledge" to a dog? Courtesy of that ancient compact, a dog is born with a singular desire to please its human, but . . . what pleases any particular human? That is the knowledge the puppy seeks—nay, craves.

It's up to the human to define what pleases. That means that the human needs to be able to think through what is desired and then communicate that to the dog—most training failures, the experts say, are failures to communicate. If the dog understands what the human wants done, the dog will do or die.

But to make the dog understand, it's necessary for the human to, for lack of a better phrase, "speak dog." The dog, we have discovered in recent decades, has a definite language, mostly body language. A "play bow," for example, means "Everything that follows is play." Two dogs can bow and then engage in what looks like a battle to the death, but neither will emerge the worse for wear.

Woe be to the human who fails to learn dog language. Uninstructed, the puppy will figure it out itself, and it will do so on the basis of signals it understands—emotional signals. That's why so many dogs end up reflecting their humans' basest behaviors. In different words, you may despise your neighbor, but you won't bite him. Your dog, however, will.

By necessity, all this means that the dog, by right, practice, and practicality, has a legitimate claim on its human's time and attention. For a dog, merely being with its human is a reward; most dogs like dog cookies, but if you watch closely when the human awards a dog a cookie, it's not the cookie that really pleases the dog the most. Its happiness comes most from the momentarily undivided attention of its human. A corollary to this is that the dog wants to work, however work is defined by the human. Herding sheep is "work," though the dog loves it. So is herding and protecting children. Paying attention to its human when the human has the blues is another form of work.

If the responsibility for teaching is the human's, it's the dog's job to learn. From puppyhood on it will plunge into this challenge with humor and enthusiasm, and never mind that the human rarely takes this business seriously or makes its instructions clear. Insofar as we fail in this task, we are reneging on the compact—which is why the human must justifiably be held responsible for the actions of the dog.

If a dog is a biter, the one with the nasty temper is usually the owner. If a dog intimidates a person, the bully is not the dog but the owner, and it's the owner who is morally accountable. Laws banning pit bulls will never work; laws penalizing humans for intimidating other humans *by any means, including a dog,* just might. A superficial observation shows that blaming the dog clearly doesn't work.

It is really a rather odd situation, if you think about it. A dog is a wolf in a different persona, under the control of a human. It is at least as dangerous as a knife and sometimes may approach the dangerousness of a gun, in that it acts at a distance. In most civilized societies, the carrier of a deadly weapon has to be licensed. The dog license, though, is not a license in that sense; usually the only thing it means is that the animal has had its rabies shot. You don't really need a license to own a dog. At least not in most places.

In Japan, where people are packed together and the standards for civilized social standards are high, some jurisdictions have gotten practical about the dog. Sacrificing the fantasy, and putting the responsibility where it belongs, they have taken to licensing not the dog but the human. To receive a license, the human has to undergo a rigorous training course and pass an exam—this before he is allowed to purchase a puppy. That is much more consistent with the terms of our ancient compact with the dog, and just might be a harbinger of the future.

Putting the responsibility on the human would also help us escape the rather preposterous assumption that a dog is a dog is a dog. When our local recreation center adopted its no-dog policy, for example, an administrator justified himself by saying that if they let in one dog, they'd have to let in all dogs.

That attitude overlooks the fact that dogdom composes a spectrum from the junkyard dog, a biter who might even be rabid, to a dog that has a Canine Good Citizen certificate and even the dog trained specifically to be around, and even perform with, human children. But the root difference between those dogs is not the dogs but the humans.

Lately I've been hearing talk (though no concerted action) that dog owners should be certified at a progression of levels. A motel, then, might allow dogs but demand to see its good citizen certificate. Or it might demand some other, higher level of certification—whatever will reassure the hotel management that the dog won't bark all night, tear up the room, defecate on the carpet, and scare the other guests. The same system would work for airplanes, trains, and restaurants.

In fact, not having been to France or eaten at a fine restaurant where there were dogs present, I suspect that some less formal version of the same system is at work there. That is, the dog owner is acutely aware that if the dog misbehaves he, his date, and his dog will be summarily ejected by an outraged maître d'. Public humiliation can sometimes work better than laws.

◇

As for Lynn and me and the new puppy, Sam, the rest was as it had been for twelve thousand years. For the first few days, he was an object of fascination, but before long he was simply a member of the family.

His training began almost immediately. When we slept he slept beside us, in a wire pen lined with blankets and amply supplied with toys. He didn't mind the pen; dogs evolved from den animals, and don't tend to be claustrophobic. It is also true that den animals don't relieve themselves in their den. They go outside. Lynn, housetraining Sam, mimicked this instinct by taking him directly from the pen to the backyard without giving him the opportunity to relieve himself on the rug. Sam caught on in a few days. He also learned to sit on command, to come when called, and to heel. He grew, and life went on. I won a professorship at the University of Maryland's College of Journalism and we moved again, this time to a timbered house in the woods south of Washington, D.C. Sam had five acres of woods to romp through and ample squirrels to chase. He loved it, of course. But then, he loved everything. He loved life—he loved his life so much, and so visibly, that he made us love ours all the more.

Time passed. Sam got his shots, and Lynn set up a grooming area in the house so she could keep him trimmed. He passed through his first birthday, then his second, as he approached poodle maturity. Lynn took him to an obedience class, and then to one that taught dog dancing. With his black wool he looked quite sophisticated in a sparkling white bow tie.

No, I'm not kidding. Charlie sang, Sam danced. That was his life and, of course, mine got dragged along. The joy of it all transmitted from Sam's brain to the audiences. He assumed standing ovations were his right. He *was* The Poodle, wasn't he?

◇

Washington, D.C., was built on a swamp, and indeed there was a swamp in the back of our house. Swamps made for humidity. Sam loved the swamp, of course, much to the chagrin of the woman who had to pull the burrs out of his coat, but to the human members of our family the swamp was the source of much misery. In the summer the humidity often climbed so high that there seemed to be little distinction between the black swamp water and the steaming air above it.

Few air-conditioning systems could handle such weather, and the one that came with our house was twenty-five years old. We normally slept on the top floor, but that summer we sought cooler air by moving our bed down into the walk-out basement.

The night of July 23, 2003, was like any other summer night in these parts, which was to say hot and muggy. I had been working on a writing project that day, and by evening I was tense and jumpy. That was a recipe for insomnia, at least for me, so I took a sleeping pill before I went to bed. Lynn, who was suffering from a sore shoulder, took a muscle relaxant. So we slept the chemically induced equivalent of the sleep of the innocent.

Sam, as always, slept lightly, as is a dog's nature.

At about 6:30 in the morning something woke him. He rose and stuck his cold nose into Lynn's face. Lynn pushed him away.

Sam persisted. Irritated, Lynn snapped at him to go lie down.

In response, Sam grabbed the sheet that covered us, and pulled it off.

Lynn pulled it back.

Sam grabbed her upper arm in his jaw and literally pulled her out of bed. She awoke on the floor, with Sam barking frantically over her.

I don't know if it was the barking that awakened me, or Lynn's screams. There was a loud, unworldly noise coming from the utility room. *BRRRRRRRT! BRRRRRRRT! BRRRRRRRT! BRRRRRRRT!*

My first thought was that someone was drilling through the basement wall. Then, as I fought myself into consciousness, it sounded more like a Hollywood representation of an electric chair.

BRRRRRRRT! BRRRRRRRT! BRRRRRRRT! BRRRRRRRT!

I ran toward the sound and threw open the door to the utility room. What I saw made me step back in surprise. A big, roiling orange cloud boiled in the air three feet in front of the breaker box; it seemed to be dancing on the breaker box with lightning-bolt legs. As oxygen poured in through the door I'd opened, the whole room burst into flame. It reached for me with long, scalding fingers. I ran. We all three ran. Moments after we exited the front door, windows began to explode from the heat. I had to restrain Lynn from going back to get her purse. It was too late.

We called the fire department from our next-door neighbor's telephone. Meanwhile, other neighbors rallied around. One of them handed me a shirt and pair of pants, so I could change out of my robe. There were offers of food and shelter. At some point there was a blurred conversation with the insurance adjustor.

Lynn sobbed out her heart on the shoulder of a neighbor lady. I just stood there, numb, full of events without meaning or understanding.

"The dog?" people asked. "The dog saved you? The dog?"

Yes, the dog.

That, too, was a fact.

Then, by some instinct, I returned alone to the house. I knew I couldn't do anything, but it drew me there. I sat on the wood rick and watched the flames lick out of the burst windows and crawl up over and through the roof, consuming wood and dreams alike.

Adrenaline wrecks the human time perception, so I don't know how long this all took. Minutes, I think. I doubt that five minutes elapsed between my rude awakening and my arrival back at the house. My head was a chaos of confusion and disbelief.

Wave after wave of heat washed over me. I heard a siren, far off in the distance, but then it disappeared. The firefighters, I would later discover, had gotten lost. It didn't matter. By that time flames were swirling fifty feet above the house and there was smoke everywhere. The house was gone.

I tried, dumbly, to absorb what had happened. The important thing was that we were alive; that much I knew. The house, the possessions—they were nothing. We would survive.

My mind worked sluggishly, but it worked, fact by fact.

Five more minutes and it would have been too late for us as well as for the house.

Sam had saved our lives.

Were it not for the dog, Lynn and I would both be dead.

The intensity of the moment evoked all those years of research. How many times had this very same thing happened, in the past? How many times had dogs saved people from fires, tornados, floods, wild beasts? How much effect had that had on the reproductive capacities of people with dogs, as compared to people without dogs? Such events might seem random in an individual case, but in aggregate they drive evolution, and drive it hard.

Eventually the red and yellow engines came rushing up the street and turned down the drive. But they couldn't do anything until the local power company sent someone to turn off the electricity. So the fire burned on, bright and all-consuming. An eternity seemed to pass before the first hose swelled and water poured into the flaming maw. Suddenly the smoke was laced with steam and it was difficult to breathe. The firemen were shouting and pulling hoses; one man ran by, with his mask on. I couldn't see the house, but I could still see the glow.

That was when I realized that Lynn and Sam were beside me. I hugged her and Sam squeezed between our legs. A wave of smoke washed over us; Sam sneezed and I began to cough. Together, as if choreographed, we turned and walked back down the long driveway leaving the shouting men, snaking hoses, and collapsing walls behind us.

Lynn reached across Sam, who was trotting between us, and took my hand. I squeezed her fingers. Life would go on.

And so, as it had always been, the woman, the man and the dog walked out of the haze to begin a new life.

INDEX

About the Author

Jon Franklin is the winner of the Pulitzer Prize for Explanatory Journalism and the Pulitzer Prize for Feature Writing, among numerous other awards. He was a science writer for the *Baltimore Evening Sun* and is now a journalism professor at the University of Maryland. He is also the author of *The Molecules of the Mind*, a *New York Times* Book of the Year.